W9-BCV-402

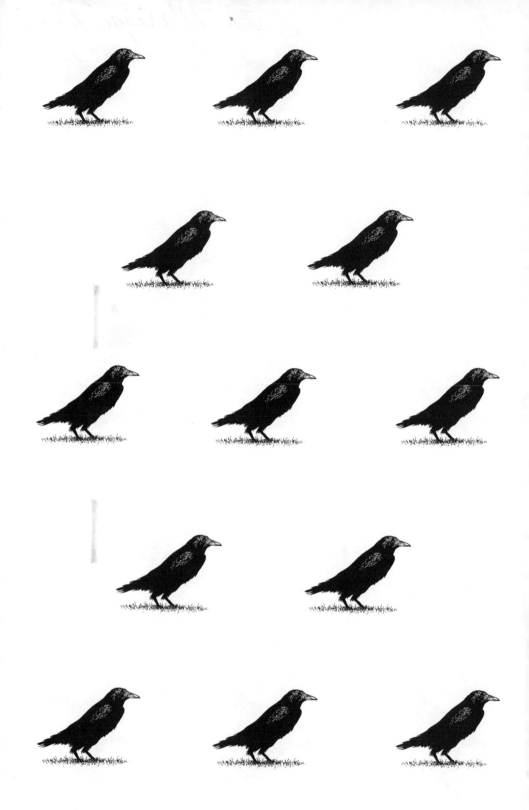

"*The Crow Eaters* is a book of exceptional charm and insight. Besides painting a portrait of an exotic culture—the Parsees of Pakistan—it is constantly entertaining, very funny, intelligent and unexpected. It has everything a novel ought to have, plus a lot of surprises."

—Laurie Colwin, author of
Another Marvelous Thing
and *Family Happiness*

Also by Bapsi Sidhwa

The Bride
Cracking India
(*originally titled* Ice-Candy-Man)

THE
CROW EATERS

A Novel
by
Bapsi Sidhwa

MILKWEED EDITIONS

The title is borrowed from an idiom which belongs to the sub-continent: anyone who talks too much is said to have eaten crows.

© 1978, Text by Bapsi Sidhwa
© 1992, Drawings by R. W. Scholes

Printed in the United States of America.
Published in 1992 by Milkweed Editions by arrangement with Jonathan Cape Ltd.
The hardcover edition of *The Crow Eaters* was originally published in Great Britain by Jonathan Cape Ltd. (1980) and later in the United States of America by St. Martins Press (1983).

Milkweed Editions
528 Hennepin Avenue, Suite 505
Minneapolis, Minnesota 55403
Books may be ordered from the above address.

ISBN 0-915943-78-6

95 94 93 92   4 3 2 1

Publication of this book is made possible by grant support from the Literature Program of the National Endowment for the Arts, the Cowles Media / Star Tribune Foundation, the Dayton Hudson Foundation for Dayton's and Target Stores, Ecolab Foundation, the First Bank System Foundation, the General Mills Foundation, the I. A. O'Shaughnessy Foundation, the Jerome Foundation, The McKnight Foundation, the Andrew W. Mellon Foundation, the Minnesota State Arts Board through an appropriation by the Minnesota Legislature, the Northwest Area Foundation, and by the support of generous individuals.

Library of Congress Cataloging-in-Publication Data

Sidhwa, Bapsi.
   The crow eaters : a novel / by Bapsi Sidhwa.
     p. cm. — (Alive Again! series)
   ISBN 0-915943-78-6 (pbk.)
   I. Title.   II. Series.
  [PR9540.9.S53C7   1992]
  823—dc20   92–3509
                             CIP

*This book is dedicated
to my parents,
Tehmina and Peshotan Bhandara*

Author's Note

The Parsees are an endangered species. Less than 100,000 in the entire world, each year finds their numbers further diminished. *The Crow Eaters* grew out of my affection for my community and the wish to portray the robust spirit and exuberance that have served the Parsees so well since their migration to India as refugees 1,300 years ago.

I take this opportunity to thank Emilie Buchwald for giving *The Crow Eaters* a new lease on life in the U.S.A. and for the affection and excitement with which she has published my novels. I thank Randy Scholes for designing the enchanting jackets for both *The Crow Eaters* and *Cracking India*, and Teresa Bonner for promoting the books with a determination one observes only in parents promoting their children.

And all at Milkweed, and the Friends of Milkweed, who work with Emilie to publish "literate" poetry and fiction . . . My blessings also on the inhabitants of Minnesota for enabling bookstores to multiply and small presses to flourish!

I thank Laurie Colwin and Phillip Lopate for their constant good will. And, since family always comes last, my husband Noshir, my brothers Minoo and Feroze, and my children for their encouragement.

—Bapsi Sidhwa
1992

THE CROW EATERS

Chapter 1

Faredoon Junglewalla, Freddy for short, was a strikingly handsome, dulcet-voiced adventurer with so few scruples that he not only succeeded in carving a comfortable niche in the world for himself but he also earned the respect and gratitude of his entire community. When he died at sixty-five, a majestic gray-haired patriarch, he attained the rare distinction of being locally listed in the "Zarathusti Calendar of Great Men and Women."

At important Parsee ceremonies, like thanksgivings and death anniversaries, names of the great departed are invoked with gratitude; they include the names of ancient Persian kings and saints and all those who have served the community since the Parsees migrated to India.

Faredoon Junglewalla's name is invoked in all major ceremonies performed in the Punjab and Sind—an ever-present testimony to the success of his charming rascality.

In his prosperous middle years Faredoon Junglewalla was prone to reminiscence and rhetoric. Sunk in a cane-backed easy chair after an exacting day, his long legs propped up on the sliding arms of the chair, he talked to the young people gathered at his feet:

"My children, do you know what the sweetest thing in this world is?"

"No, no, no." Raising a benign hand to silence an avalanche of suggestions, he smiled and shook his head. "No, it is not sugar, not money—not even a mother's love!"

His seven children and the young visitors of the evening leaned forward with popping eyes and intent faces. His rich deep voice had a cadence that lilted pleasurably in their ears.

"The sweetest thing in the world is your *need*. Yes, think on it. Your own *need*—the mainspring of your wants, well-being and contentment."

As he continued, the words "need" and "wants" edged over their common boundaries and spread to encompass vast new horizons, flooding their minds with his vision.

"Need makes a flatterer of a bully and persuades a cruel man to kindness. Call it circumstances, call it self-interest, call it what you will, it still remains your need. All the good in this world comes from serving our own ends. What makes you tolerate someone you'd rather spit in the eye? What subdues that great big 'I,' that monstrous ego in a person? Need, I tell you, will force you to love your enemy as a brother!"

Billy devoured each word. A callow-faced stripling with a straggling five-haired moustache, he believed his father's utterances to be superior even to the wisdom of Zarathustra.

The young men loved best of all those occasions when there were no women around to cramp Faredoon's style. At such times Freddy would enchant them with his candor. One evening when the women were busy preparing dinner, he confided in them.

"Yes, I've been all things to all people in my time. There was that bumptious son-of-a-bitch in Peshawar called Colonel Williams. I cooed to him—salaamed so low I got a crick in my balls—buttered and marmaladed him until he was eating out of my hand. Within a year I was handling all traffic of goods between Peshawar and Afghanistan!

"And once you have the means, there is no end to the good you can do. I donated towards the construction of an orphanage and a hospital. I installed a water pump with a stone plaque dedicating it to my friend, Mr. Charles P. Allen. He had just arrived from Wales and held a junior position in the Indian Civil Service, a position that was strategic to my business. He was a pukka sahib then—couldn't stand the heat. But he was better off than his memsahib! All covered with prickly heat, the poor skinny creature scratched herself raw.

"One day Allen confessed he couldn't get his prick up. 'On account of this bloody heat,' he said. He was an obliging bastard, so I helped him. First I packed his wife off to the hills to relieve her of her prickly heat. Then I rallied around with a bunch of buxom dancing-girls and Dimple Scotch. In no time at all he was cured of his distressing symptoms!

"Oh yes, there is no end to the good one can do." Here, to his credit, the red-blooded sage winked circumspectly. Faredoon's vernacular was interspersed with labored snatches of English spoken in a droll, intent accent.

"Ah, my sweet little innocents," he went on, "I have never permitted pride and arrogance to stand in my way. Where would I be had I made a delicate flower of my pride—and sat my delicate bum on it? I followed the dictates of my needs, my wants—they make one flexible, elastic, humble. 'The meek shall inherit the earth,' says Christ. There is a lot in what he says. There is also a lot of depth in the man who says, 'Sway with the breeze, bend with the winds,'" he orated, misquoting authoritatively.

"There are hardly a hundred and twenty thousand Parsees in the world and still we maintain our identity—how? Booted out of Persia at the time of the Arab invasion 1,300 years ago, a handful of our ancestors fled to India with their sacred fires. Here they were granted sanctuary by the prince Yadav Rana on the condition that they did not eat beef, wear rawhide sandals or convert the susceptible masses. Our ancestors weren't too proud to bow to his will. To this day we do not allow conversion to our faith—or mixed marriages.

"I've made friends—love them—for what could be called 'ulterior motives,' and yet the friendships so made are amongst my sweetest, longest and most sincere. I cherish them still."

He paused, sighing, and out of the blue he suddenly said, "Now your grandmother—bless her shrewish little heart—you have no idea how difficult she was. What lengths I've had to go to, what she has exacted of me! I was always good to her though, for the sake of peace in this house. But for me, she would have eaten you out of house and home!

"Ah, well, you look after your needs and God looks after you . . ."

His mellifluous tone was so reasonable, so devoid of vanity, that his listeners felt they were the privileged recipients of a revelation. They burst into laughter at this earthier expatiation and Faredoon (by this time even his wife had stopped calling him Freddy) exulted at the rapport.

"And where, if I may ask, does the sun rise? No, not in the East. For us it rises—and sets—in the Englishman's arse. They are our sovereigns!

Where do you think we'd be if we did not curry favor? Next to the nawabs, rajas and princelings, we are the greatest toadies of the British Empire! These are not ugly words, mind you. They are the sweet dictates of our delicious need to exist, to live and prosper in peace. Otherwise, where would we Parsees be? Cleaning out gutters with the untouchables—a dispersed pinch of snuff sneezed from the heterogeneous nostrils of India! Oh yes, in looking after our interests we have maintained our strength—the strength to advance the grand cosmic plan of Ahura Mazda—the deep spiritual law which governs the universe, the *Path of Asha*."

How they loved him. Faces gleaming, mouths agape, they devoutly soaked up the eloquence and counsel of their middle-aged guru. But for all his wisdom, all his glib talk, there was one adversary he could never vanquish.

Faredoon Junglewalla, Freddy for short, embarked on his travels towards the end of the nineteenth century. Twenty-three years old, strong and pioneering, he saw no future for himself in his ancestral village, tucked away in the forests of Central India, and resolved to seek his fortune in the hallowed pastures of the Punjab. Of the sixteen lands created by Ahura Mazda and mentioned in the 4,000-year-old Vendidad, one is the "Septa Sindh," the Sind and Punjab of today.

Loading his belongings, which included a widowed mother-in-law eleven years older than himself, a pregnant wife six years younger, and his infant daughter, Hutoxi, onto a bullock cart, he set off for the North.

The cart was a wooden platform on wheels—fifteen feet long and ten feet across. Almost two-thirds of the platform was covered by a bamboo and canvas structure within which the family slept and lived. The rear of the cart was stacked with their belongings.

The bullocks stuck to the edge of the road and progressed with a minimum of guidance. Occasionally, having spent the day in town, they traveled at night. The beasts would follow the road hour upon hour while the family slept soundly through until dawn.

Added to the ordinary worries and cares of a long journey

undertaken by bullock cart, Freddy soon found himself confronted by two serious problems. One was occasioned by the ungentlemanly behavior of a very resolute rooster, the other by the truculence of his indolent mother-in-law.

Freddy's wife, Putli, taking steps to ensure a daily supply of fresh eggs, had hoisted a chicken coop onto the cart at the very last moment. The bamboo coop contained three plump, low-bellied hens and a virile cock.

Freddy's objection to their presence had been overruled.

Freddy gently governed and completely controlled his wife with the aid of three maxims. If she did or wanted to do something that he considered intolerable and disastrous, he would take a stern and unshakable stand. Putli soon learned to recognize and respect his decisions on such occasions. If she did or planned something he considered stupid and wasteful but not really harmful, he would voice his objections and immediately humor her with his benevolent sanction. In all other matters she had a free hand.

He put the decision to cart the chickens into the second category and after launching a mild protest, graciously acceded to her wish.

The rooster was her favorite. A handsome, long-legged creature with a majestic red comb and flashy up-curled tail, he hated being cooped up with the hens in the rear of the cart. At dawn he awoke the household with shrill, shattering crows that did not cease until Putli let the birds out of their coop. The cock would then flutter his iridescent feathers, obligingly service his harem and scamper to the very front of the cart. Here he spent the day strutting back and forth on the narrow strip that served as a yard or standing at his favorite post on the right-hand shaft like a sentinel. At crowded junctions he preened his navy blue, maroon and amber feathers and crowed lustily for the benefit of admiring onlookers. Putli spoiled him with scraps of leftover food and chapati crumbs.

Quite hysterical at the outset of the expedition the cock had, in a matter of days, grown to love the ride. The monotonous, creaking rhythm of their progress through dusty roads filled him with delight, and each bump or untoward movement thrilled his responsive and joyous little heart. He never left the precincts of the cart. Once in a while, seized by a craving for adventure, he would flap across the bullocks and, juggling his long black legs dexterously, alight on their horns. Good-naturedly, Freddy shooed him back to his quarters.

Freddy's troubles with the rooster began a fortnight after the start of their journey.

Freddy had already devised means to overcome the hurdles impeding his love life. Every other evening he would chance upon a scenic haven along the route and, raving about the beauty of a canal bank or a breeze-bowed field of mustard, propel his mother-in-law into the wilderness. Jerbanoo, barely concealing her apathy, allowed herself to be parked on a mat spread out by her son-in-law. Sitting down by her side, he would point out landmarks or comment on the serenity of the landscape. A few moments later, reddening under her resigned and knowing look, he would offer some lame excuse and leave her to partake of the scene alone. Freddy would then race back to the cart, pull the canvas flaps close and fling himself into the welcoming arms of his impatient wife.

One momentous evening the rooster happened to chance into the shelter. Cocking his head to one side, he observed Freddy's curious exertions with interest. Combining a shrewd sense of timing with humor, he suddenly hopped up and with a minimum of flap or fuss planted himself firmly upon Freddy's amorous buttocks. Nothing could distract Freddy at that moment. Deep in his passion, subconsciously thinking the pressure was from his wife's rapturous fingers, Freddy gave the cock the ride of his life. Eyes asparkle, wings stretched out for balance, the cock held on to his rocking perch like an experienced rodeo rider.

It was only after Freddy sagged into a sated stupor, nerves uncurled with languor, that the cock, raising both his tail and his neck, crowed, "Coo-ka-roo-coooo!"

Freddy reacted as if a nuclear device had been set off in his ears. He sprang upright, and the surprised Putli sat up just in time to glimpse the nervous rooster scurry out between the flaps.

Putli doubled over with laughter—a phenomenon so rare that

Freddy, overcoming his murderous wrath, subsided at her feet with a sheepish grin.

Freddy took the precaution of tying the flaps securely and all went well the next few times. But the rooster, having tasted the cup of joy, was eager for another sip.

Some days later he discovered a rent in the canvas at the back of the shack. Poking his neck in he observed the tumult on the mattress. His inquisitive, little eyes lit up and his comb grew rigid. Timing his moves with magnificent judgment he slipped in quietly and rode the last thirty seconds in a triumphant orgy of quivering feathers. This time Freddy was dimly conscious of the presence on his bare behind, but impaled by his mounting, obliviating desires, there was nothing he could do.

His body relaxed, unwinding helplessly, and the cock crowed into his ears. Freddy leaped up. Had Putli not restrained him he would have wrung the fowl's neck there and then.

When the whole performance was repeated a week later, Freddy knew something would have to be done—and quickly. Afraid to shock his wife, he awaited his chance, which came in the guise of a water buffalo that almost gored his mother-in-law.

At dawn they had stopped on the outskirts of a village. Jerbanoo, obedient to the call of nature, was wading into a field of maize with an earthenware mug full of toilet water when out from behind a haystack appeared a buffalo. He stood still, his great, black head and red eyes looking at her across the green expanse of maize.

Jerbanoo froze in the knee-high verdure. The domestic buffalo is normally very docile, but this one was mean. She could tell by the defiant tilt of his head and by the intense glow in his fierce eyes. Cautiously bending her knees, Jerbanoo attempted to hide among the stalks, but the buffalo, with a downward toss of the head, began his charge.

"Help!" screamed Jerbanoo, dropping her mug. Lifting the skirt of her sari with one hand, she fled towards the cart.

"Get to one side, change your direction!" yelled Freddy, gesticulating with both arms.

17

Terrified into imbecility, Jerbanoo continued to dash in a straight line ahead of the buffalo.

"Move this way, move away!" shouted Freddy, waving his arms east and west and running to her.

Just then a man popped up from the maize stalks and bellowing for all he was worth, waving his shirt to attract the attention of the buffalo, diverted the stampeding animal. Being the owner of the beast, he quickly brought it under control.

Distraught and disarranged, Jerbanoo fell sobbing into Freddy's arms. It was the last time he ever felt a wave of tenderness and concern for his mother-in-law.

Putli was grateful and pleased with Freddy's gallant effort in rushing forward to help her mother. Taking advantage of her sentiments, Faredoon delicately presented his case for the elimination of the rooster.

"God has saved us from a great calamity today," he declared after supper. "We owe Him thousands, nay millions of thanks for His grace in preventing bloodshed. As soon as we are settled near a Fire Temple, I will order a *jashan* of thanksgiving at our new home. Six *Mobeds* will pray over enough holy fruit, bread and sweetmeats to distribute amongst a hundred beggars . . . but it might be too late! We have been warned, the earth thirsts for blood! I intend to sacrifice the cock tonight."

Putli gasped and paled. "Oh, can't you sacrifice one of the hens instead?" she pleaded.

"It has to be the cock, I'm afraid," said Freddy, permitting his lowered head to sink sadly. "We all love the charming fellow, I know, but you cannot sacrifice something you don't care for—there is no point in it."

"Yes, yes," agreed Jerbanoo vehemently. After all it was her blood the earth thirsted after—her life they were talking about!

Putli nodded pensively.

Next day they ate a succulent chicken and coconut curry.

But the dashing sprint had proved too much for Jerbanoo's sluggish muscles. Her body ached horribly, and her initial gratitude was replaced by a sullen rancor. She blamed Freddy for having undertaken a journey that exposed her to the buffalo charge and to many subsequent vicissitudes.

Jerbanoo had been against the journey from the very start. Unnerved by the uprooting and by the buffalo, by the imperturbably polite stance adopted by her unfeeling son-in-law, she had ranted, moaned and finally resigned herself to martyrdom. Arms akimbo, black, vindictive eyes snapping, she never failed an opportunity to castigate him. And the journey, fraught with mishap and mild disaster, had given her plenty.

As on that pitch-black night when the wooden wheel of the cart collapsed on the outskirts of the Rajastan Desert and a jackal suddenly howled into the stillness.

Jumping from the cart, palms on hips, Jerbanoo planted herself solidly before Freddy. Her winged eyebrows almost disappeared in her hairline. "So, now we are to be devoured by wolves! Why? Because your majesty wishes it! We are to spend the night in this forsaken place, at the mercy of wild beasts! Why? Because our simple village ways were not good enough for you! But don't imagine I'm going to dance to your tune all the time. I've come for my daughter's sake and I'm not going to stand this nonsense any longer! You turn right back! You hear me?" she bawled, her eyes shining triumphantly in the glow of the lantern swinging from Freddy's hand.

Freddy turned away silently.

"You obstinate fiend, have you no idea how we are suffering? Have you no care for your wife and child? Oh, how can they live at the mercy of your whims . . . you heartless demon!" she cried.

Putli slept through unconcerned. Her mother's screeching tirades had grown so commonplace that the uproar hardly stirred her dreams.

Ignoring Jerbanoo, Freddy set about repairing the wheel. The slighted woman bounced back into the cart and sat quivering on her mattress.

The jackal bayed, his mournful notes amplified by the nocturnal stillness.

Jerbanoo's spine grew rigid and out of sheer disgust and frustration, she howled back.

The jackal caterwauled eerily.

"Owoooo!" went Jerbanoo.

Excited by the discovery of a mate, the jackal launched an abysmal moan.

"Yieeee!" yowled Jerbanoo, and between the two rose the most ghoulish duet imaginable.

His flesh creeping, his beautiful, white teeth on edge, Faredoon leaped onto the cart and scrambled into the hut. Hurling himself within an inch of his mother-in-law's face he hissed, "Stop it . . . Stop that horrible noise or I'll leave you right here . . . I swear!"

Jerbanoo subsided at once. Not so much at the ominous pledge as at the demented gleam in his eyes.

Within two hours they had resumed their journey, soothed and lulled by the hollow toll of the bell hanging from each bullock's neck.

At other times the child had dysentery, Jerbanoo got cramps bathing in a canal, and Putli, stung by a scorpion, almost fell into a well. On these occasions, attracted by Jerbanoo's strident, scolding outcries, the entire populace of several villages was entertained mercilessly to the shortcomings of her son-in-law.

Tiring of this, Freddy addressed himself exclusively to his wide-eyed, diligent wife, and Jerbanoo slumped into a restive, martyred silence.

Two dust-grimed, mosquito-bitten months later, Freddy led his worn beasts into the fertile land of the Five Rivers.

They passed through several villages, green with wheat and gold with mustard. They spent a few days in the golden city of Amritsar and finally came to Lahore.

Faredoon Junglewalla fell in love with Lahore straightaway. His mother-in-law, the corners of whose set mouth had drooped progressively as the journey had gone on, surveyed the bustling, steaming city with bleak eyes. She withheld her comment for the moment, glad of a chance to rest her rattled joints.

Freddy toured Lahore all day, and each hour strengthened his initial love of the ancient city. That evening they parked the cart beneath a shady tree near the Badshahi Mosque. The horizon cradled the sun in a pink fleece, touching the poetic assembly of white domes with a blush, filling Freddy's senses with serenity. The muezzin's cry, suppliant, plaintive and sensual, rose in the hushed air among the domes. Bells tinkled in a diminutive, Hindu temple, snuggled in the shadows of the mosque. A Sikh temple, gold-plated, gleamed like a small jewel in the shadows, and Freddy, responsive to all religious stimuli, surrendered his heart to the moment.

In the morning, having decided to adopt the city and try his luck, Freddy approached his wife for the gold. Putli, who had been laying out feed for the bullocks, glanced around with wary eyes.

"Even trees," she advised sternly, "have ears."

Placing a cautionary hand on Freddy's arm, she led him into their room on the bullock cart.

The baby slept in one corner and Jerbanoo sat cross-legged on her mattress, battling the enervating heat with a palm-leaf fan. At Freddy's entrance she wrinkled her nose at the bazaar smells assailing her nostrils and, fanning herself into a froth, mutely advertised her displeasure of the city.

Freddy's heart trilled in his chest. Jerbanoo's disfavor set the seal on his inspired decision. Like hens settling on eggs, Freddy's mind settled on a smug clutch of smiling thoughts. Right there he took a silent oath that he would never leave Lahore so long as he lived.

Turning his back upon his mother-in-law's pointed histrionics, Freddy watched his wife unbutton the tight bodice beneath her sari blouse. Putli barely came up to his chest. Secure from prying, thieving eyes, she removed the cache that had pressed the flesh of her breasts from the onset of their travels. Carefully handing the cache to Freddy, she began buttoning herself back into her flattening, cotton bodice. Freddy eyed with chagrin the buoyant, little breasts as they disappeared. He reached stealthily for a last-minute touch, but her censorious stare, warning him of his mother-in-law, stayed his hand.

There was a certain fixed quality to Putli's humorless eyes, set well apart in the stern, little triangle of her face, that often disconcerted and irritated Freddy. The only time he saw her unwavering gaze dissolve was in bed. Then her long-lashed lids grew heavy with sensuality and there was such dogged and hedonistic devotion in her eyes for him, such a readiness to please and be pleased, that he became her slave.

As soon as Freddy left, Putli flung herself into an energetic orgy of work. In no time at all she had watered the bullocks, started a fire in the coal brazier and set a colander of vegetables and lentils to simmer. All this she did with such economy of motion and efficiency that her mother roused herself guiltily to give a hand. Taking the plate of rice from Putli she began to feed the child.

Freddy systematically found his way to the homes of the four Parsee families settled in Lahore: the Toddywallas, the Bankwallas, the Bottliwallas and the Chaiwallas. None of them practiced the trades suggested by their names. The Toddywallas, a large extended family, were the proprietors of a prosperous tea stall, and the Chaiwallas ran a bar. Mr. Bottliwalla was a teller in a bank, and Mr. Bankwalla conducted classes in ballroom dancing.

An endearing feature of this microscopic merchant community was its compelling sense of duty and obligation towards other Parsees. Like one large close-knit family, they assisted each other, sharing success and rallying to support failure. There were no Parsee beggars in a country abounding in beggars. The moment a Parsee strikes it rich he devotes a big portion of his energies to charity. He builds schools, hospitals and orphanages, provides housing, scholarships and finance. Notorious misers, they are paradoxically generous to a cause.

The four families were delighted by Freddy's visit and enchanted at the prospect of another family come to swell their ranks.

In two days Freddy had ensconced his family in a flat atop his brand-new provision store in one of the most busy and commercially prosperous areas in town.

The very next evening, rigged out in a starched white coat-wrap that fastened with bows at the neck and waist, crisp white pajamas, and a turban, he drove his cart to Government House.

Parking his splendid bullocks next to restive tonga horses, Freddy strode confidently up to the resplendent guards at the huge iron gates. The guards allowed him in almost at once and Freddy signed his name in the Visitor's Register.

Having thus paid homage to the British Empire, established his credentials and demonstrated his loyalty to "Queen and Crown," Freddy was free to face the future.

Chapter 2

Faredoon's manly bearing and soft-spoken manners quickly found their way into Punjabi hearts. He had a longish, nobly contoured, firm-chinned face. His slender nose was slightly bumped below the bridge, and, large and heavy-lidded, his hazel eyes contained a veiled, mystic quality that touched people's hearts. His complexion was light and glowing. All this, combined with the fact that he was a Parsee—whose reputation for honesty and propriety is a byword—made him a man of consequence in the locality. His sales picked up almost at once and he began to live in reasonable comfort. He was even able to save a bit.

Faredoon made a point of giving small alms every Friday, and his wife and mother-in-law never appeared in public without *mathabanas*—white kerchiefs wound around the hair to fit like skullcaps. The holy threads circling their waists were austerely displayed, and sacred undergarments, worn beneath short blouses, modestly aproned their sari-wrapped hips. Stern-visaged, straight-backed, the two women faced the world with such moral authority that Hindu, Muslim or Christian, all had profound respect for the man and his family.

Putli was content. She fulfilled herself in housework and in the care of her children and husband. But her unblinking, seemingly inane eyes saw more than Freddy ever realized. They instinctively raked the depths of him and, often enough, surfaced somewhat uneasily. Of one thing, though, she was sure: whatever else he might do, he would never stray. Blissful in her knowledge, she would, over the years, produce seven children. From the joyous climax of conception to the delivery, Putli would enjoy it all.

But for all his steady progress at the start in Lahore, Freddy's happiness was marred. Jerbanoo was a canker, a thorn in his side that blighted his life. She had not stopped moaning, sighing, muttering and quarreling for a moment. His wife bore her mother's eruptions stoically, attributing them to her uprooting and her widowed state. But Freddy, whose sensitive soul was more impatient of her rowdy outbursts, found her vitriolic presence increasingly unbearable.

She took a malicious delight in needling him, of this he was sure. She complained, had headaches, snored, wept and raved for the sole purpose of irritating him. Often he struck his head in despair, bemoaning his fate and wondering what monstrosities he had committed in previous births to merit this punishment.

He could not bear the way she appropriated the largest, choicest portions of food when they sat at table. Every time she pounced on the chicken dish, prying out bits of giblet and liver with her fingers and popping them into her mouth, he winced. The more he flinched, the more she delighted in swiping these delicacies from beneath his very nose and stuffing them into her voracious mouth. She would then sink back contentedly in her chair and pulling all the dishes closer to her plate, proceed gluttonously to help herself to second favorites.

But there is only so much a man can take. One lunchtime Freddy exploded. Taking firm hold of her plucking hand, he guided the giblet-pinching fingers across Putli to Hutoxi, who was now three years old. Ordering the startled child to "Eat!" he quietly restored the plundered hand to its dumbfounded owner.

Wagging a long, retributive finger across the table, wildly misconstruing the English text, he thundered, "Out of the mouths of babes and sucklings! Yes, you are eating out of the mouths of babes and sucklings!"

Not understanding the words but impressed nevertheless, the table waited in nervous suspense for him to continue. Jerbanoo squirmed in her chair, hatefully conscious of his stern, ascetic eyes and wagging finger. Whatever it was he said, there was no doubt in her mind that the thundering sentences were meant to vilify, condemn and annihilate her.

A solemn moment later, he demanded, "Are you a growing child? Must you eat all the liver and fat from my babies' mouths? Look at them—see how thin they are!" He pointed his quivering finger at Hutoxi and her year-old brother, Soli. They were rosy-cheeked and sturdy.

"As a Zarathusti I am not permitted to look upon a crime and remain guiltless. My children are being murdered beneath my very nose and—"

Putli chimed a warning: "Mind the Demon of Wrath."

"The Demon of Wrath! Murder is being committed before my eyes and you want me to do nothing? I shall be as guilty in God's sight as this glutton! There ought to be a law to flog greedy grandmothers like her," he proclaimed.

"Freddy!" squeaked his shocked wife.

"You heard him! You heard what he said to me!" squealed her mother. "Oh, that I should live to hear *him* say that to *me*! Oh God, rip the earth apart and swallow me alive!"

Jerbanoo surged mightily to her feet, knocking back her chair with a crash. For a fearful moment Putli believed the Deity, having taken her mother's plea to heart, had sundered the floor of their dining-room.

Kicking the fallen chair aside, Jerbanoo stormed out and shut herself up in her room with a shattering detonation of slammed doors and bolts. She lay down, flat on her back, panting furiously.

An hour later she tiptoed to the kitchen and polished off the dinner prepared for the evening.

For two days Jerbanoo ate sparingly. Thereafter her hunger grew voracious and, undaunted, she gorged herself before her son-in-law's burning gaze. She appeared to expand beneath his very eyes. And the fatter she grew the leaner he became, and the leaner he became the more Jerbanoo ate to vindicate herself—until both felt quite ill.

Her sudden expansion awed the household. Jerbanoo threw her newly acquired weight about with avenging zest. Not knowing what to make of her, Putli, the servants and the children allowed her domination. She swaggered all over the house, roaring commands and bequeathing counsel. She took complete charge of their lives, and Freddy, too weak and bewildered to counteract her bullying, allowed the situation to slip out of hand.

Increasing her circle of acquaintances, Jerbanoo invited droves of plump, middle-aged ladies to long sessions of morning gossip and emotional unburdening. Nodding with sympathy, these Hindu, Muslim,

Christian and Parsee ladies exhorted Putli to stand up to her tyrannical husband and take better care of her own mother. Freddy sensed that his good name and standing were being criticized publicly and he was resentful, but the more harried he became the less he was able to cope.

Not satisfied with commandeering the household, Jerbanoo extended her sway to the store. Whenever Freddy was away, riding roughshod over the salesman's scruples, Jerbanoo appropriated huge quantities of chocolate, biscuits, perfume and wines. These were used by her and her friends at their leisure or magnanimously bequeathed. Harilal the clerk and the two salesmen were constantly popping in and out of the store on errands. While they carried coyly decorated trays bearing gifts, invitations and messages back and forth, Freddy found himself handling the store alone.

One particular evening, after a day spent in attending to customers, indenting ledgers and unloading a cartload of biscuit cases single-handed, he trudged up wearily and told Putli, "This Olympic relay race has got to stop."

"What relay race?" she asked, surprised.

"This running to and fro of my staff. I have to cope with the work of three men single-handed. Harilal returns and the salesman is off, the salesman barely shows his face when Krishan Chand is off—carrying my chocolates, my peanuts, my potato-crisps, and my biscuits to her friends! What is she up to, anyway?"

"Oh, come now, you don't grudge her a little social life of her own, do you?" chided his matter-of-fact spouse. "After all, you can't expect her to go up and down running errands herself."

Faredoon felt a dangerous pulse throb in his temple. Of late he had the depressing feeling that his wife had ganged up with her mother.

Later that night, rearing up weakly in bed, he startled Putli by suddenly shouting, "And while I'm at it, let me warn you—this looting of my store has got to stop! I tell you, I'll have no stocks left. Who does she think she is, some goddamn princess?" he demanded, close on tears.

"Whatever has come over you these days?" remonstrated his wife, getting out of bed to light an oil lamp. "I've never seen you so mean and petty. What if she takes a little something now and then to entertain her friends? After all, don't forget, we have uprooted her."

"A little something?" shouted Freddy, interrupting her. "You call that a little something? Why, she eats like a horse at meals and then swallows enough sweet chutneys, candied fruit and liqueurs to give an elephant diarrhea—or haven't you noticed her bloated dimensions of late?" he spluttered sarcastically.

"Not bloated," amended Putli, "puffed up. She is just puffed up with sorrow."

"What?" exclaimed Freddy incredulously.

"It's been known to happen," she countered defiantly. "People have been known to puff up with sorrow—and God alone knows she has enough cause, the way you treat her."

"That robust ox has puffed up with sorrow?" repeated Freddy, at his wits' end.

"And," corrected his spouse, "she is not as robust as she looks—for all her size she's as weak as a twig. She is quite unwell, really."

"I suppose all that muscle on show is just a puff of air," mumbled Freddy faintly, feeling the bottom falling from his world.

And in fact Jerbanoo was really ailing. All in their turn the kidneys, the liver, the gall bladder and her joints upped and temporarily ceased the unequal struggle against layers of fat. A few years later even her uterus, under the strain of merry-making, overeating and boisterous exertions, turned over. She was subject to a pain that none but an "English doctor" could rectify.

"Get an English doctor. Oh, I'm dying. Get an English doctor," she howled for an hour, waving aside all other suggestions. Freddy, faint at the thought of the enormous fee he would have to disgorge, was compelled to fetch one.

The doctor, a ferocious, undersized Englishman with a sandy moustache and bald head, won Freddy's eternal gratitude by declaring, "There's nothing wrong with you that a little dieting won't cure—stop all that 'pure butter, pure cream, pure fat' nonsense."

Five minutes later, Freddy found himself plunged into a well of despair from which he never really emerged.

"Doctor," Jerbanoo asked with piteous hesitancy, "I have not revealed this to my child even, but I often get a pain in my chest, here, right here. I know it is my weak heart . . . I've known it a long time. What am I to do? Oh, doctor, am I to die so young?" she sobbed, her compelling, attractive eyes sparkling with tears.

"Now, now Mama—ooooh my poor Mama!" cried Putli, rising gallantly to the occasion. Freddy tried to disguise the happiness that Jerbanoo's revelation had occasioned in him. Lowering his lids he looked grimly in the vicinity of Jerbanoo's weak heart.

After thumping the barrellike chest and listening through his stethoscope, the doctor pronounced sentence on Freddy's happiness.

"It must have been a touch of heartburn—overeating again. Your heart's as tough as a steam engine. It'll see you through eighty years if something else doesn't pack up first."

In retrospect, Freddy realized that his stars had been particularly feeble at the time. Everything went wrong collectively. His health deteriorated, his thinking was confused and his energy depleted. So effective was the malignity of Saturn in his horoscope that he weakly watched Jerbanoo usurp his authority in every sphere, impotent to counter the topsy-turvy turn of domestic events.

Jerbanoo stomped around with a smug, challenging look in her snappy eyes that Freddy dared less and less to meet. At the slightest hint of protest, at the mildest countersuggestion, she would cannonade into an injured fury and scream at the very top of her voice for the benefit of the neighbors. Or, popping her offended eyes, she would sag into a melancholy fit of weeping so prolonged that Freddy, terrified of the resultant effect on his perpetually pregnant wife, was forced to appease and calm her with presents.

Bullied and blackmailed, Freddy felt himself sink into a muddy vortex.

Once, striking his forehead in exasperation he remonstrated, "For God's sake, keep your voice down—must you always bray like an ass? Can't you keep your voice human? What will the neighbors think?"

The retaliation to this impulsive rebuke was so severe that he never repeated his mistake.

"And now my own son-in-law is calling me a donkey!" shrieked Jerbanoo. The frizzy knot at the back of her neck came loose and the braid settled thin and quivering on her shoulder. "And now I'm forbidden even to talk in this house! Oh, Putli, take me back. Oh, my child, take me back to my childhood village. I will not spend a single moment in this house. Not any more . . . not any more!" she cried, flinging her arms around Putli and sobbing on her breast.

Putli glared at Freddy with tight-lipped censure. The exhortations of her mother's friends having taken effect, she flatly intoned, "How dare you call my mother a donkey. How dare you! I would like to see anyone try and stop her from speaking in this house!"

"Look, I'm not telling her to stop talking," explained Freddy wearily. There was a plea of despairing confusion in his eyes. "I'm merely requesting her not to shout so loud."

"Requesting? Requesting?" snorted Jerbanoo, rearing her head like a cobra from Putli's bosom. "You are always calling me names. Don't do this, don't do that, don't touch this, don't touch that. You go on and on until I feel frightened even to open my mouth, even to drink a drop of water in this house!"

Freddy choked with fury. The accusations were absurd and unjust. He was the one condemned to prowl around the house stealthily, not daring to speak for fear of touching off a revolution. Her statement that she feared even to drink water in his house stung him. Wheezing with subdued rage he said, "Of course you don't drink water. A drop of water wouldn't know where to lodge in your stomach—not with all that port wine, milk, sherbet and cognac you've pumped into it!"

He would have carried on but for the glacial, wide-eyed glower from Putli. Shriveling hopelessly beneath her look, head downcast, he slunk down the stairs.

And his stars, not content with the domestic havoc they wrought, struck blow upon bewildering blow on his business as well. He lost a contract to retail wine to the Lahore Gymkhana Club. An army canteen suddenly switched over to a store in the cantonment for its weekly provision of sugar and whole wheat. His daily inflow of customers dwindled, preferring stores where the salesmen, not having to contend with mothers-in-law, were free to dance attendance on them. A deal to get sole agency for Murree Brewery's beer, on which Freddy had set his despondent heart, fell through at the very last moment.

Then Freddy made a weird discovery. The intransigence of his luck was directly related to his squabbles with his mother-in-law. Her hatred for him was palpable and there was no doubt in his mind that she wished him ill. When he discovered that her curses and lachrymose scenes coincided with setbacks in his business, he grew fearfully alarmed. Languishing beneath the gargantuan weight of these conjectures, he became desperate.

It was five years since Freddy had come to Lahore.

Chapter 3

Hollow-cheeked, glazed-eyed, a shadow of his former self, Freddy decided to consult a mystic.

Late one chilly afternoon (Lahore can be as cold in winter as it is hot in summer), he slipped out of his store and, shivering in his overcoat, walked dismally to the seedy tenement in which the mystic was known to dwell. The fakir was reputed to be in touch with spirits and well versed in the arts of his esoteric profession.

Freddy walked through the dingy corridors of the building, too dispirited even to ask directions. He climbed an unlit flight of steps to the first floor. Wandering at random, he finally located the mystic through the open doors of his dwelling. Wild-haired and long-bearded, he sat cross-legged in his loin cloth upon a grimy mat on the floor.

Covering his head with a handkerchief, Freddy stood deferentially at the threshold of the small, bare room, which reeked of incense.

The mystic was in a yogic trance. Freddy studied the dusky, ash-covered, strong-featured face with its closed eyelids. The mystic's upper arms were decorated with silver bracelets and his chest bristled with an assortment of amulets and colorful beads. He sat within a semicircle of vials, pounding-bowls and scraps of parchment marked with astrological signs. Impressed by what he saw, Freddy drifted into a reverie.

All at once the mystic opened his huge, black eyes. His face gathered itself into a ferocious scowl and, glaring at Freddy, he thundered, "Come in, you murderer!"

Freddy's constitution was in no condition to withstand this greeting. Nearly jumping out of his overcoat, springing erect and bumping his head against the doorpost, he stumbled into the room.

Freddy crumbled to his knees and touched the divine's dirty toe. The fakir shied back like a nun pinched by a drunkard. Retracting his toes, fastidiously placing a disturbed tatter of parchment back into line, he shooed Freddy back with a rapid flutter of his fingers.

Freddy staggered back and settled trembling on his haunches. The semicircle of vials and pounding-bowls stood like a wall, sternly demarcating their territories.

"Well, murderer?" asked the mystic, graciously inviting Freddy to speak his errand.

Freddy blanched and cowered. A thousand thoughts clamored in his mind. Was the man clairvoyant? No, he thought. The thought of murder had not as much as crossed his mind. Maybe the fakir saw beyond—into a man's future—actions that were yet to be. "God forbid," he said to himself, shuddering. Pulling himself together with a tremendous effort, he mumbled, "No, not a murderer, but your humble servant who is in distress."

The mystic held aloft his jeweled arms and rolled his murky eyeballs heavenward. So effective was this performance that Freddy, convinced of the man's terrible powers, prostrated himself within the boundaries of his own territory and sobbed, "O saint, you must help me. Have mercy on me!"

"Sit up," commanded the fakir, and Freddy, looking into his dilated, snake-still eyes, was filled with an overpowering urge to unburden his soul, to dig out and spill all the hot and monstrous secrets that sometimes crept even into his consciousness. A faint warning signal flashed in his befuddled mind: what if the man dispossessed him of his soul . . . ?

The mystic had Freddy exactly where he wanted him. Practiced in the psychology and histrionics of his trade, he relied on shock tactics to unnerve a man into taking the tricky leap across the credibility gap. He addressed only the most respectable looking of his clientele as murderers, scoundrels, thugs and adulterers. He startled ruffians and professional murderers into undying devotion by calling them misunderstood saints or reincarnations of past divines. In either case his tactics worked. And it is to Freddy's credit that he had called him a murderer.

Freddy, meanwhile, was engaged in a desperate struggle to maintain possession of his soul. Bravely, determinedly, he looked straight at the terrible eyes, daring them to deprive him of his psyche. Matching his will against the other's cunning powers, he fought a pitched and fiendishly lonely battle.

The fakir, oblivious to all but the smell of money on the man, had not the remotest idea of his client's qualms on behalf of his soul. He continued glaring mechanically, his ferociously pitted face framed in a stiff tangle of black, unkempt hair.

After a full minute, pregnant with unspeakable horrors for Freddy, the fakir snapped the unholy connection by commanding, "*Bollo!*" (Speak).

Quaking on his haunches, Freddy's voice quavered, "I have reason to suspect my mother-in-law has sold herself to the devil. She torments me with evil curses and I cannot sustain the loss to my business any longer. She has also worked a spell on my wife and children—even they are turning against me. O Fakir, you must help me," he pleaded in hushed agony.

Extending his hand across the boundary of vials, the mystic held out an incense burner. Freddy gratefully smeared some ash on his forehead. Discreetly removing a crisp ten-rupee note from his pocket, he placed it in the incense tray.

The fakir's hypnotic eyes flickered an appreciative second. His demeanor underwent a subtle change. Without any noticeable alteration in his harsh, domineering manners, he managed artfully to convey an aura of compassion and sympathy.

"Go," he said gruffly, pointing a stiff finger to the exit. "Go now and get me a coil of her hair."

Freddy stood up and salaaming gratefully, backed towards the door.

"Be sure to snip the hair yourself," added the fakir in a surprisingly conspiratorial voice.

The moment Freddy emerged from the dank, stifling tenement into the twilit street, his buoyant assurance in the mystic's competence vanished. It was as if the chill evening air had lifted the smog of incense and artifice from his confused mind. For an instant his customary common sense prevailed, and he wondered at himself for having visited the charlatan at all. But then he recalled the seminaked man's mesmeric glower—why, the fellow had almost sneaked off with his soul! Where would he be now had he not clung to it with all the strength of his will! No, the bedraggled fakir had something in him. It would be foolish to discredit him entirely.

Perplexed and preoccupied, Freddy bumped into a sauntering, decorated cow. The Brahmin priest accompanying the sacred animal cried, "Watch your step, *babooji*," and sidestepped nimbly to avoid the preoccupied Parsee's contaminating touch.

The fakir was not a phony, Freddy decided, recollecting the enigmatic display of vials, powders and parchment. The man had almost certainly been in communion with the spirits, unsavory ones no doubt, when Freddy had looked into the room hesitatingly from the threshold. He never had doubted that black magic and witchcraft existed, and he was convinced a little ordinary "magic" would not be amiss under the calamitous circumstances. Of course, he would take the precaution of counterbalancing any risk to his relationship with God with extra prayer and alms-giving.

He wondered what mysteries would be perpetuated on his mother-in-law's hair once it was handed over to the Mystic. It might be reduced to gray ashes in the incense burner, to the accompaniment of appropriate chants and spells, or, wrapped up with abominable magic potions, the hair might be buried in some unholy spot. He had noticed *things* strung up with halved lemons and daggerlike green peppers dangling from the branches of a banyan tree overhanging a grave.

What then? Freddy shivered, though his part in the whole business was completely innocuous. All he was required to do was snip a bit of hair—a childish prank—and hand it over to the mystic. What the divine did with it thereafter was not his worry.

Crossing over to his shop, Freddy just missed being impaled by the spokes of a tonga as the cursing driver rammed his two-wheeled horse carriage into a clangorous, ox-drawn fire engine.

Intent on all the angles and complexities of his mission, Freddy labored up the stairs of his home and came face to face with the object of his meditations.

"Oh hello, Mother," he cried, with a guilty start.

Jerbanoo blinked at the unaccustomed and vehement greeting.

"'Ello," she mumbled doubtfully. Turning her copious back to him, the frizzled rat-tail of her hair dangled sinfully before his eyes.

Chapter 4

Freddy was a patient and meticulous man. He bided his time, and three days later an opportunity to implement his mission rewarded his patience.

It was Friday. Putli would spend the afternoon in a little washroom on the roof of the building scrubbing linen. The servant boy, who kept an eye on the flat while Jerbanoo had her afternoon siesta, had gone off in a huff. She had boxed his ears that morning for dipping into her jar of boiled sweets.

Freddy was sure his victim was blithely snoring her head off in her room.

Down below in the store, the Hindu clerk idly browsed through some bills. Few customers came at this hour, and Freddy, knowing that the moment had come, steeled himself for his task. Telling the clerk he would be back shortly, he mounted the wooden stairway.

Freddy slipped past the kitchen, which opened directly on the landing, and tiptoed through the dining room into his own room. Quietly he opened the drawers of the carved walnut sewing chest, selected an efficient-looking pair of scissors and tried them out by snipping off a bit of thread from the tasseled ends of his bedspread. Next he removed his shoes.

Stepping cautiously in his stockinged feet on floors that vibrated at the slightest movement, he stood outside the teak door to Jerbanoo's room. He paused, breathing softly, listening to the reassuring rumble of snores that filtered through the solid teak.

Freddy had taken the precaution of oiling all the hinges the day after his visit with the mystic.

Patiently, soundlessly, he lifted the latch. When the door gave a bit he let his breath go. Luckily Jerbanoo had not shot the bolts. The door eased open on its well-oiled hinges, and closing it carefully behind him,

Freddy tiptoed to her bed. The taut strings of the charpoy sagged like a hammock beneath her weight.

The square, darkened room was bare except for a rickety clothes stand, a large almirah and the charpoy. A high-backed chair to one side of the closet was untidily draped with the sari Jerbanoo had removed before retiring. A coal fire hissed gently in a small grate by her feet.

Jerbanoo lay flat on her back, the precious rat-tail of braided hair buried beneath mounds of heaving, snoring flesh.

Freddy leaned over gingerly, fascinated by the slumbering body. The room was warm and the blanket Jerbanoo had kicked off lay crumpled at her feet. She slept in a tight-sleeved, scoop-necked blouse and sari petticoat (a long, cotton skirt gathered at the waist with a tape). A film of moisture gleamed between the fat folds of her neck. Freddy studied the hated face intently. The well-defined, strongly arched eyebrows dominating the narrow forehead epitomized for him the menace and treachery of her nature. Anyone less prejudiced than Freddy would have found Jerbanoo's rounded jaws and small features rather attractive or interesting. Her skin was smooth, her slightly parted, fluttering mouth small and full-lipped. The braid Freddy was after was nowhere in sight.

Hanging helplessly over her, Freddy was wondering what to do when an angry snort exploded in his face. Jerbanoo had no more than brought to order a recalcitrant bit of air attempting to sneak out through the wrong nostril. Another snort followed, and Freddy, who was often scolded by Putli for staring at the babies and so disturbing their sleep, ducked with a terrified start. Like a drop of water in a desert, he disappeared beneath her charpoy. The bare, brick floor was icy.

The snorting and whistling stopped. There was a moan. A laborious upheaval took place on the hammock above him as Jerbanoo turned. The four slender legs of the string bed creaked and groaned.

Faredoon broke out in an icy sweat. What if she got out of bed? He felt as exposed beneath the spindly legged bed as a coy hippopotamus trying to hide behind a sapling. For the first time in his life, he wished he were a smaller man. He thought his cramped limbs were sticking out in twenty directions. Any moment now his elephantine mother-in-law would let go a trumpeting shriek.

Holding his breath and interlocking his trembling fingers, Freddy prayed. The charpoy creaked again. Freddy let his breath out only when the volcano had resumed its rumble.

A little after, bobbing up for a quick reconnaissance, Freddy peeked over the edge of the bed. Jerbanoo lay to one side, and the enormous, white expanse of her hips and shoulders rose like a wall before his glance.

There it was! Long and thin as a snake, the black braid nestled in the trough between her back and the sagging mattress. Pathetic ends of hair, tied with a red ribbon, curled like patterns plastered to her blouse. Crouching, scissors poised, Freddy caught the ends and gingerly pried the hair clear of the cloth.

Freddy could have sworn there was no untoward touch from his fingers, no pressure at all on the roots of her hair, yet Jerbanoo suddenly shot up and, emitting a quack like a duck, swinging blindly, struck Freddy a mighty blow across his face. Freddy staggered back. Jerbanoo's jaws dropped open. Sleep-glazed eyes popping, she looked at Freddy in amazement.

From some mysterious reserve of his addled wits, Freddy brought forth an apologetic simper. He could have wept instead. Nursing his cheek with his left hand, he cautiously pumped the other in a gesture intended to reassure the astonished woman. "It's all right, it's all right, it's only me," he cooed, fearing Jerbanoo would scream.

But Jerbanoo had followed the quick movement of his hand when Freddy hid the scissors in the waistband of his pajamas. She didn't see what was in the hand—perhaps a thin-bladed knife intended for her throat . . . She was on the verge of screaming when the scissors slipped into the fork of Freddy's pajamas and, plummeting down the inside of his leg, tinkled to the floor.

Jerbanoo's mind whirled ominously. She recalled the slight pressure on her hair, and a glimmer of understanding dawned. The awful knowledge gripped her heart in terror. The man had been monkeying around with her hair and she knew what that meant! Bringing her plait forward, she scrutinized the ragged ends anxiously. A quiver of triumph danced through her.

"Now, now, don't go getting any silly notions into your head," warned Freddy hastily, once again pumping a conciliatory arm. "I only looked in to see if you were quite all right and . . ."

But before Freddy could explain the benevolent motives for his visit, Jerbanoo let off a curdled bellow that shook the house. The clerk and salesman came bounding up the stairs, and Putli came flying from the terrace.

In the ensuing chaos, Freddy tried desperately to clear himself.

"She was making a noise like a thunderstorm; how was I to know she was only snoring? I thought something was terribly wrong with her—her breath was choking her or something. I merely came to help, and look at the thanks I get. I might as well have left her to die unattended!"

He explained this in turn to Putli, the store attendants and a curious customer, while Jerbanoo brayed her woes at everyone collectively.

"Oh God, I cannot stand it any longer! Take me in Your arms and lift me up to Your heavenly abode!" she stormed, glaring at Freddy with accusing, malevolent eyes.

Putli shooed the customer and attendants back to the store, packed Freddy off to his room and, after a good deal of clucking and commiseration, succeeded in quieting her hysterical mother.

This episode brought Jerbanoo's halcyon reign to an end. Putli felt things had been allowed to drift too far. She had noticed Freddy's deteriorating and gloomy state for some time, but the scene in her mother's room brought home the magnitude of the change in him. His behavior had certainly not been normal and she was concerned for his sanity. Although she pretended not to credit Jerbanoo's version of the tale, Putli suspected that her husband, pushed beyond endurance, had staged the performance to scare her silly. For her husband's welfare, Putli prudently took the domestic reins into her hands. She put an end to Jerbanoo's extravagant gossip sessions and firmly controlled her ransacking of the store.

Jerbanoo padded about her former domain listlessly, sour-faced and as surly as a deposed monarch. Freddy had succeeded, if in nothing else, in terrorizing her. She threw nervous, little glances over her shoulders like someone who expected a bee to sting her. She took to wearing

her *mathabana* at all times, even during her afternoon siestas. Each milli-
meter of hair, combed back in a tight knot, was tucked away beneath
the square white kerchief as in a steel safe. She blackened her eyes and
pressed two large spots of soot on her temples to protect herself from the
envious and evil eye. Putli, who diligently blackened her children's eyes,
protested, "Mother, no one's going to evil-eye you at your age!"

"You'd be surprised," rejoined Jerbanoo, and, in full view of
Freddy, handed Putli a tattered bit of meat membrane dipped in tur-
meric, commanding, "Here, protect me from evil spells!"

Putli resignedly circled the membrane seven times over her
mother's head and flung it out of the window to the crows.

Freddy knew there was no hope for his mission. He wondered what
would have happened had he actually succeeded in snipping Jerbanoo's
hair, and the chilling result of his speculations made him thankful he
had not succeeded. As it was, she reserved for him a special code of conduct. He could not creep into her range of vision without inspiring the
most mournful, suspicious and unforgiving look in her reproachful eyes.
The moment he stepped in, she would waddle out of a room. When
compelled to tolerate his presence, as at mealtimes, Jerbanoo would sidle
in with shifty eyes and crinkled nose, as if she was in the most infectious
ward of a hospital.

"Do I smell like a dead rat?"

"No," said Putli, perplexed, sniffing Freddy's Johnson's-Baby-
Powdered armpit.

"Then why does the old woman wrinkle up her nose every time she
sees me?"

"Oh, come now," said poor little Putli, wondering when all this
nonsense would come to an end.

And it became natural to Freddy to say "old woman" and equally
natural to Putli to hear him say so, for Jerbanoo, unabashed by the usur-
pation of her empire, resiliently shifted gears and, within a matter of
months, adopted the role of the proverbial "little old lady."

This politic switchover fitted Jerbanoo's indolent nature like a
sweater. There she was: naïve, frail, unschooled in the ways of a changed
world. How helpless she became, how delicate. The slightest exertion

exhausted her. She was no longer able to do for herself or for others those little things she was used to. It suddenly broke her back to bathe the baby. She got dizzy spells if she so much as stepped into the smoky little kitchen, and palpitations threatened when she attempted to tidy her room or almirah. All she could do was spoon-feed the kiddies, shell peas and pry out tiny stones from rice and lentils.

Of course, when it suited her fanciful little heart, she would run up and down the stairs and shift heavy pieces of furniture. If someone noticed these bursts of energy or commended her vitality, she explained how she suffered later for these impulsive actions. After all, she was getting on to sixty—she had been a hard-working woman all her life and was not yet used to the frailty of her aged body.

Jerbanoo was no closer to sixty than any woman of forty-two. But very few in India keep track of their age. People are as young or as old as they wish, depending on their health and circumstance. There are gracious old grandmothers of thirty and virile young fathers of seventy. And if Jerbanoo chose to declare herself sixty, sixty she was! Jerbanoo could no longer bathe by herself, so a maid came for two hours every morning. The maid poured mugs of water over her rigid body, lifted the soap when it slipped and soaped those parts that Jerbanoo couldn't reach. She rubbed her dry with towels, powdered her and, supporting her by the arm, led her to roost on her charpoy. After putting things in order, the maid squatted before the bed and pressed Jerbanoo's plump, dangling legs. Jerbanoo spent a good part of the day at her roost on the charpoy, brooding like a philosophical fowl.

The part of an "old lady" provided a lot of subsidiary joys. Jerbanoo turned excessively religious. All at once she recalled the death anniversaries of her departed relatives and ordered costly masses for each of them. She prayed five times a day and each time, imitating the example of temple priests, plied their kitchen fire with sandalwood. Every morning and evening she trudged piously from room to room with the family fire altar, fragrant with lavish offerings of sandalwood and frankincense. Freddy supposed this was good for his family, but as far as he was concerned the good was countered by the damage to his pocket.

Another interesting offshoot of her chosen role was her

42

martyrdom. It surged up and bubbled to the surface. If Freddy so much as looked at Jerbanoo, she cowered visibly. If he looked at her censoriously, she added a visibly trembling hand to her cowering bosom, and if he dared reprimand her, she sank to the floor in a clumsy swoon.

Freddy, terrified lest she really damage herself with her clownish collapses, rarely spoke. However, once he risked making a suggestion or issuing a reprimand, Jerbanoo made a point of obeying him.

She carried her unforgiving obedience and martyred docility so far that even Putli was irritated.

And her trump card: Imminent Death! Age brought her closer to heaven, and the prospect of death opened exquisite new vistas to Jerbanoo's ingenious virtuosity. It was always, "Ah well, now that I'm to die soon—what does it matter?" or, "You can do as you wish when I'm dead—you'll all be rid of me soon enough. All I wish is a little peace and respect in the few years left me."

Freddy watched the dismal transformation with amazement. It was like the shifting of a burden from his left to his right shoulder.

That Jerbanoo had not forgiven him was obvious. She worried him with a new and dangerous subtlety. He was compelled to put on a show of concern and commiseration. Jerbanoo would talk of death and dismals until Freddy felt a superstitious dread creep up his spine and shroud his existence.

Within a month Freddy was looking back nostalgically upon bygone days. He definitely preferred the riotous, hedonistic hooligan of the pre-hair-snipping episode era to this lachrymose and jinxed monster.

Chapter 5

Parsees are a tiny community who leave their dead in open-roofed enclosures atop hills to be devoured by vultures. The British romanticized this bizarre graveyard with the title "Tower of Silence."

Just a word or two about the Tower: the marble floor slopes towards the center where there is a deep hollow. This receives the bones and blood. Underground ducts from the hollow lead to four deep wells outside the Tower. These wells are full of lime, charcoal and sulphur and provide an excellent filter.

The outer rim of the floor is made up of enough marble slabs to accommodate fifty male bodies, then comes accommodation for fifty females, and the innermost space, around the hollow, is for children. It takes the birds only minutes to strip the body of all flesh.

Now, the height of the Tower is precisely calculated. The vultures, taking off at full throttle, are only just able to clear the Tower wall. If they try to get away with anything held between their claws or beaks they invariably crash against the wall.

Understandably, only professional pallbearers are allowed to witness the gory spectacle inside the Tower.

At a time when arable land was too precious to be used as a graveyard, this system was both practical and hygienic. The custom originated in the rocky terrain of Persia. Since then the Parsees have moved to the Indian subcontinent and to cities like Bombay and Karachi. Bombay, where Parsees live in substantial numbers, boasts four Towers. Parsees who choose to settle in far-flung areas have to be content with mere burial.

When they first came to Lahore, Jerbanoo had been mildly troubled by the discovery that there was no Tower of Silence in the city. Now that her imagined age brought her so tragically close to death, this worry became an obsession. What would happen to her remains when she died? Surely they wouldn't allow her to be buried like a Muslim or a Christian. She told them once and for all, she absolutely refused to be shoved beneath mounds of maggot-ridden earth! By bringing her to Lahore, Putli and Freddy had damned her soul to an eternal barbecue in hell. She would not permit the sacred earth to be defiled by her remains; and though she was prepared to die for them, she would not perjure her soul for anyone! She would leave her grave, she promised Freddy, and, riddled with worms and weeds, walk to the nearest Tower!

The vision of his obese, worm-sprouting mother-in-law trekking cross-country presented so grotesque an image that Freddy turned green and vowed he'd transport her body a thousand miles to Karachi and deposit it in the Tower himself.

Freddy preferred any conversation to this odious topic, but Jerbanoo channelled the talk with astounding versatility and persistence.

"Do you remember how fond your father was of eggplant, Putli?" she might inquire innocently. "But how could you? I think you were only eight when he died. He was no beauty of course—but such a fine man!

"They deposited his remains at Sanjan. What a gorgeous Tower of Silence they have there. The beauty of the estate still swims before my eyes. Ah ha! Ah ha!" she smiled in remembered ecstasy. "Such an arbor of greenery. The entire hill belongs to the *Dungarwadi* . . . full of mango trees, eucalyptus and gul-mohur. It was like paradise—a fit setting for the Tower that rises like a granite jewel amongst the trees. Truly a foretaste of heaven! And the vultures, plump, handsome creatures, roosting like angels on every tree!"

Poor Freddy, by no stretch of imagination could he transform vultures into angels. He thought her comparison in poor taste, and the food turned to ashes in his mouth.

And he couldn't very well stage a walkout, for the deceased gentleman was rather special. Putli's face glowed with awe at any reference to her departed father, and Freddy could slight that hallowed name only at his peril.

"It was his final act of charity! Every Parsee is committed to feeding his last remains to the vultures. You may cheat them but not God! As my beloved husband Jehangirjee Chinimini said, 'Our Zarathusti faith is based on charity.'"

One evening, after the fish and egg sauce was served and Putli went to the kitchen to help dish out the next course, Freddy hastily delivered his long-suffering little piece. Matching Jerbanoo's somber tone and reverent mien he said, "I remember the time of your dear husband's death. My maternal aunt died a month later, and I went to Sanjan for her rites. Those vultures were so fat they could barely fly. One of the pallbearers told me that your beloved Jehangirjee Chinimini's right leg was still sticking out heavenward—uneaten a month after he was placed in the Tower! After all, there's a limit to how much those overfed birds can eat!"

Jerbanoo, who had had her fill of fish and did not much care for the okra that was to be served, stalked away from the table in a tearful huff.

"Where's Mother?" inquired Putli on her return.

"Guess she doesn't like okra," explained Freddy quietly.

Putli, knowing there was more to it than that, went to unearth the mystery after dessert was served and the leftovers safely locked away.

Freddy performed his toilet, changed into his night pajamas and awaited her return calmly. He wasn't unduly concerned. Putli permitted poor Freddy to blow his fuse once in a while.

Jerbanoo's old belligerence also erupted occasionally. She restrained herself before Freddy and Putli and vented her feelings on the servant boy and on the woman who cleaned out their primitive bathroom tray twice daily.

Chapter 6

It was the beginning of autumn, and Lahore started to smile again. It was still warm outside in the sun but pleasant indoors. October can have unpredictable days, and this particular Saturday was hot. By about one o'clock it became quite sultry. Jerbanoo decided to get the boy to work the fan strings while she had her siesta. The fan was a stiff, quilted stretch of cloth the length of her bed. It was affixed to the ceiling. The boy would squat on the floor and diligently pull the fan string down and up, down and up, until Jerbanoo dozed off. He then nodded at his monotonous post.

Jerbanoo toddled off to the kitchen to fetch the boy, and she caught him smoking a biri. The room was acrid with tobacco smoke. He was the same boy she had cuffed two years back for pinching her sweets.

Hauling him up by his ears, Jerbanoo slapped him and yelled for Putli to come and witness the crime. More excitement followed, and Freddy was called from the store to deal with the outrage.

He was shocked.

In a house fragrant with sandalwood and incense, the smell of tobacco is an abomination. Fire, chosen by the Prophet as the outward symbol of his faith, is venerated. It represents the Divine Spark in every man, a spark of the Divine Light. Fire, which has its source in primordial light, symbolizes not only His cosmic creation but also the spiritual nature of His Eternal Truth. Smoking, which is tantamount to defiling the holy symbol with spit, is strictly taboo—a sacrilegious sin. Theirs was a household in which candles were snuffed with a reverent pinch of the fingers. The cooking fire was never permitted to be extinguished: it was politely preserved in ashes at night and fanned alive each morning. To blow upon fire is vile. Priests tending the temple fires cover their mouths with cloth masks lest spittle pollute the *Atash*.

The shameful crime hurt everyone deeply and each thrashed the boy in turn. Later, to soothe his family's ruffled sentiments, Faredoon

47

suggested a drive in the colorfully varnished tonga that had replaced his bullock cart. Clip-clopping sedately over the Ravi Bridge, the horse pulled the two-wheeled carriage and its occupants into the countryside.

The evening was cool and welcome with the promise of winter. Flat fields of young, green wheat trembled daintily in a languid breeze, and, brushing past as they rode, the breeze brought to them the fragrance of rice and spices, of new beginnings in tender, sprouting things.

Freddy had not felt so tolerant of his mother-in-law in a long time. That afternoon they had been united in a cause and agreed upon principles. She wasn't such a miserable old so-and-so, he mused with whimsical magnanimity, when suddenly Jerbanoo exclaimed, "Look there," and excitedly pointed out a tree. The rotten top branches of the sheesham were covered with vultures.

Infected by her excitement, the children chattered and delightedly discovered cluster upon cluster of the brooding, ungainly birds.

Clucking her tongue sympathetically, Jerbanoo commented on their rather lean and mangy appearance. Warming to the theme, she shook her head sadly and said, "What a pity. What a shame. These poor birds are permitted to starve despite all the Parsees we have in Lahore."

Putli reasonably pointed out that one or two bodies a year could hardly be expected to fatten the multitude.

"Still," sighed Jerbanoo wagging her head, "all these vultures are going to waste—such a pity."

Freddy's skin became as prickly as an army blanket.

Jerbanoo eyed the vultures as if she were witnessing an inspiring sunset. She swiveled her head, ducking this way and that, squashing the children to look admiringly over the brim of the carriage.

Freddy desperately racked his memory for a suitable English quote.

"Water, water everywhere and not a drop to drink!" he cried at last, venting his agony. His family, so used to these alarming, erudite outbursts, turned to him for enlightenment.

Freddy stamped savagely on the warning-bell pedal by his feet. Then he stood up and, turning to Jerbanoo, once again shouted, "Water, water everywhere and not a drop to drink!"

"Uh?" asked Jerbanoo.

"Vultures, vultures everywhere and not a body to share!" he translated with an accompanying clamor of bells from the depressed pedal.

"I'll leave your remains on top of that hill there," he said, pointing out a small brown mound on the flat landscape and wishing feverishly to deposit her there right away.

"Leave my remains where you wish. At the first peck of the vultures the angels will rush forth to escort me safely across the bridge."

Faredoon felt positively sick. The old hag is getting more sinister, morbid and weird each day, he thought.

"Rush forth to push you over into hell more likely!" he said aloud.

"The man is stark, raving mad," whispered Jerbanoo, sliding closer to Putli. "He's getting dangerous. There's no telling what he might do. I tell you, you'd better watch out."

The drive back home was not a success.

Freddy's penchant for quoting scraps of English not only relieved his feelings, but it was a source of pride to him and his family. He memorized proverbs—not always quite accurately—and hauled them up like genies from a bottle.

How much store he set by these sayings can be judged by the hallowed position occupied by his book of "Famous English Proverbs." It stood on a shelf right above the prayer table, snug between the Bible and the Bhagavad-Gita. Other books on the shelf were a translation of the Holy Koran and Avesta (the holy book of the Parsees), the complete works of Shakespeare, Aesop's Fables, *Das Kapital*, and books representing the Sikh, Jain and Buddhist faiths.

Beneath the shelf, on the prayer table, burnt the holy lamp with a likeness of the Prophet Zarathustra stamped on its glass shade. The Prophet held aloft his finger to remind his followers of the One and Only God.

The table once again echoed his reverence for all faiths, a tradition dating back 2,500 years to the Persian kings Darius and Cyrus the Great, who not only encouraged religious tolerance but, having freed the Jews held captive by the Babylonians, rebuilt their Temple. The Torah, written at this time, testifies to the influence of Zoroastrianism on Judaism, and the influence of the ancient religion of the Parsees on other Semitic religions can be dated to this period. A Hindu scholar says that "the Gospel of Zarathustra, the *Gathas*, covered all the ground from the Rig-Veda to the Bhagavad-Gita, a period extending over 1,500 years at least, in the short span of a single generation . . . Zoroastrianism lies, thus, at the center of all the great religions of the world, Aryan and Semitic . . . "

Other scholars, European and American, say much the same thing; and it is little wonder that Faredoon Junglewalla's yearning heart discovered an affinity with all religious thought.

A picture of the Virgin Mary was framed with an inset of the four-armed, jet-haired goddess Laxmi. Buddha sat serenely between a sinuous statue of Sita, provocatively fixing her hair, and an upright cross supporting the crucified Christ. Photographs of Indian saints crowded the table. Then there was the sacred silverware: rose-water sprinkler, pyramid shaped *pigani* and anointing bowls. Fresh coconuts, joss sticks, flowers, figs, prayer beads and garlands of crystallized sugar completed the ensemble.

Freddy, who normally approached the prayer table once a day for a brief benediction, found himself attracted oftener as his woes increased.

The burden that had shifted to his left shoulder became unbearable. His business steadily diminished, for how could anything be expected to prosper in a household committed to death, disease and vultures? He was sure they were jinxed. Jerbanoo had got them to a point where even the children considered these topics commonplace and suitable for airy and animated chit-chat.

In desperation Freddy frequented once more the fortunetellers. He took his horoscope from one sage to the other for interpretation.

The birth of a Parsee infant is timed with the precision of an Olympic contest. Stopwatch in hand, anxious grandmothers or aunts note the exact second of delivery. This enables Hindu pandits to cast the horoscope with extreme exactitude. It is an enigmatic diagram of circles and symbols, quite beyond the scope of the layman, hence the need for interpretation.

Freddy learned of the devastating influence of Saturn on his stars. The worthies clucked sympathetically and told him to take heart. Saturn was on its way out and better days lay ahead. "Your life will blossom in unexpected ways," they told him. "Once you get started you'll never look back." Of all the predictions, Freddy was most taken by what a gypsy told him. Sitting on the pavement dealing out a strange deck of cards, the gypsy said, "A tall, slender charmer will come your way soon. The person will have a very fortunate influence on you and change the course of your life."

Who can blame Freddy for the dreams this prophecy sparked in his despondent heart? He envisaged a willowy angel with soft, black eyes and blush-brown lips. She came to him in a hundred ways from a hundred places. From the far-off mountains of Iran she came, and from the depths of the Indian Ocean. She was part of a chance encounter—dramatic with his heroism, and glamorous with her gratitude. Full of sympathy and tenderness, she touched their hearts—Freddy's, Putli's and the children's—but not Jerbanoo's. Oh no, that flinty heart was impervious to love.

She saw all, knew all, understood the whole complex and agonizing situation. Befriending him, her voice quivering with emotion, she told the world of Faredoon's worth and kindness, of his grueling and silently endured ordeals, of his courage in face of unmentionable tortures at the hands of his satanic, vicious, demented and hypocritical mother-in-law.

And in a final act of sacrifice, the lady of his dreams invariably throttled Jerbanoo with her bare hands and fled, heartbroken at the separation from Freddy, to her remote and mysterious habitat.

As was to be expected, the dark and charming stranger figured in a cornucopia of sexual fantasies. Her hands, like perfumed garlands, circled his neck . . . they wandered . . .

But the blackest cloud has a bit of silver, and when things were at their worst, a glib, dark and long-nosed insurance agent arrived from Karachi.

Mr. Dinshaw Adenwalla, long and lean, visited Lahore in December and changed the course of Faredoon Junglewalla's destiny. Unbeknownst to Freddy, the prophesied charmer had stepped into his life.

Visiting Parsees were rare. When they did steam into the city station, the community mood became festive. The Toddywallas, the Bankwallas, Chaiwallas, Bottliwallas and Junglewallas vied with each other in making the visitors welcome. They were wafted from home to home for breakfast, brunch, lunch, tea, drinks and dinner. The festivities ended with a gala farewell shindig in which the whole community participated. The morning after, fortified with enough roast chickens and hard-boiled eggs to feed the entire train, the hung-over wrecks were seen off at the station. Grandmas, grandpas, aunts, uncles and children waved until the little fluttering handkerchiefs faded from view.

Hospitality was accorded even to those Parsees who merely passed through the city. It did not matter if no one knew the travelers. As long as news spread, and it invariably did, that a Parsee was on a train, some family or other was sure to meet him. Bearing gifts of food and drink, they helped pass the time for the duration of the stop.

It is little wonder then that Mr. Adenwalla was welcomed with open arms and lavishly entertained.

This sleek, fast-talking insurance agent whirled ecstatic children through the air. He disarmed their strait-laced mammas with flattery and called their grandmothers "little girls." Jerbanoo hung about him like an overfed puppy, and Putli was transformed into a breathless, pink-cheeked hoyden. Well, not hoyden really—but at least she acquired a fetching animation. He treated the whole jing-bang assembly to mildly off-color stories and had the men roaring at smuttier ones.

Mr. Adenwalla distributed his charms impartially, paying as much attention to Mrs. Chaiwalla, who was almost bald, as he did to Mrs. Bankwalla, who was green-eyed and merry. He slapped shy Mr. Bottliwalla as heartily on the back as easygoing and witty Mr. Toddywalla. Everyone loved him. They talked and laughed, and Freddy, together with all the others, was swept off his feet.

Mr. Dinshaw Adenwalla, silver-tongued and loving, spent a full week in Lahore. He arrived on Sunday and left the following Sunday. They begged him to stay longer. But he just had to get back to his family for the New Year, you know. Ooh, what a shame. They'd let him off just this once if he'd promise to stay longer next time!

The Parsees, who celebrate every festival under the sun with all the attendant customs and spirit, understood his need to be united with his family over the New Year.

Saturday, the day before Mr. Adenwalla's departure from Lahore, was a very busy day. Man after man signed on the dotted line. Women signed with intent faces and labored pens. Jerbanoo preferred to give her thumb impression.

En masse, they flocked to the station to see Mr. Adenwalla off and he steamed away, energetically waving a white handkerchief at the end of his long, lean arm.

After the train left, the Parsees huddled in a tight little knot talking animatedly about Mr. Adenwalla. They attracted a barrage of curious glances as they drifted in a throng towards the exit. A bunch of bearded Sikhs with curving swords and the hockey sticks that showed off their prowess in World Cup matches stood by to gape. The Parsee women whom they ogled tied their heavy silk saris differently, with a triangular piece in front displaying broad, exquisitely embroidered borders. The knotted tassels of their *kustis* (the sacred lamb's wool thread that Parsee women wear around their waists) dangled as if pajama strings were tied at the back, and white *mathabana* kerchiefs peeked primly from beneath sari-covered heads. The men wore crisp pajamas, flowing white coats fastened with neat little bows, and flat turbans. They looked quite distinctive.

Freddy glanced at the Sikhs. The muscles in his jaw grew tight when he noticed the lewd direction of their eyes. He couldn't stand his women being stared at. For that matter, no one in India appreciates strangers looking at their women. He threw the Sikhs a fierce glower. The men averted their eyes and moved away, trailing their hockey sticks on the platform. A shorn Brahmin with a strand of hair looping from his crown shuffled by, saluting Mr. Bankwalla. What connections did a Brahmin priest have with a dancing instructor? asked his merry friends of Mr. Bankwalla. Mr. Bankwalla, enjoying the merriment, parried the question. A venerable Muslim, with a beard like a bib around his chin, passed with properly averted eyes. He was followed by a train of children and burqa-veiled women. Two of the children stayed to dance a jig and sing, "Parsee, Parsee, crow eaters! Parsee, Parsee, crow eaters!"

Jerbanoo took a threatening step forward and they scampered away. The huddled knot smiled with tolerant indulgence. This little ditty was a well-earned tribute to their notorious ability to talk cease-lessly at the top of their voices like an assembly of crows.

The platform was almost deserted by the time the merrymakers reluctantly dispersed.

The happy mood continued all the way home, and Freddy resumed his chair at the store till with a light heart.

He sat back, musing idly, and calculated the returns on his insur-ance policies. His lips parted in a dreamy smile and his fingertips drummed a merry tattoo. He'd be rich . . . in his old age perhaps . . . when he'd need money most. Aglow with a sense of security and achievement, he daydreamed.

After a while, when Harilal approached the table, Freddy sat up and guiltily wiped the smirk off his face. He leaned forward and, assuming a busy air, picked up a pencil. For want of something better, he noted down the figures of the premium he was committed to pay. He added the figures absently—and then it struck him! He felt as if, stepping on a safe-looking crust of ice, he had plunged into the chill depths of the Arctic Ocean. The full weight of his commitment to the glib stranger sank in. Astronomical figures reeled before his eyes, and crushing the paper, he buried his head in his arms.

"Anything wrong, sir?" asked Harilal anxiously. Freddy shook his head and the clerk walked away quietly.

No doubt Mr. Toddywalla, Mr. Chaiwalla, Mr. Bottliwalla and Mr. Bankwalla were in an identical state of shock.

Blinking back his tears, Freddy wondered what had come over him to make him behave so foolishly. His straitened finances were in no condition to meet even a fraction of the premium. The honey-tongued gentleman had talked him into a lot of trouble—they had unwittingly harbored a snake!

Freddy had insured everything insurable. His children, his wife and his mother-in-law, the last in consideration of the age she kept flaunting at them. The fellow had implied Freddy would reap rich harvests on her demise—he'd made it sound as if Jerbanoo's flight to heaven was just around the corner. "Hah!" he grunted bitterly. Freddy felt like kicking himself for his idiotic impulsiveness. The English doctor's pronouncement rang dismally in his ears. She might outlive him, for all he knew . . .

As for his store, there was not the remotest chance of its catching fire, being looted or caving in. Freddy plucked at his quivering, chalky lips and groaned.

Chapter 7

Freddy's cloud of despair thickened as the week progressed. He did not even notice Jerbanoo's presence. He allowed her to corner all the drumsticks and liver without comment. Putli grew alarmed. She tried to draw him out, but he snapped at her peevishly.

Freddy was already in debt, a condition both stigmatized and loathed by Parsees. Although he owed a very small sum, his secret debt assumed all the harrowing proportions of mendicancy, disgrace and ruin. He saw himself charged and jailed for insolvency, his property and possessions auctioned, his destitute family shuttled from one kindly home to the next . . .

And Jerbanoo didn't help any. Her dismal pronouncements weighted the scales of his imagined doom catastrophically. He was sure her malign intent and ill-starred tongue were at the root of all his misfortunes. Sinister forces were at work undermining all his efforts. She was the jinx. He once again felt hopelessly sunk in a quagmire, with one difference—this time he was further trapped by the weight of a mountain.

Freddy's misfortunes found an outlet. As always, Jerbanoo was the catalyst. Before supper she had piously trudged through the house with the sandalwood fire, wearing her *mathabana* open and austerely tucked behind her ears like an Egyptian head-dress. She had not bothered to knot it at the back when she sat down to dinner. Glancing at her, Freddy thought she looked like an Egyptian mummy.

This was a momentary diversion, and soon he lapsed into his world of premonitions and envisaged calamities. He picked at his food abstractedly and in silent gloom.

The Egyptian mummy, meanwhile, both gobbled her food and mouthed her words with enviable dexterity. Her monologue fell on deaf ears, for Freddy had stopped listening to her altogether. She disturbed him no more than the flies buzzing round their food. Putli busily juggled the dishes, poured water into glasses and served the children.

Jerbanoo's soliloquy droned on and on, but towards the end of fifteen minutes she said something that pierced right through Freddy's preoccupied stupor.

She had said, " . . . can you imagine how I feel? I may never see my sisters and brothers again! One by one they will die off and I won't ever again see their faces! What does he care? Look at him—chewing unconcernedly like a cow. Poor, dear innocent, he can't hear a word of what I say—does he care if I live or die?"

Live or die! Live or die! The words reverberated dizzily in Freddy's mind. And this vibration sparked the germ of an idea that had Freddy quaking in his chair. He turned pale. His legs beneath the table went limp. His hands trembled so violently that in desperation he flung his napkin on the table and, pretending to be offended by what Jerbanoo had said, marched stiff-necked from the room. He had never done this before. Jerbanoo had provoked him much worse without such a display. Putli and her mother exchanged bewildered glances and fell silent.

Freddy locked himself in his room and flung himself on his bed, trembling. The havoc wrought by the soundless detonation in his mind had shaken the foundations of his being. He felt sapped and dazed.

An hour later he opened the door to Putli's insistent knock. Retreating like a zombie to his bed, he covered his head with a pillow.

After a few anxious inquiries that met with granite silence, Putli fell asleep and Freddy spent a restless night quarreling with his conscience.

The die was cast.

The following months kept Freddy in excruciating mental turmoil. His mind seethed with weird ideas and searing doubts. His conscience alternately roared, jeered, applauded and scorned. He had never thought so hard, and his head throbbed with pain. He swallowed huge quantities of aspirin and wandered about with a handkerchief knotted in a tight band round his aching forehead. The idea produced on that fateful evening at the dinner table, that insidious little germ, grew and grew. Feeding on his misery, on his dire monetary circumstances and on his horror of Jerbanoo, it intoxicated his soul.

57

Try as he might, he could think of nothing else. He prayed, endeavoring to quiet the interminable discourses in his mind. But his relentless brain worked despite himself, sorting, combining and forcing his thoughts. He became an insomniac, defining principles and guidelines that were to serve him the rest of his life.

It did not take Freddy long to connect the gypsy's prophecy with the insurance agent's visit. If it was ordained that the man would favorably influence the course of his life, who was he to stand in the way of his own good fortune? The idea had come to him with a devastating impact, and God would take care of the rest.

In all, Freddy surmounted his mental crisis rather well. He had come to terms with his conscience, and there was nothing on his mind now but the implementation of his plans. After two grueling months of self-doubt, Freddy once again faced the world with confidence.

The plan was exquisite in its simplicity. He went over the details carefully, examined all the angles and, in a self-congratulatory frame of mind, marveled at his brain. As usual, a proverb wormed its way into his consciousness: "Two birds with one stone . . . kill two birds with one stone," it whispered sagely out of the pages of his thick books. With this omen, he knew he could not fail.

Chapter 8

Mr. Adenwalla had departed for Karachi in December, and by the end of February Freddy was ready for action. The plan was to be executed on Sunday, March 15th, 1901. He began an elaborate countdown.

Freddy had only twenty-one days in hand. The bulk of the action called for preparatory work, and Freddy inaugurated the scheme with a subtle change in his attitude towards Jerbanoo.

Day by day, unobtrusively and suavely, he evinced more interest in Jerbanoo's ailments and in her well-being. His polite glances now included her when he addressed his family. It was hard for him and embarrassing, since he had made a fine art of avoiding her eyes. Freddy proceeded so gradually, it was almost a week before Putli noticed that the relationship between her husband and her mother had somehow changed. It was more than she had hoped. Yet, she was troubled. Searching Freddy's face with her candid, knowing eyes, she sometimes caught a look which disturbed her. She wondered what he was up to.

One day, Freddy arrested his firstborn's headlong flight from the room. He rebuked her, saying: "Can't you see your grandmother is still talking to you? Hasn't anyone taught you to respect your elders? Go to her and hear what she has to say. Do as she tells you."

Putli, entering the room at that moment, was so astonished she stopped dead in her tracks.

Freddy turned his head and caught her eye unawares. The words, so noble in their content, were charged with a special foreboding when Putli saw the sly, vindictive and triumphant look on Freddy's face.

The next morning he told Putli, "Try and keep the kids quiet in the afternoon. They bother the old lady with their noise."

"Why this sudden concern?" she asked skeptically.

"Ah, well, she is an old woman after all. I feel sorry for her. I imagine she misses her relatives, don't you think?"

59

He spoke with such obvious sincerity that Putli lowered her probing eyes.

And again when Freddy said, "I'll be sending up a bottle of port wine. See that mother has some before lunch; she needs a tonic," Putli bowed her head in shame and buried all her misgivings. He had spoken with a shy reticence that touched the very core of her loving heart.

Anxious to make amends to her gentle spouse for having doubted him, Putli rushed to Jerbanoo the moment Freddy left.

"Faredoon is sending a bottle of port wine up to you," she declared breathlessly. "See how much he cares for you? It's only that he is too shy to show it. Some men are like that I suppose. Why, he is so concerned about you, he noticed you weren't looking well. And he feels—he *really* feels for you—that you have been parted from your dear ones. Oh dear, how much he cares for us all . . . I hadn't realized it before."

Jerbanoo eyed her daughter's enthusiasm with bleak, unmoved countenance. She could not bear to hear Putli praise that abominable man.

"He does seem to have changed a bit," she conceded cagily, "but let's see how long it lasts."

"Oh Mother! Give him a chance. He has his own way of showing his love for you. Try and overlook his little faults . . . won't you?"

Jerbanoo averted her eyes. "You cannot clap with one hand only," she intoned sagely. "If your husband is suddenly being nice to me, it is because I have made such an effort to please him. I have sacrificed so much for you all, stood so much for your sake. Maybe God at last sees fit to reward my labors."

"God is just. He will always reward those who work for Him," said her daughter, matching Jerbanoo's high-mindedness. And upon this pious note mother and daughter parted, the one to bathe and the other to cook.

Freddy, shrewdly aware of his limitations, did not risk his equilibrium too far. He was polite and convivial only when Jerbanoo was not in one of her more sour-faced and morbid moods. Then his face grew tight and he sometimes succeeded in stemming the tide of her moribund discourses with a stern glower.

Preparatory step two: Freddy's love of the outdoors became an obsessive passion.

He all at once discovered that his four children and Putli and Jerbanoo were too pale. Vowing, "I'm going to put some color into our cheeks," he threw open doors and windows, taught them breathing exercizes and at every opportunity, bundling them into the tonga, took them for long drives.

One Sunday Jerbanoo, drowsy with port wine, politely declined the airing. "I'll accompany you in the evenings, but I must have my afternoon rest. This is getting a bit too much for me. After all I am not as young as I once was, but it's good for you young people. You must get out in the fresh air. Carry on. Don't worry about me. I'll be all right on my own."

Putli protested kindly, "Come on, Mother, we won't be gone long. I'll massage your back afterwards."

But she didn't press when Freddy intervened with an understanding murmur, "It's all right, Mother. Do as you wish. We will go out together tomorrow evening."

Putli, who had protested because she felt Freddy might be offended by her mother's refusal, instructed the children to kiss their grandmother good-bye. Casting a diligent eye over the flat to see if everything was in order, she shooed the family, including the servant boy, down to the tonga.

Jerbanoo was quite alone in the flat.

Step three: In a matter of days the store was filled up with fresh stocks. Staid rows of coffee, honey, Italian olives and pickle jars gleamed on the glass-encased shelves. Rich oaken boxes of Havana cigars, liqueur chocolates, saffron and caviar were tiered decoratively in the show windows. The main bulk of space was taken up by biscuit tins, tea and other staple items. The floor to one corner was neatly stacked with small unopened crates.

Freddy's shop was at one corner of a long row of commercial establishments facing the main street. A metalled road ran along the front of the buildings, and between it and the main street was a cheery strip of grass and trees maintained by the municipality. Freddy's immediate neighbor ran a successful brokerage. Then there was a toy shop, a shoe shop, a sari shop, and so on down the line, each with its own proprietors visible through the entrance.

Around the corner, across a busy thoroughfare, was the huge square block of the General Market, the main meat, fowl and vegetable bazaar.

Freddy's immediate neighbor, the broker, called in one evening.

"What's going on?" he asked with a glad, meaningful smile.

"Oh, I just seem to be getting busier. Every day there is more and more work to be done."

"Business appears to have picked up?"

"Yes, a bit," said Freddy modestly.

"Good, good," the broker beamed.

Another time, the toy shop owner standing at the entrance to his shop salaamed as Freddy passed by.

"How's business these days?" he called.

"Seems to have taken a turn for the better. Got some new supply contracts—by the grace of God. A few new agencies also."

"Good. May God's grace always be with you," the toy shop owner called encouragingly after him.

All in turn congratulated Freddy on his apparent success.

A narrow, brick-paved alley ran along behind the store, between the commercial flats and the back of a long tenement. The downstairs landing opened directly into this alley. Horse carts brought goods to this entrance and cases were carried through the landing door to storerooms at the rear of the shop.

Then, one day, a mountainous load of stocks arrived at the front entrance. The bullock cart carrying the load was too wide for the back alley. Envious neighbors drifted closer to watch precious, choicest cognacs, liqueurs, whiskey and vintage wines being unloaded.

Supplies started arriving at night. Cart drivers shouted up from the alley, "Junglewalla sahib, Junglewalla sahib," until Freddy appeared at the dining room window overlooking the alley. Peering into the pitch-black alley, he answered, "Wait, I'll be down in a minute."

Taking a small bunch of keys hanging from a nail and borrowing the kitchen lantern, Freddy scurried down to open the landing door.

Neighbors on either side of the alley grew accustomed to these nocturnal disturbances. At such times, Freddy worked late into the night, carefully entering each item in his inventory book. He also spent long hours in his storeroom quietly prizing open packing cases and removing their contents. Exhausted by his labors Freddy crept up the stairs, reverently pinched out the wick of his lantern and fell into a deep, contented sleep beside his slumbering spouse.

On March 9th, Freddy hired a warehouse near the railway station, explaining to the apathetic landlord that he was expecting a very large shipment of goods from England. He paid three months' rent in advance.

That night again men called up from the alley after the household had gone to sleep. Freddy crept to Putli's bed and whispered, "I might be a little late getting back. A large consignment has arrived."

"All right," mumbled Putli sleepily.

Freddy went down the stairs quietly and opened the door. Night lay like a thick mattress over the alley. Only one window far down the line showed a dim, lamplit glow. He beckoned the men in. Large gunny bags of the sort used by a local brewery were piled all over the storeroom floor. Packing cases towering in the background were barely visible in the anemic sphere of light thrown by the lantern. Two men lifted a sack between them and, staggering beneath its weight, carried it to the landing door. Freddy gave a hand as they carefully hauled the sacks into the cart.

No one knew or cared that the cart, instead of delivering a consignment, was being loaded. Springing atop the freight, Freddy directed the *rehra* to his newly rented warehouse by the station. They made three trips that night and Freddy crawled into bed around two o'clock in the morning.

This activity was carried on for three nights, until the packing cases in the storeroom, stamped with expensive brand names, were quite empty.

Chapter 9

Only three days were left.

Freddy had been too busy to feel anxiety. But now that the preliminary work was done, he began counting the hours to the final moment. He was suddenly as tense as an overwound clock. Climbing wearily up the stairs on the third night of his clandestine forays, he sat down for a moment. Endeavoring to soothe his nerves, he systematically ticked off the things he had so far accomplished. His psychological assault on Jerbanoo had worked as well as could have been expected in the time allowed, and the tasks he had set himself regarding the store were satisfactorily concluded. Now only the books remained: the account books, ledgers and receipts. He would take everything over to his auditors on Saturday. They were due for checking anyway, and, most important, the books would be safe. He sat on the steps a full hour before tiptoeing to his room.

Although Freddy slept soundly, he got up feeling completely enervated. It was already past eight and Putli's string bed alongside his was empty. He peered at himself in the mirror, stroking his stubbly cheeks, and fancied his face showed telltale traces of guilt and tension. He splashed himself with cold water from a bucket until the shock numbed his nerves and revived his spirits. Refreshed and alert, he changed into a fresh pair of pajamas and a starched muslin coat wrap.

He called to Putli but there was no answer.

Emerging from the room, Freddy walked straight to the prayer table. Covering his head with a black skullcap, he softly chanted prayers. As he held a match to the wick of the holy lamp, Jerbanoo came into the dining room and he asked, "Where's Putli?"

"She's retired to the *other room.*"

"What! When?" he gasped.

"This morning. Didn't you know?"

Mutely he shook his head. Strength drained from his body. The match in his hand burnt through to his skin and he flung it away with a tiny sob. The room grew hazy and swam before his eyes. He saw Jerbanoo's bulk hover about the table as through a mist. Somehow managing to keep himself erect, he groped his way back to his room.

Freddy locked the door and sagged limply on the rumpled bed sheets. He stared at the wall before him. A lizard slithered across the whitewash and snapped up a moth. Crossing his hands tightly over his fluttering stomach he rocked back and forth and moaned, "Oh my God. Oh my God."

Translated into plain English, Jerbanoo had only said that Putli, being in one of her rare non-pregnant phases, had started her monthly cycle.

Now, you must wonder, why all this fuss about a healthy woman's very natural condition? It meant a postponement of Freddy's plans.

Unnerved as he was, it appeared to signal to him the end of everything. It was an unexpected hitch. No, he thought, striking his forehead in self-disgust, not a hitch but a careless oversight. Despite all his careful thinking, planning down to the minutest detail, he had overlooked this one obvious factor. His timing had misfired and he had only himself to blame. Putli would not be able to step out of the house for five days at least, starting from the 13th—and Sunday, the 15th of March would come and go forever.

"You damned fool, you stupid donkey!" he hissed bitterly, swearing at himself in English. Freddy had been coiled into a precise little ball of unfolding action and the unexpected caught him off balance. It wasn't until the next day that he once again regained his poise. The plans would have to be postponed for a week. But the agony of waiting a week seemed to Freddy a year of slow torture.

Putli retired to the *other room* for five days. It was a tiny windowless cubicle with an iron bedstead, an iron chair and a small steel table. The room opened directly onto the staircase landing opposite the kitchen.

Every Parsee household has its *other room*, specially reserved for women. Thither they are banished for the duration of their unholy state. Even the sun, moon and stars are defiled by her impure gaze, according to a superstition that has its source in primitive man's fear of blood.

Putli quite enjoyed her infrequent visits to the other room. It was the only chance she ever had to rest. And since this seclusion was religiously enforced, she was able to enjoy her idleness without guilt.

Putli spent her time crocheting or tatting. She left the room only to use the bathroom. Then she would loudly proclaim her intention and call, "I am coming. I want to pass urine," or, as the case might be, "I want to wash."

In either case, if Jerbanoo or Freddy were at the prayer table they anxiously shouted, "Wait!"

Hastily finishing their prayers, they scurried out of the room and called back.

"All right, you can come now."

Once the all-clear was sounded, Putli made a beeline for the bathroom, carefully shading her face with a shawl from the prayer table.

She was served meals in her cubicle. A tin plate and spoon, reserved for the occasion, were handed over by the servant boy. She knew she couldn't help herself to pickles or preserves for they would spoil at her touch. Flowers, too, were known to wilt when touched by women in her condition.

The family was permitted to speak to her through closed doors—in an emergency they could speak directly, provided they bathed from head to foot and purified themselves afterwards.

Freddy spent five harrowing days. Without Putli, the strain of being courteous to Jerbanoo was almost unbearable. However, his mind was functioning once again, and the extreme stage of depression passed. He set a new date for the target: Sunday, March 22nd. This would see the New Year through merrily at least. The New Year was on the 21st.

By the time Putli emerged from the *other room*, Freddy was convinced that the delay had been for the best. Given another seven days, the plans he had set in motion had time to jell. Yes, he reflected, the 15th might have been a trifle premature.

Freddy prudently told his auditors that the books were not quite ready and he would bring them the following Friday.

The 21st passed happily. They started the New Year with a visit to the Fire Temple, lunched with the Chaiwallas and, after a long drive, congregated at the Bankwallas for dinner.

Next morning, worn out by the excesses of the previous day, the family slept late. It was Sunday, the 22nd of March.

Chapter 10

Freddy alone was up early. He went down to the store and, working behind closed shutters, quickly packed two large cardboard cases with all the cigars, caviar and other costly items he could lay his hands on. Placing the cartons by the landing door downstairs, he went up and had a bath. Only then did he hear the household stir to life.

Now that the moment was upon him, Freddy was calm. And more than calm—in a mild state of elation. Just before lunch was served, he announced merrily:

"We are all going to the Toddywallas after the meal. They are expecting us for a game of cards. We'll take the boy along—he will keep an eye on the children."

The children were overjoyed. They loved playing with the Toddywalla brood.

"All right," assented Putli.

"I'm not coming," said Jerbanoo.

"But you like cards! Come on, you'll enjoy yourself," pleaded Putli.

"I'm too tired from yesterday. You all carry on. I'll catch up on my sleep."

"Oh, just this once, Mother! You can catch up on your sleep tomorrow. We're still in a holiday mood. Do come along."

Freddy, unperturbed by Putli's coaxing, refilled Jerbanoo's glass with port wine. He knew Jerbanoo would never accompany them.

Freddy had singled out Mr. Toddywalla for an invitation because he knew Jerbanoo did not get along with Soonamai, Mr. Toddywalla's mother-in-law. He did not know the exact cause of the enmity between them but made a shrewd guess.

At first the two mothers-in-law got along like a house on fire. Soonamai's relationship with her son-in-law was conspicuously cordial. Capitalizing on this to point out to Putli and Freddy how well

Mr. Toddywalla treated his mother-in-law, Jerbanoo had enjoyed many a glorious scene at the cost of Freddy's discomfiture. She had poured out her tales of woe to Soonamai, who had listened patiently and with sympathy.

Then Jerbanoo made the fatal mistake of according the entire credit for their halcyon relationship to Mr. Toddywalla. Soonamai could not bear it any longer. She subtly suggested that it was she who did so much for her son-in-law; in fact, the happy state of affairs had been brought about by her.

Jerbanoo did not take the hint.

Then Soonamai, angered by her dense, unfeeling friend's chatter, took to giving Jerbanoo pointed little tidbits of advice. It was their duty as women to win over their menfolk. Naturally, men were tired and irritable after a hard day's work, and it was the little things that mattered: like her fixing Mr. Toddywalla's breakfast with her own hands, pressing his shoulders of an evening, handing him his tea in his room, agreeing with his views. Jerbanoo ought to try a little tact . . . she might try to do those little things men liked so much . . . save choice bits of food for Faredoon, show him special deference, consider him before her daughter and herself in everything. After all, he was the breadwinner . . .

At last Jerbanoo realized what her friend was up to. She, Jerbanoo, was being blamed for not getting along with Freddy! She was astonished.

"You want me to dance to the tune of that infernal toad?"

"Well, why not? If it keeps everyone happy," said Soonamai.

"*You* may be a hypocrite and a toady—that is your lookout and your family's concern—but don't expect me to join you!" said the forthright and indomitable lady. The two women sat in glum silence, avoiding each other's eyes, until Freddy fetched Jerbanoo home. They had not spoken since.

As soon as the children had eaten, Putli bustled about getting them ready for the outing. Freddy generously poured more wine into Jerbanoo's glass. Jerbanoo was almost nodding at the table. Freddy glanced at his watch. It was ten past one.

"We're ready," announced Putli, ushering the children before her towards the staircase. "You'd better get to bed before you fall asleep right here," she told her mother.

"Yes, I feel I could sleep forever," agreed Jerbanoo.

"Now, now, that's no way to talk on an auspicious day," admonished Putli affectionately.

Freddy's hair prickled all the way from the base of his neck to his ankles. The damn woman was uncanny! He rubbed his hand on his spine to erase the hairy caterpillar and stood up.

"Carry on. I'll be down in a minute," he said to Putli, and Putli instructed the children to go down and wait in the tonga.

Freddy washed his hands and, tying neat bows on his coat, followed the family downstairs. At the landing he beckoned the servant boy and between them they hauled the two cartons into the front of the tonga.

"Got to make this delivery today," he explained.

The servant boy jumped onto the cases. Two of the youngest children sat in front next to their father. Putli, snugly holding the baby in her arms, sat at the back of the tonga with Hutoxi. The horse swished his tail, and a few bristles, escaping over the wooden dashboard, tickled the children in their faces. They squealed with delight. Freddy leaned over to smooth the tail down.

The wind stung fresh against their faces and brought them the fragrance of flowers blooming all over Lahore. Fifteen minutes later they arrived at the Toddywallas. The children ran to join their friends in the garden, and Mr. Toddywalla led the Junglewallas into his study. A group of friends were already gathered around the large, circular table playing cards. Freddy and Putli were greeted effusively. There was a lot of scraping and shifting as two more chairs were fitted into the expanded circle. Freddy seated Putli on a chair and standing behind her, lightly placing his hands on her shoulders, said, "I'll join you a little later. I've got to make an urgent delivery. The cases are lying in the tonga."

"Oh, come on now," said Mr. Toddywalla, taking Freddy by his arm and leading him to a chair. "Sit down. You can't work on Sunday. What will the padres at Saint Anthony's say if you do business on a Sabbath? They will throw the children out of school!"

There was a titter of laughter. Freddy affectionately loosened the grip of the other's arm and, slipping out of reach, waved, "I'll be back soon."

Freddy went straight to the rented warehouse and deposited the crates. Then he headed home. There was very little traffic on the streets. He parked the tonga in a lane two blocks from the back alley and walked to his own lane. The narrow alley was deserted. Putting a key in the lock he quickly opened the door and stepped inside. As far as he could make out no one had seen him.

Now everything would have to be done in split seconds. He had rehearsed these few moments so often that he found himself moving like a robot.

Freddy removed two gallon-cans of kerosene oil, a pair of rubber gloves and an old oilskin coat from a storage closet beneath the steps. Deftly rolling up his sleeves he put on the gloves and the long coat. Unscrewing the caps on the cans he poured some oil over the heap of old newspapers in the closet. One after the other he opened the storerooms and sprinkled oil on a few crates and gunny bags, counting on the cheap stock of spirits and rum to do the main work.

Stepping into the main storeroom, Freddy felt trapped by a sudden grip of sentimental sorrow. This would never do! Wrenching his mind back to his task, he doused the old desk and counter. He sprinkled oil on shelves, painfully averting his eyes from the discoloring labels on biscuit cans, tea and honey jars as the oil spread.

He led a trail from the desk, through the passage, to the closet.

He crept up the wooden steps, pouring a steady trickle of oil. When he reached the landing on top he listened. The house was absolutely quiet. The dining room door was closed. He held his breath. He thought he heard the faint vibration of Jerbanoo's snores coming through the rear of the house, behind the *other room*. Quickly, stealthily, he climbed down.

Freddy entered one of the musty, lightless storerooms. He struck a match and held it briefly to a sack reeking of oil. The room lit up in a flash. There was a great billow of smoke that stung Freddy's eyes. Stepping out quickly, he locked the door. Rushing at a frantic pace, his movements economical and precise, he repeated the performance in the other two storerooms and locked the doors. His eyes streaming, he sprinkled the remaining oil all over the floor and flung the empty cans into the closet. He tossed a lighted match in behind them and as the closet exploded in a blinding flare, Freddy shut the door and threw himself against it in a crazy, heart-pounding jolt of panic. He heard a subdued, hissing roar. Shedding his coat and gloves he fled to the landing. Composing himself, he stepped out into the alley and locked the door with trembling fingers.

A short while later he was dealing out a deck of cards and bluffing his way to a tidy little pile of chips.

But why did Freddy, obviously shrewd and farsighted, attempt something as commonplace as arson and murder in order to benefit through insurance? A timeworn scheme—but not in India in the year 1901 among a semistarved mass of superstitious people. Here a religiously conditioned, fatalistic people were unconditionally resigned to the ups and downs of life. They were an obedient and spiritually preoccupied race, used to being governed, slavishly subservient to their masters, to law, order and decree. In other words, an oriental people as yet quite unused to the ways of the West and its political, industrial and criminal practices.

Insurance in India was in its infancy. Its opportunities struck Freddy as brand-new, a creative thought without precedent. In its own way, Freddy's brainwave was as unique as the discovery of the wheel.

Chapter 11

Jerbanoo tossed on her charpoy. Noise disturbed her dreams. There was
a faraway thunder. Now she knew what it was: a buffalo, black, long-
horned and mean, galloping, galloping, galloping unseen towards her.
She knew it would find her. She ran in futile, fatalistic panic, with a
familiar sinking pain in the pit of her stomach. Down a narrow lane,
through a maze of rooms—but the thunder drew inexorably nearer.
With a loud crash, the buffalo broke through the door of the bare room
in which she was hiding. Horrible bloodthirsty eyes glared at her. Rushing at her with smoking nostrils, the enormous, demonic beast gored
her, pinning her against the wall.

Jerbanoo half awoke, fighting her way to consciousness. Still in the
throes of her nightmare, she opened frightened eyes. Her heart was
pounding. She lay in a numb stupor. Slowly her natural world shaped
itself around her. Noises intruded into her consciousness. What was the
shouting and yelling going on in the streets? An accident? Some religious procession? A queer haze clouded her vision. The ceiling appeared
to recede. Lying on her back she rubbed her eyes. The haze was still
there. She became aware of a ringing in her ears, a hoarse, crackling roar.

Again she sniffed and again, trying to make out the acrid stench.
Smoke, she thought, the room was full of smoke! That idiotic servant
boy had left something on the fire. She couldn't make out why Putli tolerated the scoundrel.

Swinging her legs laboriously over the edge of the charpoy, she sat
up. Her feet fumbled their way into a pair of slippers. A thick, yellow
wave of smoke floated up behind her. Jerbanoo turned her head. Smoke
was pouring in from a crack at the base of the door in a series of undulating waves. The door, separating her room from the *other room*, was
bolted from either side and never used. A rickety clothes stand stood
before it. Their dinner for the night was burned to cinders, she knew.
The smoke definitely came from the direction of the kitchen. Hastily

shuffling through the children's room and through the smoky hall, she opened the door to the dining room.

Smoke was pouring in black clouds through the open windows facing her, from the flaming landing to her left. She stood rooted in the door, eyes smarting, mouth agape. There was a splintering report and the landing door burst open, scattering its burning fragments throughout the room—on chairs, sideboard, tablecloth and bookshelf. A bloodred, glaring, scorching fire roared like a gigantic blowtorch into the room. An angry swirl of smoke choked her.

Jerbanoo slammed the doors shut, drew the bolt and, lifting her petticoat clear off her fleshy knees, ran through the rooms. The house vibrated in the wake of her heavy, flat-footed passage. Coughing, twisting and turning her way through the house, she ran into Putli's and Freddy's bedroom. Here there was only a thin film of smoke. Crashing through a door she burst out on to a semicircular balcony overhanging the pavement twenty feet below.

She had never seen so many people. A swarming, crawling mob of humanity swayed beneath her gaze. Clenching the wrought iron railing on the balcony, she screamed a piercing series of ghoulish shrieks.

In that eerie moment, the stunned throng turned their faces to the balcony. Then a clamorous roar rose from the crowd that had supposed the house to be empty. Grubby street urchins turned up beaming faces. Their favorite gods, mischievous and flamboyant, were treating them to an engrossing spectacle of a fat lady beautifully screaming her head off on a balcony.

Chapter 12

Bicycle wobbling dangerously, the clerk pedaled up the long pitted drive. Serious and harried-looking at the best of times, at that moment his swarthy face was pitiful to behold. Almost falling off the bicycle, he came to an abrupt stop in front of the long bougainvillea-covered veranda.

"Junglewalla sahib, Junglewalla sahib, Junglewalla sahib!" he shouted in sweating urgency.

Putli's alert eyes sought Freddy's across the card table.

"Junglewalla sahib, Junglewalla sahib!" called the voice.

"Damn it! Can't they let me alone even on a Sunday?" Freddy swore mildly. Reverting his attention to the cards he told the servant who was pouring tea, "Tell the fellow to wait."

"It's Harilal," said Putli, recognizing the clerk's voice. "I think you should find out what it is."

"Some mighty English gentleman must have run out of Scotch, what else! Why don't they worry another fellow? No, they must come to me. Well, I won't open the shop for anyone today."

Just then the clerk, followed by the servant, burst into the room.

"Sahib," he panted, his eyes distended, his limbs trembling, "the shop is on fire. You must come quickly."

Consternation.

Freddy leaped from the table, knocking his chair over. He caught the undersized man by the shoulders and shook him like a bottle of medicine. "Speak up man. Speak up!" he bellowed.

Putli tried to restrain her husband, murmuring, "Take it easy, please calm yourself, please calm yourself."

At the card table the players hastily gathered in their chips while the harried clerk was trying to wriggle out of Freddy's grip. "Leave me, sahib, please. Come on, let's get to the store. We must hurry. Oh Bhagwan, save us . . ."

Taking control of the situation, Mr. Toddywalla ordered his servant, "Bring Junglewalla sahib's tonga to the front. Quick, be quick."

The servant pattered barefoot across the veranda and, jumping off the edge, ran to the rear of the house. Freddy, clutching the pocket of his coat so the loose change in it wouldn't spill out, galloped after him. The clerk, Mr. Toddywalla, Mr. Gibbons, an Anglo-Indian Deputy Superintendent of Police, Mr. Azim Khan, a Mohammedan professor, and the other Parsee gentlemen ran in single file behind Freddy.

The horse, patiently quivering his hide and swishing his tail at the flies, was quickly untethered. Servants pulled the light carriage forward and between them the men harnessed the horse. Freddy leaped into his seat and the men piled in, four up front and three at the back. Slackening the reins and lightly touching the horse's flanks with his gold-threaded whip, Freddy drove around to the front of the house.

Putli ran down the veranda steps calling, "I'm coming with you. Wait for me!"

"You'd better stay here!" shouted Freddy.

"I'm coming. Mother, my mother," she screamed, running down the drive after them.

Freddy tugged at the reins, bringing the tonga to a halt. Stepping high, inadvertently showing a shapely bit of leg, Putli lithely hauled herself into the front of the carriage and unthinkingly sat down on Mr. Bottliwalla's lap. There was no other place for her. Mr. Bottliwalla, shy, pale, liquid-eyed, blushed and tried to keep his features matter-of-fact and bland. Freddy whipped the animal to a gallop and Mr. Bottliwalla, placing his hands on either side of Putli's slender waist, supported her gallantly.

Open frock coat flying, Freddy raced through the streets. When he took a turn to the main street, traffic suddenly increased. Cycles, carts and carriages filled the road. But all eyes in the tonga were riveted to the huge black mushroom of smoke far up in front.

Freddy overtook a bell-clanging fire engine composed of three bullock carts. The leading cart was jammed with smartly uniformed firemen and thick pipes fitted with gleaming brass nozzles. Behind it, two carts groaned beneath the weight of gargantuan water tanks.

Traffic grew dense. The men in the tonga sniffed anxiously at the smoky air. Tears rolled down Putli's face. Delicately shifting his weight, Mr. Bottliwalla dug into his pajama pockets and handed Putli a handkerchief.

A slight curve in the road brought the tonga abreast of the commercial buildings. They were still on the main road, separated from the row of shops by the strip of municipal lawn. The fire was at the General Market end, two furlongs up. A monstrous red glow could be glimpsed through the trees.

People swarmed up the road. Ragged, barefoot men leaned against bicycles, stood upon stalled carts and idly drifted between stationary carriages.

Holding his foot pressed on the bell pedal, Freddy fought through as far as he could. Then abandoning the tonga, they forced their way through the crowd.

Freddy, followed by Mr. Toddywalla, pushed diagonally through the dusty, trampled grass. The rest of their party was scattered by the multitude. Suddenly, looking up between a clearing in the trees, they had a clear view of the balcony—of Jerbanoo, crinkly-haired, petticoated, disheveled, flanked by two confused and harassed-looking firemen. Propped up against the wall was a narrow, toylike, steel ladder. As they watched, a jet of water from below drenched the three figures.

Almost simultaneously, out of the corner of his eye, Freddy spied a smooth-faced, naked-torsoed Hindu *Bania*. "Please God," he prayed, "Please God, don't let the man make a scene."

His stomach rumbled and he had an uncontrollable urge to evacuate his bowels.

Freddy had borrowed most of the money to finance his plans, to stock up his shop, from the *Bania*. The fat moneylender, watching his investment go up in smoke, was sure to kick up a row. All credibility, so painstakingly built up by Freddy regarding his recent turn of fortune, would stand shattered. Once again, out of the corner of his eye, he glanced at the man. The moneylender was looking placidly at the fire.

He didn't appear to be at all perturbed. Freddy decided to keep as far from him as possible. This definitely was not the moment to provoke the issue.

Meanwhile, a tense little drama was taking place on the balcony. A fireman climbed up the steel ladder and reaching over the balustrade placed a squat wooden stool on the balcony. He climbed down a few rungs and waited. Two firemen, holding Jerbanoo firmly beneath her short bodice sleeves, helped her climb on the stool. Gripping the ladder with one hand, Jerbanoo lifted a thick, clumsy leg over the railing and placed it gingerly on the rung. The men gave her support. Jerbanoo lifted her other leg. For a brief, breathless instant she stayed up, half-suspended over the railing, but the next instant she was down again, both legs planted squarely on the stool!

Slashing out at restraining arms, shouting, "Let go! Get away!" she jumped off. The men caught hold of her hands, trying to drag her back to the stool, but Jerbanoo strained back with all her weight. Touching her obdurate bottom to the steaming concrete, she glowered at them. Another merciful jet of water doused them and the men let go. Jerbanoo's seat bumped to the floor. Folding her arms defiantly across her chest, she remained seated. The scorched, panting men stared at her, their hands hanging by their sides.

The fireman on the ladder climbed down.

Chapter 13

The space in front of the burning house had been cordoned off. Policemen held the crowd back with a fence of lathi sticks. The edge of the clearing undulated with every pressure from the back. Tap tap, thump thump, went the policemen's batons bouncing off the skulls and bodies of those nearest the rim.

Inside the clearing, firemen rushed about with wet cloths wrapped round their faces. Two or three groups supported the hose that poured thin, sharp jets of water into the furnace. Helmeted men in the broker's office and the toy shop hacked at woodwork and flung out inflammable debris.

The fire chief, a middle-aged, sweating, red-faced Irishman, directed the operation. As the fireman stepped off the ladder, the Irishman walked up to him.

"What the hell's going on up there?"

"She refuses to climb down."

"What's biting her? Doesn't she know she'll be bloody roasted in fifteen minutes? Lucky for her the wind is blowing the other way."

"She's too scared to climb down. Besides, being a modest Indian lady, she doesn't want anyone to get a look up her petticoat."

"Bloody woman! What's to see up her petticoat anyway. A pair of cotton bloomers? We're running out of time. Throw her over your shoulders, spank her bottom and carry her down."

"You try, sir," came the laconic reply. The dispirited, soot-blackened fireman, who had just climbed down the ladder, walked away.

The sun hung red above the burning building. Freddy had lost Mr. Toddywalla and was cutting a quick passage for himself with the magic cry, "It's my house, let me through."

At the cordon a baton bounced off his thick, dark brown hair. Freddy gaped in disbelief as the policeman raised his baton a second time. "I'm the owner, I'm the owner!" he gasped, and the baton, swerving mid-course, landed on the awed head of the man holding his ground next to Freddy.

"Let me through," commanded Freddy, breaking past the policeman and running straight into the blaze. Three firemen ran after him and hauled the struggling, grief-stricken man to their chief. Freddy's hair was slightly singed and a few black-rimmed holes speckled his white garments.

"So, you're the owner . . . you poor son-of-a-bitch," said the Irishman sympathetically.

A heartrending cry hushed the throng.

"Oh, my mother! Oh, my mother!" screamed Putli, breaking through into the clearing.

The rapt crowd fell back a bit. Tears sprang into the eyes of women onlookers. They brushed their cheeks with crumpled sari ends.

The ground shook beneath their feet as Jerbanoo's agonized bellow rent the air.

"Oooh! Oooh, my child! Help me, my child!"

"Oh, what am I to do? But don't worry mother, don't worry!" cried Putli wringing her thin, hard-worked hands.

Freddy felt obliged to claim a slice of the action.

"Mother! Oh, our poor mother!" he shouted. Tears of compassion (brought on by the smoke) streamed from his eyes.

Freddy's neighbor, the broker, materialized from the crowd, and putting his arms round his stricken friend, he murmured, "Junglewalla sahib, pull yourself together . . . the gods will not abandon us." He persuaded Freddy to leave the clearing.

A drove of women, following their husbands in hired tongas, had arrived from Mr. Toddywalla's house.

One of them tore Putli away from her engrossing, though monotonous, conversation with her mother. Holding her affectionately to their bosoms in turn, they crooned, "She'll be all right—Oh you poor dear— they will get her down in no time. There, there now, don't you worry."

As soon as they spied Freddy, they swarmed around him and, depending on their ages, held him to their copious bosoms.

Seven shops and homes to the right of the fire had been evacuated. The fire was almost certain to engulf the broker's office and the toy shop. The fire chief had ordered the evacuation, assuring the shopkeepers it was just a precaution. They had the situation well in hand, he said.

Women and children who had been evacuated from their homes, sat on the grass in voluble little bunches, guarding possessions, while their men made various arrangements. The drove of ladies from Mr. Toddywalla's house descended upon each stricken family in turn, avidly ferreting details and offering solace. When did they first know of the fire? What did they do? The children must have been terrified, poor little things. What a shame! Oh dear! Is that so! Oh my goodness! they exclaimed as each new feature came to light. In turn, chattering excitedly, they related how Freddy and Putli had played cards all afternoon like innocent babies. They had been in such good spirits, poor dears. The irony of it. And they would never forget the way Freddy reacted. How he rattled the clerk who brought the news.

Eyes sparkling, they commiserated with each other in shrill, cooing voices.

Escaping them, Freddy drifted among the spectators. He saw the tenement fakir. The mystic held a rusty iron tripod above his head. His long black hair fell about his fierce eyes. Deferentially touching his fingers to his forehead, Freddy approached him.

"God be with you, my son!" roared the fakir, demoniacally probing Freddy's face. At that moment, Freddy wished the earth would crack open and swallow him. He bowed his singed brow and closed his lids. The fakir placed a grimy hand on the lowered head. Then, turning with characteristic abruptness, cutting a passage for himself with the disconcerting jingle of bells strapped to his bare ankles, he marched away. The measured jingle of his progress could be heard long after he had disappeared.

The sun dipped beneath the pall of smoke, leaving a pink afterglow. Freddy marveled at the unique color with a tinge of creative pride. The glow shone with a purple halo from the lingering sunset.

Freddy became aware of someone staring at him. Reluctantly

tearing his eyes from the sky, he focused them on a softly gleaming mass of brown flesh and came alert with a start. The black, rubberlike eyes of the moneylender bounced off his face.

"Panditjee!" squealed Freddy, squeezing the *Bania's* hands in both his and touching them to his forehead. "How good of you to come."

Then he waited, flinching, half-expectant, like a prisoner awaiting a dreaded sentence and wanting it over and done with. His stomach rumbled.

Panditjee released his hands and clasped Freddy to his plump bosom. He held him for a long, mutely sympathetic moment and stepped back.

"What a tragedy, my friend, what a tragedy," he sighed, his rubbery eyes inscrutable, his face full of the gentlest concern. "Oh dear, I see you've burned yourself. Let me fetch some excellent salve from my house. My wife has prepared it herself."

"Please don't trouble yourself, it's nothing really," demurred Freddy, adding, "When they say you know your friends in times of adversity, how right they are! You cannot imagine the comfort your solicitude gives me, my friend. By sharing my grief, you have made it bearable—you struck it in half. Oh, but look at this . . . all these years of work. I've toiled night and day like a mule, built up a little to live by— and all wiped away like that! Like that!" Freddy snapped his fingers to illustrate the point.

"What will become of us, I don't know; of my little children, of my poor mother-in-law. We are ruined! Ruined!" he cried, totally carried away by the spirit of his prose.

"Courage, my friend, courage. You are beloved of the gods— handsome, young and strong—you will easily make up for the loss. It won't take you long to establish the business again."

"With your prayers, with God's blessings, maybe," said Freddy. The explosive pressure on his bowels contorted his features and lent a pa- thetic catch to his voice. He sniffed and wiped his nose on his sleeve.

A look of genuine anxiety narrowed the moneylender's shrewd eyes. "You are a man of sense and discernment. I hope you have some insurance cover?" he inquired softly.

Freddy tried to conceal his astonishment.

"A bit," he nodded, neatly averting his eyes.

"Oh well," sighed the Pandit. "Even as a drowning man finds support on a bit of driftwood, the trifle will aid you. You may not believe it now—you are too overcome—but time, the great healer, and the strength of your prayers will get you back on your feet."

He made a small kissing noise with his mouth, the kind mothers make cajoling children. "Carry on, my friend. I will not delay you. You must be anxious to see to your mother-in-law. May the gods preserve the noble lady."

Lifting one end of the white dhoti that was tied up between his legs like an oversized diaper, the Pandit moved away. Freddy looked after him speculatively, a veiled, faraway look in the depths of his handsome eyes. Here was a man, supposedly ignorant and illiterate, a man who spoke no English beyond "yes" and "no" . . . It was amazing that the Pandit knew of insurance—that he had heard of it at all, let alone guessed that Freddy might have insured his store!

Chapter 14

"I don't care if we lose everything! Save my mother, save my mother!" cried Putli. She was hysterical. Neighboring women, forgetting their woes in the face of the impending calamity, struck their breasts and sobbed, "Hai Bhagwan! Hai Bhagwan!" and, "Hai Allah! Hai Allah!"

The fireman once again climbed the ladder. This time he held an enormous pulley basket of the kind used by housewives to haul up coal and potato sacks. He jumped onto the balcony. A strong pulley was attached to the railing and the thick rope tested. Holding the tangle of cords to one side, the fireman persuaded Jerbanoo to sit in the basket. Modestly holding her petticoat down, Jerbanoo sank into it. It was a tight fit and she leaned the small of her back against the rim. The cords, standing in a cone above her head, grew taut. She clutched the rim. Bending forward, the firemen carefully hoisted the load. About a foot off the floor, Jerbanoo suddenly screamed, straightened her legs and, slipping from the basket, stood up. A disappointed wail rose from the crowd. Tongues of fire darted up and licked the projecting balcony. The cement floor turned as hot as the bottom of a pan. The crowd roared, encouraging Jerbanoo to try again. They shouted an unintelligible jumble of suggestions.

Screaming, "Mother, Mother!" Freddy once again broke into the clearing.

"Oh my son! What am I to do? Tell me my son, what am I to do?" wailed Jerbanoo.

Rushing perilously close to the fire, spreading his arms and bracing his legs, Freddy shouted, "Jump into my arms, Mother! I will hold you. Jump into my arms! Come on, come on," he begged, his voice cracking with desperation. If only she'd jump, he prayed. If only she'd jump before a rescue was effected.

Jerbanoo looked at the hard, gleaming stretch of tarmac beneath her, and at the queer figure of her son-in-law with his eager upturned face. She nearly fainted.

"Jump! Come on, jump!" Freddy's voice begged hypnotically.

"Get that crazy bastard out of here!" screamed the Irishman.

By the scruff of his neck and the seat of his pajamas, a policeman dragged Freddy back.

Pale and stunned, Jerbanoo almost crashed through the door behind her.

The Irishman rushed about giving orders.

"Get the net. Go on, get the net!" he shouted.

"Where from?" asked the exhausted fireman whose destiny it was all evening to climb up and down the ladder.

"Where from!" exploded the chief, flinging his hands up in exasperation. "Every bloody fire department in Lahore is here, and you can't find a bloody net?"

"I'll get it, sir," volunteered another fireman, hurrying away.

"Come on. You come up with me," said the chief, buttonholing the weary mountaineer. "I'm getting that daft woman down even if I've to knock her out first."

As the determined Irishman scurried up the ladder, a group of firemen spread a net in the clearing.

It all happened quickly.

A curious huddled struggle took place on the balcony. For a brief moment it appeared as if the grim-faced Irishman was dancing a tango with the even grimmer and glowering lady. Jerbanoo's winged eyebrows almost disappeared in her hair. Then she disappeared altogether from view in a flaying tangle of arms and bent backs. A weird operatic aria rose into the sky, in which Jerbanoo's strident soprano distinctly outbid the Irishman's rich tenor.

And a moment later, with the dramatic timing of a prima donna, Jerbanoo made her grand appearance over the balustrade—swaying from the end of the rope in her basket!

One wail of a lost soul flying through space, and Jerbanoo's voice dried up. She remained as still as a statue of the Chinese Buddha swaying from a pendulum. The earth and its people down below heaved like the sea. Trees and buildings lunged forward. Jerbanoo squeezed her eyes shut. Her grip froze on the wickerwork.

Slowly, jerkily, the swaying basket, with its flaccid overflow of arms and legs, descended. The firemen, holding the net taut between them, looked up anxiously, ready in case the basket swerved out of control.

Ten feet from the net, one of the cords snapped. Losing her balance, Jerbanoo slipped from the basket, hanging on to the rope she'd had the sense to grasp. The crowd screamed once and hushed. The snap and roar of the fire came through in all its pristine majesty.

Scraping up her back, the wicker had caught in Jerbanoo's petticoat, hitching it up with the basket. Jerbanoo pivoted on the rope like a sporting trapeze artist in loose, homespun drawers. Air filled the knickers and the gathers tied round her waist with a tape. They expanded into smooth balloons. Seconds thereafter, a confused jumble of basket, rope and Jerbanoo sank into the net.

The firemen, her weight divided among them, staggered to the grass and deposited the bundle beneath a tree.

Sprawled on the net, Jerbanoo lay inert and winded. A man stepped forward with a jug of water. Someone hurried off to get salve for the burns. A glass of water was held to Jerbanoo's lifeless lips. Putli cradled her mother's head on her lap. She efficiently swabbed the blackened face and dusted singed bits of hair from Jerbanoo's head. Dusk was gathering rapidly.

Squatting by her feet, Freddy sobbed as if his heart was breaking.

"There, there, she'll come around soon . . . she's perfectly all right," soothed Mr. Toddywalla.

Jerbanoo's lids fluttered. She moaned deliriously, trying to sit up. Ten pairs of hands reached to help the mountainous heap. She glimpsed Freddy. A flicker of recognition sparked in her glazed eyes, and back she fell in a dead faint.

Soonamai put her ear to Jerbanoo's chest. "She's alive. Her heart's beating."

"Alive? Alive?" squawked Freddy feebly. He was convulsed by a fit of weeping, and some of his friends, supporting him tenderly, took him away.

"Poor fellow, it's been too much for him. He's so fond of Jerbanoo . . . " said Mr. Toddywalla to Mr. Bankwalla, Mr. Chaiwalla and Mr. Bottliwalla.

Mr. Gibbons, the Anglo-Indian Deputy Superintendent of Police, and the fire chief joined the group.

"She's OK now, so what the blazes is he crying for?" inquired the Irishman.

"He's in shock. He is overcome by the reverend lady's collapse. And then, look at what's left of his place," explained Mr. Bankwalla on Freddy's behalf.

"Blimey! You chaps really go for your mothers-in-law, don't you?" said the intrepid Irishman.

A month later he was awarded a medal for his gallant part in the rescue.

Night descended on the scene. Now that the old lady was out of the way, the firemen attacked the blaze in earnest. By nine o'clock the last flames were out. As predicted, the fire had not spread beyond the toy shop.

The crowd thinned. Evacuated families set about refurbishing their shops and homes. Everybody helped everybody. Mr. Toddywalla took the Junglewallas to his spacious home. Two rooms were quickly emptied of their occupants and allotted to the stricken family. Chicken curries and hot soups were served.

Chapter 15

Mr. Adenwalla arrived from Karachi. Five tongas loaded with Parsees went to receive him at the station. Docile and unobtrusive, Freddy hung behind the welcoming committee lined up on the platform holding garlands.

Mr. Adenwalla jumped to the platform. He clasped the men to his lean, loving chest and greeted the women with affectionate pats and smiles. Bristling with flowers, he tossed a little boy in the air and picked up a little girl. Carrying the girl, he cut through to Freddy.

Demure, deferential and becomingly forlorn, Freddy took Mr. Adenwalla's extended hand in both his hands. He didn't say a word.

Mr. Adenwalla was effusive. "Well, well, my friend, how good to see you. You've given us some anxious moments, you know, but you are looking well. I'm so glad. Everything all right? Sure, everything's all right!"

Mr. Adenwalla put his arm around Freddy and, chattering nonstop, led the procession to the tongas parked outside the station.

Five tonga-loads drove to Mr. Toddywalla's house. After a round of fizzy drinks for the children and beer for the adults, the men went into the sitting room cluttered with small tables, china figurines and any number of vases crammed with drooping red roses. After a few pleasantries they settled to the business that had brought Mr. Adenwalla to Lahore.

Mr. Adenwalla ran a hand over his sleek, oily hair and deft fingers over the pencil-thin moustache beneath his long, hooked nose.

"I am so glad to see you all again, but I wish it were in happier circumstances."

Everyone glanced at Freddy. In a room full of sofas he sat quietly in the only straight-backed chair.

Mr. Adenwalla cleared his throat. "Now my friends," he said, "I want you to remember I am your friend first and foremost, but I am also a representative of my company. I eat their salt. So now, if you will not take it amiss, I will talk to you as a company officer."

Understanding heads wagged their consent, and Mr. Adenwalla continued in a clipped, official voice that seemed to issue straight from his nose.

"Gentlemen, you are perhaps thinking, 'here is a house burned down and valuable stocks destroyed, but the man who insured it will write out a check for an enormous sum of money.'

"It is not as simple as that. First of all, I am not authorized to sign a check. If I were, naturally, there would be no problem. But the company is not going to fork out a huge amount of money just because they hear a house has been gutted."

The gentlemen listening to Mr. Adenwalla were taken aback. However, they quietly waited for the agent to lay all his cards on the table.

Mr. Adenwalla proceeded to do so.

"First of all, you have to establish—prove to my company—that the fire was accidental. Then they must find if the claim is truthfully calculated."

Freddy turned pale. His friends looked apprehensive.

"If it cannot be proved that the fire was accidental—if the company is not satisfied—then, of course, I cannot help you."

Mr. Chaiwalla, middle-aged and corpulent, drummed his fingers on his stomach. Studying the horizontal beams on the ceiling thoughtfully, he said, "What if the cause of the fire cannot be traced? Who knows what happened. What caught fire first? When? How? The whole place has been burned to cinders. After all, it was a provision store, all flammable stuff: rum, wine, kerosene, wood, paper."

"Well, I'm afraid the company will not clear the claim in that case."

"What do you mean?" demanded Mr. Toddywalla leaning forward. "Mr. Chaiwalla has just told you all the stuff in the store was flammable. I think that's proof enough. Any little thing could have sparked it."

"But that's no proof. Millions of stores are crammed with the same stuff, but how often do they catch fire?"

Mr. Toddywalla flung his arms out in exasperation and sank back in his sofa. He had a dark, oval face decorated with bell-bottom sideburns and a bristling moustache.

"Then why the hell were you so eager to get us all insured?" he cried. "Why pay all the premiums and whatnot, if in the time of our need we have to prove sisterf—ing this and motherf—ing that? It doesn't look like your company is going to be satisfied with truth and facts and the word of a gentleman! They just want some damned excuse to wriggle out of their commitment. If I might speak as plainly as you, it is nothing but a swindle. I don't think any of us need your damned insurance!"

Mr. Adenwalla's straight, slick moustache agitated pathetically. "I don't see the need for this ill-feeling. Please hear me out first," he begged.

Mr. Toddywalla had scored a direct hit. What if they decided to withdraw their patronage? They were valuable clients: generous and prompt. Besides, two new families had arrived in Lahore, the Coopers and the Paymasters, and both were represented in the sitting room. Mr. Adenwalla had his eye on Mr. Paymaster in particular. Mr. Paymaster was an engine driver, a profession invested with much glamour and status. Through Mr. Paymaster's influence, Mr. Adenwalla hoped to acquire a heap of railway insurance.

"Now, please," he said in his most suave and persuasive manner, "try to look at this from my company's point of view. I will tell you something which may surprise you. Insurance is fairly new here, but it is not uncommon in Britain for some rascal to set fire to his business to present a large claim. It has been proved over and over. And the company is worried. Which is why it must have proof. It is the way insurance companies work. I am not saying the company will not honor its claim. Of course it will if the claim is legitimate, and I have been sent here to investigate. I am putting it to you straight because I don't want to waste your time or mine."

But nobody understood anything. Mr. Adenwalla had put it to them much too straight, straighter than behooved a well-bred Parsee.

"Do you mean to imply that the fire was deliberate?" said

Mr. Bankwalla sternly. "Are you accusing our friend Mr. Faredoon Junglewalla, here, of purposely setting a torch to his own house? Do you know that his mother-in-law was in the house? The poor woman was charred, bruised and half-dead. Do you mean to say he willfully and purposefully set fire to his house, knowing his own mother-in-law was in there? Do you mean to call my friend a murderer also?"

"For God's sake!" exclaimed Mr. Adenwalla. "I am not saying or denying anything, but as a representative of my company, I am responsible. I have to answer to them."

"Mind your tongue," warned Mr. Toddywalla, thrusting his pugnacious whiskers to the forefront. "We are not going to sit around having our friend insulted. You have accused him of murder. That's going too far . . . too far."

A grandfather clock ticked solemnly in the sudden quiet. The scent of the red spring roses was stifling. Freddy's lids were closed. He sat on his straight-backed chair, the incarnation of exploited innocence, meekly allowing his friends to champion his cause.

"What rot! Who's saying anything about murder?" protested Mr. Adenwalla. His sharp eyes raked Freddy briefly. It suddenly occurred to him that, but for the grace of God, there might have been two claims to settle. He offered a silent prayer for the absent mother-in-law's longevity.

"Now, please, let's not get carried away. Look, I never said you will not get the claim—there's no question of it. But there are certain formalities to be gone through. They are just formalities, but of a legal kind. You understand? Legalities."

Freddy felt the time had come for him to speak up, to give the "charming stranger" of the gypsy prophesy a little assistance. He sat forward purposefully, and Mr. Bankwalla, who had been about to speak, checked himself.

All heads turned to Freddy.

"I understand your anxiety on behalf of your company. You are quite right. Please proceed as you think best and do everything as legally and properly as possible."

"Yes, you're quite right, quite right," said the grateful insurance agent. "We must do everything properly. Now, I'm afraid, there has got to be a proper police inquiry. It's part of the law. Even if my firm wants to help, they cannot do so without police clearance.

"Next, we must go through the books. Each entry will have to be investigated, you understand? It is my duty, and it is to your advantage. But I must warn you—I suppose the books were destroyed in the fire? In that case the company will settle on what it considers reasonable, and you can be sure—"

"They are not burned," said Freddy quietly. "They were due for checking and I gave them to my auditors just before the fire. You are welcome to see them anytime—and also talk to my suppliers and agents."

"Oh, I see," said Mr. Adenwalla lamely. In all the long, intimidating session of the evening he had not felt quite so shaken. "I see," he repeated. "It is interesting—providential, I should say—that you thought to hand the books over to your auditors just before the fire."

"Providential, yes, providential. You see, my friend, my intent and my conscience are clean. God has seen fit to protect me. I have always been content with my lot. I have never envied anyone—nor have I coveted my neighbor's wife," said Freddy modestly, quoting the commandment to pointless but good effect.

A servant entered the room. Leaning over Mr. Toddywalla, a duster thrown over his shoulder, he whispered, "Gibbons sahib is here."

"Ask him in, ask him in!" exclaimed Mr. Toddywalla heartily and, surging to his feet, went to receive his guest.

Mr. Gibbons, who often dropped in of an evening for a drink, was warmly shaken by the hand. "My friend, I'd just been thinking of you!" said Mr. Toddywalla, leading him into the room.

Mr. Gibbons was introduced to Mr. Adenwalla.

Freddy rose from his chair and embraced the policeman.

Mr. Adenwalla, pale as a sheet, knew he was worsted.

Fortifying himself with a long draught of beer, graciously accepting defeat, he set about entertaining the company with some of his engaging stories.

Three days later Mr. Adenwalla received a letter from the Punjab

Police Department. The very next day he left for Karachi.

The letter read:

Dear Sirs,

In accordance with the inquiry registered by your Insurance Company, we have investigated the fire at the Provision Store and house belonging to Mr. Faredoon Junglewalla.

We are satisfied that the fire was entirely accidental. I will quote from the report presented by our investigating officer, Mr. R. Gibbons:

> There is no doubt that the store caught fire when a bottle of fizzy soda exploded and knocked over a lamp that always burned on the counter nearby. Running along the oil spilled from the lamp, the fire quickly engulfed the store and storerooms.
>
> Like all stores, the shop was full of flammable stuff. Furthermore I have investigated Mr. Faredoon Junglewalla's character thoroughly. He is known to be an upstanding man of integrity and virtuous habits. There is nothing in his past to indicate that he would stoop to so base a felony as arson.

We trust the matter is closed to your satisfaction.

From the office of the Inspector General,

Punjab Police.

Mr. Faredoon Junglewalla received a sizeable check.

Chapter 16

Following the fire, Jerbanoo ceased to be a problem. Freddy, electrified by a series of successful enterprises, had little time to brood on her irksome ways.

For her part, Jerbanoo was subdued beyond recognition. In Freddy's presence she was as quiet and unobtrusive as a fat little mouse. Not that she was convivial or full of kindly forgiveness. Not at all. She hated his guts. But her terror of his unprincipled methods outdid her loathing. Her terror was such that she had not let out even a peep of her suspicions. Not even to Putli. She was convinced of Freddy's true intent but shrewd enough to know that no one would believe her.

But her lot was not altogether pitiful. Her dramatic rescue from the jaws of death had given her glamorous renown, and she was sought after and made much of by her friends and her daughter.

Freddy, though disappointed that the stone he had so carefully aimed had secured only one bird, was nevertheless content. Years later, when Jerbanoo gradually returned to her former ways, he found refuge in the comforting axiom, "What cannot be cured must be endured."

Putli, now that things had worked out so well, contentedly went on producing her babies, four daughters and three sons in all, of whom Behram, Billy for short, was the second to last.

Behram Junglewalla was an ugly child. His mother, looking at the dark, large-nosed, squalling infant, remarked, "I can hardly believe he is mine. He is so different from the others. Look at the funny amount of hair he has!"

"What does it matter? Haven't you produced enough good-looking brats? Don't worry, by the time he grows up he'll look all right," consoled Freddy.

But Behram Junglewalla was one of fortune's favorites! Years went by. Freddy expanded his business. He hobnobbed with Maharajas and Englishmen. As opportunity beckoned, he dabbled in a variety of trades, deftly "buttering and marmalading" the Colonel Williamses of his acquaintance and obliging others like Mr. Allen with Scotch and dancing girls.

Hutoxi was married off, and then Ruby. Jerbanoo, succinctly cramming all the wisdom of her short married life into two incomparable strictures, advised each on her nuptial night.

"Now don't you go around stripping yourselves naked and lying flat on your backs like plucked chickens. Mark my words, you will lose your husbands that way. Show as little as you can, as slowly as you can. If you remove your drawers, leave your blouse on, and if you remove your blouse, never remove your drawers! That will intrigue him all his life and keep his interest and virility intact.

"And remember, always keep yourself busy with housework. Stop reading storybooks—they have been invented by the demons of indolence. Idleness will make you brood. As for me, I was never idle. Even when your grandfather was making love I busied myself removing blackheads from his neck and shoulders."

How far the blushing brides followed these injunctions, I cannot say.

Freddy merely remarked, "Poor Mr. Chinimini. He didn't have much to live for, did he?"

Chapter 17

"And from then on, I never looked back," said Faredoon, coming to the end of a story. His enraptured audience continued to look at him. Faredoon was comfortably ensconced in his cane-backed armchair, his legs propped up in a v on the sliding arm rests.

"What year was it?" asked Ardishir Cooper, breaking the spell. The slight young man was Faredoon's son-in-law. He had been married four years. Hutoxi sat primly on the sofa with her husband.

"The fire took place in 1901," said Freddy. "I thought my world had come to an end. I cried, literally sobbed, like a baby. You can ask your father; he'll tell you. Of course, I did not know then how things would turn out—I didn't know it was a blessing in disguise.

"I used to pray daily, asking God's blessing, and when the fire struck, I struck my forehead and cried, 'o God, why have You done this to me?' But God works in mysterious ways. He never forgets those who remember Him."

"What became of the adjoining shops?" asked Soli. He and his friend, Jimmy Paymaster, were sitting cross-legged on the Persian carpet. Billy, fourteen years old, undersized and scrawny, sat next to them, leaning against the sofa.

"They repaired and painted their premises like I did. They'd had time to remove everything. There was very little damage to the toy shop in any case. The broker was quite well-off. He's moved to Mall Road now—he's doing all right."

"When did we start the store in Amritsar?" asked Soli. Faredoon smiled at his son. It was a special smile, proud and adoring. People likened Soli to him, but he felt his son was better-looking than he'd ever been. Pausing for a moment, he allowed his eyes to feast on the long, golden limbs, on the intelligent, red-lipped face. Soli was nineteen.

Billy felt a lump rise in his throat. He swallowed silently and fixed his hurt, bespectacled eyes on the soles of Faredoon's bare feet. He watched a blue vein throb in the ankle. His father never looked at any of them the way he looked at Soli.

Billy glanced at Yazdi. Lounging against the wall, his thin, endless legs stretched out before him, Yazdi was, as usual, lost in the world of his poetic fantasies.

"Now, let me see," said Freddy. "I think the store in Amritsar was opened a year or two after the fire. Oh yes, I remember now, it was the same year Billy was born—1903. A few years later I opened up in Peshawar. The one in Delhi was established only a couple of years back."

Faredoon liked to explain his business to Soli. The boy was interested and eager to learn. Being the eldest male, he would inherit everything some day, and Faredoon was happy that it should be so.

Ten-year-old Katy, their youngest child, suddenly chirped up, "Oh, Papa, please tell us about grandmother and the basket. Please!"

Faredoon ran a hand over his thick, graying hair.

"Ask your grandmother to tell you sometime. She loves relating that story."

Jerbanoo appeared in the door, filling it completely. "Dinner's ready," she announced.

Freddy made no move to get up. Reclining majestically, his legs propped up, he gazed at her. Her arms, bulging through tight sleeves, were like barrels. She stood sturdy and defiant in the short, thick column of her sari. Jerbanoo's face sagged a bit at the jowls, but her skin remained smooth and taut. Her eyebrows were as striking as ever.

She raised them. "Come on, come on. It can't wait all evening. The food will get cold while you lie with your legs up in the air."

Freddy lowered his feet good-naturedly and slipped them into his slippers.

"We were just talking of you when you came. That means you'll live very long, doesn't it?" cried Katy.

Freddy rose from the armchair. The others stood up, smoothing out their clothes.

"Yes, yes, your grandmother will live forever. She hasn't half the gray hair I have," he said.

"That's right. And we are none of us growing any younger either," snapped Jerbanoo, her shrewish eyes mean with envy. For Freddy, if anything, looked handsomer than in his youth. He would grow into a gracious and kindly looking old man, and no one would know how diabolically wily, unscrupulous and false he really was.

Chapter 18

At the first glimmer of dawn, Freddy sat up. He looked at the row of charpoys, humped and shadowy in the faint light. His family was sound asleep. It was a hot night in June, and they slept on the roof. There were still a few stars in the sky. Putli's charpoy was next to his, then the charpoys of the five children and, last of all, Jerbanoo's.

Each summer they slept on the roof. And each year the row grows shorter, thought Freddy with a painful twinge of loss and loneliness. Hutoxi and Ruby were married. One by one the others would get married . . .

Jerbanoo stirred at the other end, and the strings of her charpoy creaked rebelliously.

Freddy knew she also had spent a restless night. It was incredibly hot and incredibly dry. The terrace still radiated the heat absorbed during the day. Twice that night Freddy had sprinkled water on his bed sheets. He had heard Jerbanoo splash water over herself in the washroom and, following her example, had drenched himself and returned dripping to his damp charpoy. When he drifted off to sleep, he knew the hot air would suck up the moisture in minutes.

Freddy stood up. It was time for dawn prayers. Stepping quietly, he crossed over to the staircase and went down to the kitchen. He was thirsty. Summer thirsty. It was the kind of thirst quenched only when the weather cooled.

Freddy dipped his silver glass into the brown earthenware water jar. The round-bellied container stood on a stool. The servant filled the *matka* at night, and by morning the water was miraculously cold. The porous texture of the fragile clay worked as a refrigerating agent.

The glass felt deliciously cool in Freddy's hand. He took a long, eager swallow and was almost through by the time he realized the water tasted of salt. He took a small sip and swished the water intently between his teeth . . . Yes, it was definitely brackish.

Freddy rinsed the glass, and the water again tasted salty. He stood a moment, wondering. Then he lifted the jug and drained the water into the sink. He filled it fresh from the tap and replaced it on the stool. It would be hours before the water cooled again.

"I've never known such heat," remarked Putli at breakfast. "The water in the *matka* is still lukewarm."

The next morning Freddy awoke with a curious sense of anticipation. He knew he had to do something . . . and he remembered. Slipping down quietly, he dipped the glass into the jar and took a cautious sip. No doubt about it! The water was faintly brackish. He wondered if he should leave it be. At least the water was cold, and the taste of salt was barely perceptible . . . No, he had better change it.

Why did it always have to be summer? he said to himself fretfully. Couldn't they choose a cooler time of year to broadcast their passions? He could be mistaken though. The water might be brackish at its source. He had better wait and be sure.

For three days the bewildered family drank lukewarm water.

"Everybody else says their *matkas* are quite all right. What's wrong with ours?" demanded Putli.

Freddy sipped his tea tranquilly.

"Must be that Krishan Ram! He probably forgets to fill the *matka* at night and does it early in the morning. I'll find out soon enough." Putli rushed into the kitchen to cross-examine the unfortunate and mystified servant.

On the fourth morning Freddy sipped the water. It was pure, cool and delicious to his taste. He smacked his lips significantly.

Freddy lingered over his tea. The children had gone. The servant cleared the breakfast dishes and Putli got up to follow him to the kitchen.

"Just a minute," said Freddy, calling Putli back. He motioned to her to sit down.

"What was the water like today?" he asked.

"All right, of course! Didn't you hear me give that clod a good scolding yesterday? If he'd do one thing by himself, but no! I've to be at him all the time. I don't know—"

"It is not his fault," Faredoon interposed gently. "I changed the water every morning myself."

"You? Why?" gasped Putli.

"Because it had salt in it. For three mornings it was brackish and today it was quite all right."

He looked at Putli as the words sank in. His heavy-lidded, brown eyes smiled.

"Oh," she said. Putli's features softened. "I wonder which one it is?"

"Whoever it is, I wish they wouldn't go about falling in love in summer. Can't they choose autumn, winter, spring? I can't stand luke-warm water in this heat."

"Yes," agreed Putli absently. "It's the heat I suppose—they have so little else to do . . . I wonder who it is though," she mused aloud.

"Either Soli or Yasmin. Katy and Billy are too young and so is Yazdi—he's only sixteen, isn't he?"

"Fifteen," corrected Putli.

"Well, as I said, that leaves only Soli and Yasmin. I've seen Soli eye the Toddywalla girl once or twice . . . Anyway, I'll tackle him. You tackle Yasmin."

Putli nodded. "Yes. But please be tactful. You know how shy they are at this age."

"Don't you worry," replied Freddy, dredging the last drops of syrupy tea from his cup.

After school the children returned, and Freddy summoned Soli to his office. "I think there is some shortage in the stock—I want you to check the spirits store," he said, handing Soli a bunch of keys.

Soli was used to this. Taking the stock register from the counter drawer, he went into the storeroom.

He loved working in the cellar. The dank, twilight air was saturated with the mellow odors of pinewood packing cases, of jute sacks and packing straw. Commingling with these was the heady, exotic scent of wine and liqueurs seeping through damaged bottles. He counted the cases, meticulously ticking them off against the columns in the stock book.

He had been at it ten minutes when Freddy came in.

"I'll help you," he said.

Father and son were closeted in the cellar for two hours.

After dinner Freddy asked Soli if he would like to come along for a stroll.

"I'll come with you, Papa," volunteered Yazdi promptly.

"I didn't ask you, did I? You had better finish your homework first." Freddy's tone was kind but firm.

When they returned from their walk, Putli was in her room.

"What news?" she asked, sitting up as Freddy came in to change.

"None yet. I gave him every blessed opportunity to be alone with me. Two hours in the storeroom, then the walk, but not a peep from him. I wonder if it is he."

"Must be—because it's not Yasmin."

"You're sure?"

"Well, I couldn't very well ask her directly, but I mentioned the salty taste in the water, and she was surprised. I'm sure it's not her. Did you say anything—I mean, ask Soli something that would lead up to it?"

"No. But he had all the time in the world to have a go at it if he wanted to."

"There! You see! That's not enough. Soli may look bold, but he is bashful. Quite like you really, come to think of it. You must try and get him to talk gradually, tactfully. Just a few leading questions. Tell him about us—you know what I mean . . ."

"I'll do that tomorrow," agreed Freddy.

Putli picked up the lamp and they climbed up. Electricity had been introduced to Lahore, but the terrace and the steps leading up had not been wired as yet.

The children and Jerbanoo were asleep. Freddy leaned over the bed. He lowered the wick of the lamp, removed the chimney and pinched out the flame.

The night was humid. It meant the monsoons would break earlier than expected.

"I think the rains will come soon," he whispered.

"Shush! The children will awaken," hissed Putli, putting a stop to his talk.

Freddy looked at the sky. The stars appeared to have receded. There were thin, opaque clouds hazing them. "I'm right," he thought. "It will rain soon."

Simultaneously, he tried to recall how it felt to be nineteen. It suddenly appeared to be as far back as the stars.

Chapter 19

Before dinner they gathered around Faredoon in the sitting room. They knew by the way he reclined in his armchair that he was in a fine mood to talk. The electric fan whirred jerkily above them and displaced the still air enough to allow them to breathe. The open windows were screened by gauze netting to keep out the flies, mosquitoes and gnats. Freddy wore only his pajamas and his *sudreh*, the collarless, sleeveless, V-necked coarse muslin undergarment. Three strands of the holy thread girdled the *sudreh* at the waist. As he spread himself out on the chair beneath the fan, Billy marveled at the smooth, strong expanse of his father's shoulders and arms. Billy wondered uneasily that Freddy had so little hair on his chest. Only that morning a boy at school had remarked that men with no hair on their chests were heartless. He was glad that at least his father had some. He suddenly realized that Faredoon was already talking. He leaned forward to catch the words.

Faredoon said, "I'm going to tell you how I got married.

"My mother died when I was twelve. My father was around forty-five at the time. My youngest sister was only five days old! I had two other sisters, both younger than I.

"When I was Soli's age, about eighteen or nineteen, something happened to my father. He suddenly decided he was too nervous to cycle to work, too nervous to face his bosses and co-workers, too nervous even to venture out of the house after dark. In short, he was too nervous to look after his family! Since I was the eldest, and the only male, the entire responsibility fell squarely on my shoulders. I got a job in the coconut plantation where my father had worked. In two years I was promoted to overseer.

"That year the eldest of my sisters got married.

"We weren't well-off, but we were comfortable. I was twenty, successful in my work, able to support the family—and ready for marriage. The blood sang hot in my veins. It sang one tune only: marriage,

marriage, marriage. Oh, God, give me a woman!

"My sister squabbled with her husband and came to live with us for a few days. I thought, 'Here is my chance!' And every morning, for three days, I dropped a fistful of salt into the drinking water.

"Then I waited.

"No one approached me. Neither my sister nor my father. Nothing happened.

"My sister returned to her husband, and a month later my father obliquely hinted that my wish to get married was inconsiderate. We were barely able to make ends meet, he said. Thank goodness his daughter had returned to her husband—it was impossible to go on feeding another mouth! And, my unmarried sisters' dowries—he had to think of that!

"I saw his point, but I was miserable. My needs were clamoring. Anyhow, I managed as best I could—single-handed." Freddy lowered his lids and grinned.

Soli smiled, red-lipped and intimate. Yazdi blushed, Hutoxi's husband and Jimmy Paymaster (the engine-driver's son, who often visited with the family) tittered. Billy missed the innuendo. He and his sisters looked at the smiling faces with surprise. When Katy glanced towards him for illumination he put on a superior look and inclined his head to indicate he'd explain later.

"After two years, when my second sister got married, I tried again. But my family had grown too accustomed to my single state and to my salary. They imitated the three wise monkeys: speak not, see not and hear not. By this time I was in love with every woman in the village: married, unmarried, old and young. Hidden in a mango grove, near the village well, I watched them pass by—a procession of *hoories*—pitchers balanced on their heads, on saucily jacked-up hips. It drove me crazy.

"My eldest sister quarreled with her husband and once again moved in with her brood. A few days later her husband joined her. I found myself contributing to their upkeep as well.

"At twenty-two I was no longer able to bear my celibate condition —Ahura Mazda is better pleased with a married man than with an un-married man—so one evening I brought home a ten-pound sack of salt. I hid it in my room. Every morning I poured a fistful of salt into the drinking water. Afternoons, when I came home for lunch, I poured in some more, again in the evenings, and at night again. As soon as they changed the water, I sneaked in a fistful of salt. To hell with the prescribed limit of three days, I thought, and I continued pouring until the family, fed up with drinking brackish water, finally gave in.

"My eldest sister approached me.

"'Fredeee, I think I detected a trace of salt in the water this morning!' she said, as coy and insinuating as a kitten.

"A trace of salt! My word! They had swallowed ten pounds of salt in twenty days! It oozed from their bodies. I could see the chalky moustache on her upper lip where her sweat had dried. Her children ran around with salt glistening on their sickly faces. And she had detected a trace of salt only that morning!

"'You have?' I asked. 'Well, now that you have, what are you going to do about it?'

"She produced your mother. I approved. I saw her only once before marriage. I didn't care whom I married as long as the girl was young, decent and reasonably good-looking. But your mother was beautiful— one of the bewitching pitcher-bearers, veiled in maidenly modesty. I was overripe for love, and I fell passionately in love."

Freddy's lilting voice was as rich and mellow as honey.

Putli passed through the room to the rear of the house and Freddy paused, following her transit with veiled eyes. She was still whip-slender and straight, but there was a gaunt, middle-aged angularity about her elbows, shoulders and hips.

Her small, high-cheekboned, triangular face was palely etched with lines. Her hair was still jet black.

Putli went through a side door and Faredoon said, "Your mother looks stern, doesn't she? But that's just an impression. She has no guile in her, no gossip, no evil. She is honest and straight. So soft-hearted— she wears that expression to safeguard herself. I appreciate this in her, her goodness. I love her even more now than I did then. She is my one and only love. The image of her beauty is painted on my soul. But I can't tell her that. She will snap at me and tell me not to babble like a foolish child.

"Coming back to the story, that is when I realized that you have to respect your own needs! You can't go wrong! My family had been using me, and I had buried my needs. But God has fashioned man as a creature of desires, and fulfilling desires brings contentment, the driving force, the essence, of life. Such a man follows the divine *Path of Asha*. But a discontented man creates chaos! Thus spake Zarathustra!" sighed Faredoon, content at the scholarly effect he created by quoting the title of Nietzsche's book. Had he read the book, he would have crusaded to establish that its philosophical outpourings were not Zarathustra's!

"I was unhappy until I asserted myself, and we were happier all around for it in the end. I stayed with them for a year, until Hutoxi was born. I stopped giving them money. My sister's husband regained his self-respect when he started looking after his own family. My sister was happier. Then I embarked for Lahore.

"That is how I got married," said Faredoon.

Chapter 20

After supper, Faredoon and Soli went out for a stroll. The air was slightly cooler, carrying in it a promise of rain. The sky was like black felt, dotted with pinpricks of tarnished silver.

"Did you like the story?" asked Freddy.

"Yes," said Soli.

"Well?" said Freddy, pausing beneath a gaslight. His son was as tall as he, so Freddy could look him in the eye. The road was deserted.

Soli felt embarrassed. His father looked as if he expected him to hurrah and clap him on his back. He averted his bewildered eyes and said nothing.

Putli was right. The boy was shy. "Well?" Faredoon encouraged again.

Well, what? thought Soli, suspecting they were at cross purposes. "It was an excellent story," he said lamely.

"That's not what I meant," Faredoon began to walk. He decided on another approach.

"I've seen you eyeing the girls . . . The Toddywalla girl is pretty, isn't she?"

"Yes, she's OK. The Cooper girls are very pretty too. Have you noticed Shireen Bottliwalla? She isn't much to look at, but she has a lovely voice. She sings beautifully," added Soli helpfully, hoping to keep the conversation rolling until his father decided to come to the point.

"But which one do you like best?"

"I like all of them," sighed Soli, with impartial ardor.

"But you can't marry all of them!"

So, thought Soli, we have come to the point!

"I don't think I can make up my mind just yet," he said.

"Then who has been putting water in the salt, I mean, salt in the water?" said Freddy.

Oh, so that was it! His father's peculiar behavior the last few days began to make sense.

"Not me," he laughed. "I didn't even know there was salt in the water."

"It isn't Yasmin either. I wonder who it could be? Unless it's your grandmother!" exclaimed Freddy, chortling gleefully at the mischievous afterthought.

Soli's mouth curled in a wide, warm smile. His eyes twinkled and he laughed—a young bellyful of mirth. "That's a good one. But don't let Grandmother hear you."

It was too good to pass up.

Jerbanoo, Putli and Freddy sat around the breakfast table.

Freddy had called a family conference and the two women looked at him with excited and expectant faces.

Putli had already confided in Jerbanoo. The salt in the water was of too momentous a significance to be passed over lightly. Jerbanoo would have been mortally offended to discover she had not been told.

Faredoon cleared his throat.

Their suspense rose to an ungovernable pitch.

"You know someone put salt in the water?"

Jerbanoo nodded her head solemnly. "Putli told me."

Freddy turned to Putli. "And you are sure it wasn't Yasmin?"

"That's right."

"Well, it's not Soli either!"

"Oh!" the women cried simultaneously.

Freddy ran his hand over the tablecloth, thoughtfully brushing some bread crumbs. "I can think of only one other person."

Putli and Jerbanoo looked at him encouragingly.

Faredoon raised his eyes on a direct level with Jerbanoo's.

"I'm not going to beat about the bush. We are all adults here . . . no one is going to feel shy or coy. Did you put salt in the water?"

Jerbanoo gurgled, choked and glared at Faredoon with disbelieving eyes.

Putli turned and stared at her mother in astonishment. Jerbanoo's jowls were quivering as if an electric current was passing through them.

"Well?" persisted Freddy.

"How dare you! At my age! You are shameless! Absolutely shameless!" she spluttered.

"I've asked you a plain, simple question. Did you or did you not put salt in the water? All I want is a plain and simple answer."

"No! No! No!" screeched Jerbanoo.

"Oh, Faredoon! How could you!" protested Putli.

"Look! You asked me to find out, didn't you? It's not Soli, it's not Yasmin, so why not your mother? Maybe she is still over-fond of the Irishman who rescued her from the fire. How was I to know?"

"Behave yourself!" said Putli.

"What do you mean, 'behave yourself'? What else do you think I'm doing? I ask a reasonable question, expecting a simple 'yes' or 'no'—and here you two go screaming like fishwives and losing your heads. So, it's not your mother. That's all I wanted to know!"

"You'd better get to work. It's almost half past eight." Putli pushed back her chair. Jerbanoo stood up.

"All right! If that's the way you feel about it, I wash my hands of the whole affair. You can find out for yourselves," called Freddy after the two haughtily receding backs.

Faredoon skipped down the steps, a huge boyish grin wreathing his noble features.

Chapter 21

Every day a steady stream of visitors poured into the store to see Faredoon. He had converted one of the storerooms into a private office. When he was not attending to customers personally (he did this very seldom now) he sat here, busy with matters relating to his Peshawar, Amritsar and Delhi stores. He was constantly interrupted by the visitors.

This morning a thickset Sikh police officer was waiting to see Freddy. His hair, as long as a woman's, was tucked away beneath the neat folds of his khaki turban. His black beard was parted in the center and made to fan out fiercely on either side of his swarthy face. The Sikh sprang to his feet and salaamed as Freddy entered the room.

"How are you, my dear friend?" cried Freddy, clasping the policeman's hands in both of his and touching them to his forehead. The man smelled faintly of the yogurt with which he washed his hair and beard. "Get some tea for Sunder Singh sahib," Freddy told the clerk who was sitting at his small table in one corner of the room.

Harilal, old, diminutive and wiry, removed his small reading glasses and tucked them into the top pocket of his coat. He left the room with the hospitable air of a housewife accustomed to entertaining.

The police officer sat down, sheepishly adjusting the bandolier across his khaki shirt. Freddy knew the symptoms. He wondered what the man wanted.

After a few preliminaries, resting his elbows on the desk and sipping tea from the saucer, the policeman aired his request.

"Sir, there is a slight matter—I wonder if I could trouble you with it?"

Freddy looked at him kindly. "Yes?"

"I want my son admitted at the St. Anthony's School. You know how it is—those Padres have no time for a poor constable."

"By all means. It will be done! The Fathers are good friends of mine . . . I send them a hamper every Christmas. Anything else?"

"I will be very grateful, sir. I want my son to be educated at an English school."

Harilal came into the room. "Mr. Paymaster's son is here to see you, Sahib."

"Tell the rascal to wait," said Freddy.

The Sikh stood up, sending a whiff of yogurt across the desk. "I will not delay you."

Freddy walked round the table and put his arm around the policeman's shoulder. As they moved towards the door he drawled, "There is a young pup waiting outside to see me. I'd clean forgotten about him . . . He's a decent boy really—but you know this young blood. He's in a spot of trouble. Two or three nights back, he was caught in a brothel raid. The fool knocked down one of the sepoys. He is my kinsman and they expect me to do something for him. Think you can handle it?"

"Why not? Ask him to see me at the *thana* tomorrow morning."

"Thank you, your honor. I will. But don't make it look too easy—otherwise young Mr. Paymaster will not learn his lesson."

Freddy walked through the store to see the Sikh out.

Harilal followed behind with a brown paper parcel.

As the policeman kneeled to undo the lock on his bicycle, Freddy tucked the parcel into the carrier stand.

"Must you take this trouble? You never allow me to go empty-handed."

"No trouble at all. Just something for the children," smiled Freddy.

After Jimmy Paymaster also left, Freddy settled down to write out an order to a firm in England for a consignment of paste jewelry for his store in Peshawar.

Halfway through the letter, Mr. Charles P. Allen walked in with an affable "Hello, old chap," and a seductive flash of raw pink thigh.

"My lord! My lord! My lord!" cried Freddy, surging to his feet and dancing forward. He was genuinely pleased to see the huge bear of a man with his mild, clean-shaven, purple face. Mr. Allen was rigged out in the costume he had worn for the past fifteen summers with unvarying constancy: a gray, open-necked, short-sleeved shirt; loose, white duck shorts held up by elastic braces; and, though the temperatures ranged around 115 degrees Fahrenheit in the shade, a pair of thick, gray stockings of pure wool. The stockings were turned to make a thick-ribbed border at the knees. Between the stockings and the shorts was the tantalizing bit of vein-mottled, hair-fuzzed leg.

Embarrassed by the lavish battery of titles, the "My lords," "Your honors" and "Your excellencies" bestowed upon him by Freddy, he had protested and then given in to his friend's incorrigible persistence, realizing it signified little more than a desire to please. He never grew accustomed to the authority and deference unexpectedly bestowed upon him by his career as a British civil servant in India.

Mr. Allen removed his sola-topee, revealing a close-cropped, sweat-matted sphere of sandy hair, and sat down in the chair held out by Freddy. Freddy drew his own chair closer to the Englishman's, asking, "What brings your worship to Lahore to give me this glorious surprise?"

"I'm on my way to see the Memsahib off. She's already in Karachi. The ship sails on Tuesday. Thought I'd stop in Lahore for a day and say hello to you. Got to catch the train tomorrow, early morning."

"You visit Lahore after all these years for only one day? I will not allow it! I will tell the Chairman of the Railways to delay your train until nightfall. He is my friend."

"And he'll do it, too, if I know you," grinned the Englishman, his little blue eyes twinkling like gems. "But I've got to be off in the morning. Otherwise the Memsahib will come after me with a broom."

"All right then. We will have a party, a big party to celebrate your visit tonight," declared Freddy. "You occupy a special corner of affection in my heart." The corner had been occupied since the time Freddy had ministered to his friend's impotency with his own particular brand of doctoring and been rewarded with a franchise for trade with Afghanistan.

Freddy beckoned Harilal, who had been hovering around with a beaming, obsequious face. "Go, see if you can find Alla Ditta. He's bound to be at the biri shop or in the bazaar. Bring him here."

Harilal darted out obligingly.

"Where are you stationed?" asked Freddy.

"Bihar. Deputy Commissioner. Bloody boring place."

"And how is my prince?"

"Peter? He's in England. Quite a *Pukka Sahib* now."

"And my little golden-haired princess?"

"She'll be sailing with her mother too. You wouldn't know Barbara if you saw her now. She's thirteen—such a tomboy—forever teasing the old Hindu gardener . . . keeps trying to pull his loin-cloth off. You should see the poor fellow—holds on to his little bit of cloth as if it were a chastity belt or something. The Memsahib thinks the school in England will improve her manners."

Harilal unleashed Alla Ditta into the room. The pimp-cum-cart-driver salaamed, giving off an odor of sweat, grease and garlic. He was of middle height, with a massive chest and an enormous, solid stomach that protruded through his shirt like a bomb. Despite the grimy *lungi* wrapped around his legs, his gross flesh conveyed an air of obscene nudity. His close-cropped head was criss-crossed with white brawling scars. He stood proud and straight-backed before them as if before equals.

"Well, you old rascal," said Freddy affectionately. "Haven't seen you for a long time. Where are you hiding all the pretty girls?"

"At your service, hazoor," said the pimp.

"My dear friend Allen sahib is here for only one night. I want you to arrange a good party for him at the Hira Mandi. It has to be a memorable evening. Pretty girls, mind you. I will bring the Scotch. And they should be good dancers and singers. Not like the one you produced last time—she sounded like the creaking of your horse cart."

"I'll get the best," promised Alla Ditta with an assurance that recalled Freddy to the time when he had first hired him for the nocturnal trips to the warehouse just before the fire. Right away he had been taken by the youth's air of self-assurance and had found him useful and reliable over the years. They fixed on the time. Alla Ditta salaamed and swaggered from the room.

Mr. Allen and Freddy remained chatting for an hour. When Mr. Allen got up, flashing his enticing bit of muscular thigh, Freddy escorted him to his hired tonga. Mr. Allen directed the tongawalla to take him to the Nedous Hotel.

Chapter 22

Having instructed Harilal to see that no one disturbed him, Freddy sorted out a heap of work during the uninterrupted afternoon.

At about five o'clock, Harilal finally allowed Yazdi into Freddy's presence.

"Yes, Yazdi?" said Freddy, barely looking up from the letter he was reading. "Sit down."

Yazdi sat gingerly on the chair. Freddy looked up. Yazdi was rigid with tension, and his large dreamy eyes were alarmingly bright.

"I want to get married, Papa," he said, holding Freddy's gaze steadily.

"I should have guessed!" Freddy struck his forehead in a mock, self-deprecatory gesture.

Yazdi flushed, thinking of all the times he had tried to corner his father alone while Faredoon sought Soli's company.

"Don't you think you are a bit young to decide? You're only fifteen, your mother tells me. How will you support your wife?"

Yazdi remained obstinately quiet.

"Well, who is the lucky girl?" inquired Freddy, thinking to humor his son with a show of interest. He knew the romance would be short-lived. And, if the puppy love withstood the test of time—at least four years in Yazdi's case—they could get married. There was no harm in it.

"Well, who is she?" repeated Freddy, resting his elbows on the table and leaning forward with low-lidded, amused eyes. "Anyone we know?"

"No, you don't know her. She's a girl who comes to my school. Her name is Rosy Watson."

Freddy had not been prepared for this. His face stiffened visibly. "What kind of a name is that? I don't think I know any Parsee by the name of Watson."

"She's not Parsee. She is an Anglo-Indian."

Father and son were both as pale as whitewashed walls.

115

"Come here," said Freddy in a strange, harsh voice.

His face twitched uncontrollably. Yazdi came around the table and stood before his father. Freddy got out of the chair. He gave his son a hard, level look. Yazdi felt his long, stringy frame cringe involuntarily, but he held his ground. Suddenly, Freddy raised his arm and slapped the back of his hand hard across Yazdi's face. The boy staggered back.

"You have the gall to tell me you want to marry an Anglo-Indian? Get out of my sight. Get out!"

Desperately holding back the tears that stung his eyes, Yazdi left the room.

Freddy sank down in his chair, drained of all strength. His hands trembled.

This was the first time he had struck any of his children.

Putli served Freddy his cup of tea. Salted pastry, lentil cakes, and bread and butter were already on the table. She had an entire family of servants working for her now, a husband and wife, son and daughter-in-law team, but she insisted on doing all the little things for her husband and her sons herself. She rose at the crack of dawn and dutifully filled the house with song. She sang with a determined cheerfulness, inviting the spirits of prosperity and good health to her household. Then she set about adorning the landings with patterns of fish and entrance doors with garlands of fresh flowers—omens of good fortune.

Loath to see the servants idle, she kept them busy. The house was thoroughly scoured every day. Carpets were beaten, walls brushed, furniture moved aside and floors scrubbed with soap and water until they shone like Dresden china. The brick floors had long been replaced by glazed tiles arranged in flowering patterns. Putli industriously supervised all the work and then, when the daily orgy of spring-cleaning was spent, retired to the kitchen to prepare delicacies. The servants chopped onions, peeled vegetables, ground spices and kneaded the flour. Putli was left with little to do but mix recipes and stir the pans. Undaunted, she resourcefully busied herself washing potatoes and tomatoes with soap. Spare moments were devoted to making *kustis*. She spun the white lamb's wool into seventy-two fine strands and wove them into a long, thin, hollow tape. The tape was turned inside out and ceremoniously washed. Her finely made *kustis* were in great demand, not only in Lahore but in Karachi as well. Her proudest moments came when her children were formally initiated into the Zarathusti faith at their *Navjote* ceremonies. Then, invested with the outward symbols of the faith—the undershirt, *sudreh* and the *kusti*—they were girded to serve the Lord of Life and Wisdom.

Freedom of choice is a cardinal doctrine in the teaching of Zarathustra. A child born of Zoroastrian parents is not considered a Zoroastrian until he or she has chosen the faith at the *Navjote* ceremony. Zarathustra, in his Gathas, says:

> Give ear to the Great Truths. Look within with en-
> lightened mind (literally: flaming mind) at the faith of
> your own selection, man by man, *each one for himself.*

And this freedom of choice extends also to Good and Evil, aspects of God Himself. Evil is necessary so that Good may triumph. Yet Evil by itself does not exist; it is relative, depending upon the distance from God at which the individual stands upon the Path of *Asha*—the Eternal Truth—the grand cosmic plan of God.

Putli sat across the table from Freddy and, when he was almost ready for his second cup of tea, remarked, "What's troubling Yazdi? He went down to see you, I think, and when he came up his face was red and cranky. He's locked himself up in his room, and he refuses to open the door. I don't know what's come over him—did something happen between you two?"

"Yes, I slapped him."

"Oh!" exhaled Putli, wondering and solemn.

"That stupid fool wants to marry an Anglo-Indian!"

Putli turned ashen. She didn't say a word. She knew Freddy was going out later that evening. She told the maid to bring another cup of tea. Then she talked matter-of-factly of household matters and presented her daily quota of complaints regarding the servants. When

Freddy was quite calm, she timorously ventured, "You did quite right to strike Yazdi—but that won't show him the right path. It might be better if you sat down with him and talked things over."

"I've thought of doing that already," admitted Freddy, delicately dipping pastry biscuits in the tea. "Just let me finish this tea."

Freddy knocked on the door. "It's me," he announced.

The children were conditioned to obedience, more out of love and an ingrained sense of respect peculiar to their training than to any authoritative endeavor on Freddy's part.

The children sometimes defied their mother but never their father. Yazdi opened the door at once. His sensitive face was sullen. His lids and lips were swollen and red with weeping.

Freddy felt a sharp pang of remorse. He held his lanky son to his chest, kissed his swollen lids and half carried him to the bed. Sitting side by side, his arm around the boy's slender shoulders, Freddy gently encouraged him to talk. In a short while, he elicited the full story.

Yazdi, alone among his brothers, went to a coeducational school. Overly sensitive and delicate from childhood, Putli had feared for him among the rough little boys at St. Anthony's. She had meant to transfer him to the boys' school later, but when the time came, she persuaded Freddy to allow him to remain where he was.

Yazdi's gentle ways and unfailing courtesy made him a favorite with his teachers. He was more at ease with the little girls in his class, seeking them out and preferring them to the boys.

Rosy Watson had been in his class from kindergarten. She had been a pitifully skinny, aloof and sullen child, and he had gotten to know her only a year back. There was an air about her, a mysterious tragic reserve, that excited his pity. She had no friends. Sometimes, during break, the older boys talked to her. She was offhand with them and, unlike her gig-gling contemporaries, astonishingly poised. Yazdi was intrigued by her composure. It was as if she was initiated to some somber, grown-up rites that suffused her slender body with languor and carved her beautiful face into an unsmiling, withdrawn mask.

Yazdi sought her friendship with little attentions and loyalties. He broke from his friends and tried to penetrate the arid world of her lone-liness. He sat next to her in class, composing his features to match her cool insouciance. He strolled with her during break, sharing his sand-wich. Little by little the girl's reserve gave way. Responding to the sympathy in him, she offered her friendship, her embittered, unhappy confidences. She told Yazdi about her abominable stepmother, her spiteful brothers and sisters. Every day she brought a new story of suffer-ing. He felt he glimpsed for the first time the world's sorrows. He was filled with compassion.

He felt she permitted him to peer through a rare keyhole on the world of sadness.

Their relationship had changed about a month back when she returned to school after an absence of four days. There were dark circles beneath her eyes, and her wan little face, sandwiched between heavy falls of straight long hair, was puffy.

During break they went to their nook, a grassy arbor of shady hedges and trees behind the School Chapel, and there she sobbed out her anguish. Not only her stepmother, but even her father thrashed her. They had confined her to her room without food or water, strapped to her bed. They had allowed all sorts of men into the room. Yazdi thought this was done to humiliate her even further. He did not probe the cause that provoked this punishment. The immediate cause was always trivial and inconsequential, weighted down by the elemental fount of her step-mother's jealous hatred and vindictiveness.

Yazdi's heart constricted with pity. His face crumpled in an effort to contain the tears that blurred his eyes. "Don't cry, don't cry," he begged in a barely audible voice, stroking the weeping girl's light brown, silken hair. "I cannot bear to see you like this . . . you don't have to live like this . . . I will marry you and take you away from that horrible house. I will marry you," he repeated with a determination that made the girl raise her bowed head and look at him.

Taking his pale, bravely determined face in her hands she kissed him. This was Yazdi's first kiss—and the girl was beautiful.

Freddy listened patiently. His face was red. He saw much more in the simple story that his son told him. He saw the poverty of the girl's family and the faceless depravity of their existence. He was shocked when Yazdi told him of her chastisement, shocked by his straight narrative tone: "They tied her to the bed and brought men into the room," he had said, compassion flitting across his face as he pressed closer to his father, wanting him to sympathize. Only when he realized that the boy had missed the significance of the scene which he described with such unwitting candor (endowing the men with his own sensibilities, Yazdi imagined them embarrassed and reluctant to witness the girl's humiliation) did Freddy understand his son's total lack of embarrassment. Really, he's such a baby, thought Freddy.

"She is so unhappy, father. I've got to marry her. I promised, and I love her," Yazdi cried desperately.

"You love her? No, my child; you want to marry her because you pity her. But you cannot marry all those you pity. I pity the mangy dogs on our street, the beggars, the noseless leper who comes every Friday—do you expect me to marry them? Your heart is too soft. You cannot expect to marry the dogs you pity!"

"She isn't a dog."

"No, but a mongrel . . . a mixed-breed mongrel."

Yazdi stiffened and, sitting back, glowered at his father.

"What does it matter if she is not Parsee? What does it matter who her parents are. She is a human being, isn't she? And a fine person. Better than any Parsee I've met." An ungovernable rage at his father's prejudice seethed in him. His eyes wild, he sprang from the bed and paced the floor.

Freddy calmly doubled up a pillow against the wall and reclined. "Sit down, sit down, there's nothing to get excited about," he said.

Yazdi perched on the edge of the bed.

"You are too young to understand these things; maybe I am too old to understand you. But there is one thing I would like to explain to you. Now, this is not something I alone believe. It is what our ancestors professed and what our race will go on believing until the end of time. You may think what I have to say is nonsense, but once you are past a certain age, you will see the wisdom and truth of these thoughts, I promise you. May I tell you what I believe?"

Yazdi, responding to the plea in his father's voice, nodded.

Although his demeanor was respectful, Freddy could not help noticing the defiant gleam in his son's eye, condemning Freddy's bigotry and daring him to express it.

"I believe in some kind of a tiny spark that is carried from parent to child, on through generations . . . a kind of inherited memory of wisdom and righteousness, reaching back to the times of Zarathustra, the Magi, the Mazdiasnians. It is a tenderly nurtured conscience, evolving towards perfection.

"I am not saying only we have the spark. Other people have it too: Christians, Muslims, Hindus, Buddhists, they too have developed pure strains through generations.

"But what happens if you marry outside our kind? The spark so delicately nurtured, so subtly balanced, meets something totally alien and unmatched. Its precise balance is scrambled. It reverts to the primitive.

"You will do yourself no harm—you have already inherited fine qualities—you have compassion, honesty, creativity. But have you thought of your children?

"In the case of the Anglo-Indian girl, the spark is already mutated. What kind of a heritage are you condemning your children to? They might look beautiful, but they will be shells—empty and confused, misfits for generations to come. They will have arrogance without pride, touchiness without self-respect or compassion, ambition without honor—and you will be to blame."

Yazdi wondered bitterly why he had expected his father to be different. He had somehow imagined him, of all people, to be above these antiquated prejudices.

"You are as ignorant and biased as the others," he said, voicing his disappointment. His face was drawn and contemptuous. "I will never swallow such disgusting beliefs."

"I cannot force you. But you must grant me the courtesy of at least thinking about what I've said—then reject it, by all means. It will help you to realize why I will never permit you to marry that girl."

"I'd be ashamed to even think of such rubbish!"

Freddy's face congealed into something closed, hurt and unforgiving. Without a word he drew himself forward on the bed, slid his feet into his slippers and went from the room.

Chapter 23

At seven o'clock, the Nawab of Panipur's younger brother, Prince Kamaruddin, sent up word that he had arrived. Faredoon, Mr. Allen and Mr. Toddywalla hastened downstairs. As a concession to the occasion, Mr. Allen wore a pair of long, baggy duck trousers. The Prince stepped off his gleaming carriage and after embracing each other the middle-aged rakes, hell-bent on gaiety, scampered into Freddy's tonga. Alla Ditta, with a little wad of jasmine-scented cotton plugged in one ear, stroked the restive horse. At a signal from Freddy he slid onto the tonga shaft, allowing his passengers to spread out comfortably on the front seat. With a flick of the whip he started the tonga moving.

"Ah, now we sally forth on adventure," said Freddy pompously, beaming at his friends.

They spoke in English out of deference to Mr. Allen.

"Hope the girls are good, old chap," said Prince Kamaruddin, opening a jeweled snuff box and squeezing a pinch into each nostril above his enormous, stiffened moustache.

Mr. Allen, already disconcerted by the odor of jasmine, garlic and sweat given off by Alla Ditta, was completely put off by the Prince's impeccable Oxford accent. The bizarre effect of a swarthy, arrogant Indian with pearls in his ears sounding like an Englishman never failed to diminish his meagre store of self-confidence.

It was still bright. The sun sent fierce red shafts from the horizon. The tonga clipped through the Mall at a brisk trot. They turned right on Kachery Road, and their pace slowed. The street became narrower, traffic congested, but once they were past the shrine of Data Ganj Buksh the rush eased somewhat.

Soon they saw the dark brooding outline of the fort and, gleaming against it, pink in the sunset, the domes and minarets of the Badshahi Mosque.

At the entrance to the Hira Mandi streets, Alla Ditta stopped briefly to get a bundle of betel leaves.

"Are we there?" asked Mr. Allen, turning around to peer at the lights.

"Yes. You will soon see our Diamond Market—that's what Hira Mandi means," answered Freddy.

"Why Diamond Market?"

"You'll find out soon enough, old chap. Plenty of gems—walking around on two legs!" said the Prince.

It was the prime hour for visitors. Mr. Allen craned his neck this way and that to ogle the girls on either side of the narrow street. The girls, gaudily dressed and heavily made-up, reclined provocatively on silken cushions. The wide doors to their parlors were open to the street. Musicians sat cross-legged before their sitars, harmoniums and tabla drums, idly tuning their instruments and running up melodious snatches. The heady sound of ankle-bells drifted through the closed doors of girls already engaged.

Sitting next to him, insouciantly chewing on a paan, the Prince murmured, "Careful, old chap, we can't have you falling out of the tonga."

A great tide of love washed over Mr. Allen. The Prince is a dear old fellow, he thought, forgetting his earlier discomfiture in his presence. His heart brimmed over with adoration for the entire land and populace of India. The dilapidated buildings towering on either side, superficially decorated with trellises and carved wooden balconies, appeared to him incomparably beautiful. Bright lights pouring from the rooms flooded the darkening street with mysterious, sensual shadows. Mr. Allen sighed, thinking he would have to leave all this in a few years and retire to his cold, damp and colorless little country. He'd miss it—all these beautiful, tantalizing, bewitching creatures with shimmering clothes and large, darkly flashing eyes.

They drove through to the end of the street and stopped. Freddy jumped from the tonga and, gallantly escorting Mr. Allen and the Prince like delicate ladies, ushered them up a dingy flight of steps to a small sitting room. The atmosphere in the room was stale and musty. The Prince turned up his nose at the dust-coated paper flowers and at the stained, lopsided sofa. He refused to sit.

A placid Hindu woman with a roll of waist showing between her sari and blouse came into the room and greeted them. She was kindly looking and middle-aged, and the bunch of keys hooked into her sari jingled as she plopped down on a sofa.

"Would you like tea?" she asked.

"Had we wanted tea, my dear, we would have stayed at home," said the Prince. "Tell the girls to come out."

Mr. Allen blushed, looking apologetically at the woman. She wasn't the least bit affronted. Hauling herself out of the sofa, she said calmly, "Well, then come along, let's go to the parlor. You'll be more comfortable there. The girls should be out in a few minutes."

She walked to a door and held it open. Prince Kamaruddin, followed by Mr. Allen, Mr. Toddywalla and Mr. Junglewalla, went through into a long, enclosed veranda. A man dozing by the harmonium and tabla drums on the floor hastily stood up and salaamed.

Prince Kamaruddin's disdainful eyes raked the parlor. The wall facing them was punctuated by slender, arched windows. Some were open, and the room smelled fresh. The windowpanes were clear, carpets thick and dust-free, and the mosaic floor around their edges gleamed from scrubbing. The walls were a pale yellow and the curtains cheerfully printed with peacock blue elephants.

The woman led them to divans covered with white sheets at the far end of the room, and they reclined comfortably against satin bolsters.

Suddenly the gay tinkle of ankle-bells filled the room, and a short, prettily curved girl came up to them. Bending gracefully, she salaamed. She had a beautiful face with dimpled, voluptuously rounded Indian features and large, demure eyes. Mr. Allen and Freddy exchanged approving glances.

The Prince leered rakishly and smoothly engaged the girl in conversation while Mr. Toddywalla transported his fierce whiskers to a window and looked down on the colorful street. He was subdued and obliging, obviously invited to fill out his friend's party unobtrusively. Although he was Freddy's age, he looked much older.

Alla Ditta came into the room followed by a slight, pale-skinned girl holding a cloth bundle. She had on black, skintight, satin churidar-pajamas and a full-skirted, powder blue kamiz bordered with a silver braid. Barely glancing at the visitors, she removed her slippers and sat down by the musicians. Her movements were light and quick. She removed a pair of *pyals* from the bundle and deftly strapped the bells round her ankles. As she stood up Alla Ditta, who had settled in a corner behind the musicians, pulled her skirt straight. Freddy frowned, shocked to see the ruffian on such terms with the delicate creature. It suddenly struck him that Alla Ditta probably slept with the girls.

"That's Nilofer," said the madam, interrupting Freddy's thoughts.

Quickly, lightly, Nilofer ran up to them and salaamed. Mr. Toddy-walla was left breathless by the yellow glimmer of her green eyes.

"Must be Kashmiri," Freddy remarked, commenting on her light skin and eyes.

The musicians started to play, and the girls, tying their chiffon scarves around their waists, began to dance and sing in shrill, nasal voices. In turn, they danced up to each guest, sang a verse and delicately plucked the proferred coin from their fingers. Their gauzy skirts swirled high above the tight churidar-pajamas.

The fair girl was bolder. There was an excitingly depraved air about her, cynical and insensate. She went through the timeworn motions and expressions of the dancing-girl, swaying her hips, glancing provocatively through slanting eyes and smiling with an impassivity that was coarse and mechanical.

The dark girl, an exceptional beauty, was also mechanical and impassive, but her seemingly refined and demure manners and natural dignity transported her above her calling. The men were aware in them-selves, despite an uneasy insight at their foolishness, of a feeling of affection—an almost tender desire to protect and possess her.

Prince Kamaruddin stretched out on the cushions, raised his arms helplessly above his head and announced, "God be praised, but it's hot in here."

At once the girl with the bold eyes, the one introduced by the madam as Nilofer, kneeled by him to undo the buttons on his brocade sherwani-coat. But the Prince, placing a smooth hand flat on her breasts, pushed her back. "Not you. I want the other girl."

Nilofer stood up, calmly making way for her colleague. The darker girl kneeled, dimpling prettily, and dexterously unlooped the endless row of buttons from neck to knee. She helped the Prince out of his coat and hung it on a peg. Prince Kamaruddin reclined in his collarless silk kurta-shirt, and the girl admiringly fingered the chain of gold studs down the front.

Mr. Allen, consumed by envy—and by pity for the rejected girl— wished he had something to unbutton as well. He doubled his chins in an effort to glance at his person, and seeing nothing but the four plain buttons on his front, frowned ruefully. He caught the pale girl's cynical, smiling eyes.

"Wait, man, I will undo your braces," she said in English, sinking to her knees beside him.

"Oh, you're Anglo-Indian?" asked Freddy, quite surprised.

"Yes, man. What the hell did you think I was?"

"I thought you were Kashmiri."

The girl pulled Mr. Allen forward and bending over him, reached the buttons in the back of his trousers. She stood up, playfully stretching the elastic, and flicked the braces over the Prince's brocade coat.

Mr. Allen beamed. Now that he knew she spoke English he felt a special tie with her. He relaxed completely, talking easily with her, and tried desperately to focus his eyes on both girls at once.

The Prince had monopolized the other girl. Noticing his friend's cockeyed endeavors, Freddy caught the girl's eye and signaled her in Mr. Allen's direction. The girl excused herself with practiced poise and went over to the Englishman. But the Prince was having none of this. "Come here, you. Come back to me, my dove," he demanded drunkenly. Eventually, galvanized into a spurt of energy by his exasperation, he got up and lifting the girl clear off the floor like a baby, carried her to the cushions away from the others. "Now you sit right here and talk to me," he said, patting the divan with an autocratic hand.

The madam smiled indulgently at the Prince's antics. She could see he was enormously taken by the dark beauty and mentally calculated the price she would wheedle out of him in the future.

Mr. Toddywalla and Faredoon were not interested in the girls. They sat there in the capacity of glorified pimps, more or less, steadily imbibing whiskey and pretending to be lascivious.

Meanwhile, Mr. Allen could not keep his hands from touching Nilofer. She kept brushing his fat fingers off good-naturedly and chatting in her coarse voice. She liked him as she liked all Englishmen, identifying herself, however tenuous her claim, with the British.

Freddy heard a snatch of conversation as Mr. Allen teased her. Leaning forward foxily, his little blue eyes roguish, he baited the girl where she was most vulnerable.

"Go on, you're more Indian than English! I bet you eat food with your fingers at home. I bet you prefer chapaties and spicy curry."

"Of course!" the girl retorted, stung to the quick and defensive. "But we also eat English food: Irish stew, roast beef, custard, mint sauce and all that. It's tasteless, but we eat it."

"There! You see! You don't really like it. Now, if you were English, you would. And your name—Nilofer isn't an English name?"

"That's not my real name. My name is Rosy."

Something clicked, alert and angry in Freddy's alcohol- blurred mind.

"Rosy what?" he interrupted suddenly.

"What's it to you?" the girl snapped.

"Watson?" he persisted.

The girl turned to him. Her green cat-eyes narrowed to dangerous slits. Fear, anger and surprise kindled the first genuine spark of life he had seen in her all evening.

"What's it to bloody you?" she hissed.

"Nothing. I was just guessing. Watson's a common name."

The girl turned away contemptuously.

A murderous, monstrous rage straddled Freddy. He knew this was the girl his son wished to marry. And despite his anger, a strange heat surged and congealed in his loins. But she's only a child, he thought, shocked by his reaction. However much he endeavored to subdue his rage and perverse passion, he could think of nothing else.

The rest of the evening passed slowly for Freddy. He merely went through the motions of catering to his guests and of joking and laughing in keeping with the spirit of the party.

At about three o'clock he slid over to the madam. Mr. Toddywalla was sleeping as soundly as a bewhiskered baby on the cushions. The Prince had disappeared with his favorite. Mr. Allen was yelling an unintelligible pub song.

The madam led Freddy behind some curtains and through a passage to a small, dimly lit room.

He was trembling. He paced up and down, racked by a thousand conflicting thoughts and emotions. When the girl came into the room he stared at her with austere eyes. She was disconcerted. "Well, man, what d'ya want?" she snapped.

"What do you think I want?" said Freddy slowly, speaking English in his heavy accent, not removing his cold eyes from her.

The girl held his eye for a moment. His look was noncommittal. Wordlessly she went to the bed and wriggled out of the kamiz, revealing her slender, small-breasted torso. Her hair fell forward, shading her face as she struggled to pull the tight, black churidar-pajamas down her ankles. When she removed them, Freddy snatched them from her hands and flung them to a corner. Throwing her back on the bed, he flung himself upon her. He squeezed the taut, nubile little breasts until she cried out. He fumbled around feverishly, seeking ways to humiliate the girl and assuage his anger, but the girl submitted to everything he did with her usual impassive apathy. She had been through much worse than Freddy could ever dream up.

When they returned to the parlor, Mr. Allen directed his questioning eyes upon Freddy. Freddy avoided his eye.

Mr. Allen was too polite to query his friend after that. Freddy, abashed by his rudeness and neglect, sat beside him and confided, "Quite good—except her breasts have been chewed away by goats."

Mr. Allen was dumbfounded by Freddy's curious expression. Then getting the drift of his meaning he mumbled, "Fried eggs, we call them— same thing I suppose. How old d'you think she is? Fourteen?"

"About that," said Freddy gloomily.

At five o'clock they went to the Nedous Hotel to collect

Mr. Allen's luggage, and from there they drove straight to the station.

"I could easily have had the train delayed. You would have had a chance to wash and rest," said Freddy.

Stretching himself full-length on the red velvet couch in his compartment, Mr. Allen disagreed.

"Better this way. I'll sleep right through to Karachi. Best way to recover from a ripping night, old chap." A small fan directed over a tubful of ice had already cooled the compartment.

The train left the station at 6:30.

Putli had just come down from the terrace when Freddy returned.

"How was the party?" she asked her haggard-looking husband.

"Too damn tiring," he replied, heading for the bathroom.

Freddy emerged somewhat refreshed from his shower and change of clothes. Putli had his breakfast ready. His tongue felt thick. "No eggs for me," he said, pressing his throbbing forehead. "I'll just have some tea."

Putli quietly made an eggnog and placed it before him.

Freddy looked up. "By the way, Yazdi is not to go to school. I will take him over to St. Anthony's at 10:30. About time he went to a man's school. God, what a poetry-ridden, spunkless little sissy you've turned him into."

"I'll tell him to be ready," said Putli.

"It's all your fault, really. If you had let me transfer him when I wanted to, this would never have happened! God alone knows what kind of a girl has him trapped. She may be a prostitute for all I know."

Putli looked shocked and reproving.

"Why not?" Freddy continued. "What do we know about her? From what Yazdi told me I gather she is from one of the worst type of Anglo-Indian families. You know how low some of them can be." His rage flared up suddenly. He flung his napkin onto the table and said with unforgiving severity, "If only you'd listen to me sometimes!"

At 10:30 Freddy mutely transported his sullen son to his new school.

Chapter 24

Billy hitched up his pajamas and squatted on the six-inch cement parapet in the bathroom. It was Friday morning. He splashed his face at the tap and, ducking his head forward, allowed a trail of water to dribble over his scrawny neck. Still squatting, he drew a rough towel and dried himself briskly. He scoured his teeth with a walnut twig until they gleamed white, put on his glasses and replaced the skullcap on his curly hair.

Billy stood up and, solemnly turning to face the bathroom mirror, began to mumble his prayers. He dexterously undid the knots of the sacred thread and held the unraveled *kusti* in both hands. Billy did not understand a word of the ancient Avesta text except the bit "Shikasta shikasta, sehtan," which, roughly translated, means, "I shall conquer evil." When he came to this bit, he whipped the tasseled ends of the thread so that they cracked thinly at the back. Once again he wound the *kusti* around his waist, tying it in a reef knot at the front and back. Each twist of the knot was meant to remind him that God is One Eternal Being, that the Mazdayasni faith is the true faith, that Zarathustra is the true Prophet of God and that he should obey the three commandments: *good thoughts, good words and good deeds.*

The thread tied, he raised his eyes to the mirror, joined his hands in front and proceeded to sibilate through the remaining prayers.

This was his most private moment of the day. Alone with his God, alone with the mirror, Billy studied the unique details of his person. He was neither pleased nor disturbed by what he saw, merely interested.

Billy's eyes fastened on the reflection of his large fleshy ears. He was acutely conscious of them. They stuck out at absolute right angles to his face, level with his eyes, making his eyes appear even more close-set than they were. His ears were the most vulnerable thing about his person. His brothers and sisters found them handy to get hold of in a disagreement, and his elders punished him by tweaking them or by literally hauling him out or in by his ears whenever expedient.

Billy flattened them with his palms and felt he looked much better, but the moment he removed his hands they sprang back like red, scrubbed soldiers falling in line. For all their size, his ears were as soft as cotton, and the cartilage could be pinched together like lint.

Billy's wandering eye fell on the toothpaste on the dresser. The tube belonged to Freddy and no one was allowed to use it. He glanced at the bolt on the door and made up his mind to experiment.

Racing through the prayers, gulping short cuts, he quickly touched his forehead, touched his fingers to the floor in hasty salutation to God, and reached for the tube. It tasted of mint. Billy squeezed a little more on his finger and the pressure released a wiggly white worm that spilled to the floor. Nervously, he scraped the paste off the floor with a finger, which he licked clean. The taste was sharp and refreshing but there was too much of it and he felt mildly sick. He screwed the top on and carefully put the tube back where it belonged. At this moment he noticed the emerald ring.

Billy recognized the ring at once. Freddy had given it to Yasmin on her sixteenth birthday. It lay on the dresser and Billy had missed seeing it in his anxiety to get at the toothpaste.

There was an impatient knock on the door.

"Are you going to be at it all morning or what? Don't blame me if we're late for school." Yazdi sounded peevish. It was a month since he had changed schools, and now that Soli went to college, Yazdi and Billy cycled to St. Anthony's together.

"Just a minute," shouted Billy. As he ducked past the mirror he caught a glimpse of his face. His wide mouth was almost split in two by an irrepressible grin; his eyes sparkled like shiny black buttons behind round metal-framed glasses.

"You'd better hurry up," he said, opening the door and rushing past Yazdi.

Once he was in his room (Billy shared the room with Katy but she had already left for school) he unclenched his fist and examined the ring. He changed into his gray school shorts and slipped the ring into a pocket.

Freddy held Yazdi on a tight leash and Yazdi carried his sullenness around like a virus. He was accompanied to school by Billy and returned with him. In the evenings Yazdi was under the tactful surveillance of his family. If he went out, Soli made some excuse or other to accompany him. His two married sisters invited him to their homes frequently and took him out to dinner, dance-dramas or the cinema. St. Anthony's was quite far from Yazdi's former school and it was impossible for him to cycle back and forth and squeeze in a visit with Rosy during the break.

Yet a week back, he had boldly approached Brother Jones to excuse him from class before break. "It's urgent," he said, and the teacher gave him permission.

Yazdi had pedaled furiously all the way and hung around the school gate until he heard the bell. Rosy came running up as soon as she spied the gangling, forlorn boy leaning against his bicycle. Wordlessly they hurried to their private nook behind the hedges.

Yazdi barely had time to explain his absence from school and give an account of his father's unfortunate reaction.

"Please don't be so angry," he begged.

Rosy's face was flushed with rage and her eyes smarted with tears. She struck the grass with childish fists and hissed in a choked and curiously husky voice. "The bloody bastard! Who the bloody hell does he think he is, man?"

Yazdi gripped her frail arms and kissed her flushed, wet mouth. "Look, don't feel like that. Does he matter? I'll marry you. I'll find a way out. I promise. Just have a little faith in me . . . please . . . please?"

The school bell clamored urgently. Rosy moved back.

"When can you see me again?" she asked.

"Next Friday. I'll skip class again."

Yazdi looked deep into the flecked green eyes, large and bitter in the wan little face. "Don't worry, I'll get around my father . . . just give me a little time."

Rosy stood up, smoothing her pleated school skirt. "Can you carry a message for me? Tell him go bugger himself, man!"

Yazdi had alternately blushed and wept all the way back to St. Anthony's.

While Billy affectionately fingered the ring in his pocket during the math period, Yazdi went through an agony of timidity in the tenth form. Brother Jones had been in a thunderous mood all morning. Twice Yazdi had risen from his chair determined to confront him, and both times he was deterred by the unapproachable scowl on the teacher's face. "Rosy is waiting for me," he kept repeating to himself, and finally, gathering courage from the vision of her wrath and disappointment if he didn't show up, he approached Brother Jones.

"Excuse me, sir. I have to go out—it's rather urgent. Please excuse me for this class. I'll be back after recess."

Brother Jones, bald and corpulent, scowled up from the books he was correcting.

"You skipped out last Friday as well, didn't you?"

"Yes sir. I'm sorry, sir. Only this once more, sir."

"I doubt if your father pays us so that you can cut classes whenever you wish. I'm afraid I can't allow you to go. Next time you think something urgent is liable to crop up, get a note from one of your parents."

"Yes, sir," gulped Yazdi, biting his lip. Dejectedly he returned to his desk.

Billy spent the entire recess closeted in the school toilet, examining and admiring the ring. When he returned home late in the afternoon he wandered about the house hoping to catch a glimpse of Yasmin. He wanted to observe her face, knowing it would reveal, as plain as chalk on a blackboard, whether the ring had been missed—and reveal also the full satisfying measure of her wretchedness.

He sauntered casually through the rooms where his sister might be found and he climbed to the terrace. The roof, like the rooms, was bare of Yasmin. Disappointed, Billy climbed down. Seeing his mother in the kitchen, he inquired, "Where's Yasmin?"

"I told her to lie down in my room. She looked as though she'd swallowed castor oil. I hope that girl isn't coming down with something."

Billy turned away, hiding a grin.

When Yasmin, subdued and preoccupied, came to the dinner table, Billy was hard pressed to contain his merriment. He lowered his brow to his plate and, wrapping huge chunks of bread around the meat with his fingers, stuffed his mouth.

Billy found it as impossible to control the grin that split his face from one outstanding ear to the other as the tears that sprang to his eyes at the merest hint of moisture in another's. He felt his tears unmasked a shameful and sissyish softness. And, of course, one look at his grin when he'd been up to mischief, and the whole family pounced on him to discover what it was.

Halfway through the rice course, having succeeded in gaining control of his features, Billy ventured innocently, "Why are you so quiet, Yasmin?"

"None of your business," replied Yasmin dully. She remained quiet throughout the rest of the meal.

Saturday there was no school. Billy tossed drowsily in bed as Katy slipped into her clothes, combed her hair and left the room. It was already too cold to sleep on the roof, and the nip in the October air that had sent Katy hungrily to breakfast had kept Billy lazing in bed.

Katy returned to find Billy fast asleep. He was covered from head to toe by his bedsheet as by a shroud. Soothing little snores were issuing, and Katy went straight past him to the chest of drawers which served as their dressing table.

Billy's eyes were wide open beneath the sheet. His ears were cocked vigilantly to follow the sound of her movements, and he was careful to snore lightly every now and again. Katy, not caring if she disturbed her sleeping brother, set up a din that would have awakened a hibernating bear. She lifted and banged down jars, bottles, and hairbrushes. At last the clatter stopped and Billy heard her say, "Have you seen my money? I left two two-piece bits on the dresser a minute ago."

Billy emitted a little crop of snores.

There was a moment of ominous quiet. Billy wished he could see what Katy was up to. Maybe she had left the room to search elsewhere. Cheered by this reflection he gingerly lifted an edge of the bedsheet and found himself looking straight into Katy's watchful eyes. She crouched by the bed, peering at him from a distance of two inches.

Before Billy had time to seal the chink, Katy had snatched the sheet off his face. "I knew you were pretending to sleep," she cried, demanding in the same breath, "Have you seen the money? I left it on the dresser."

"Ahaaaaaahooooo," yawned Billy, as elaborately and loudly as a lion. He stretched himself full-length on the bed and, turning away with an exasperated and aggrieved rustle of sheets, he once again covered himself from head to toe.

"You have it! I know you have!" cried Katy, jumping astride Billy's buttocks and pounding on the bedsheet.

Billy cowered beneath the rain of blows from her small wrathful fists and stuck out his skinny elbows to protect his face.

"OK, OK," he temporized, but the instant Katy suspended her pummeling, he caught her off-balance and sprang upright on the strong bed. He adjusted his glasses and wagged a sticklike finger solemnly in her face.

"Serves you right for being so careless."

"Give me back my money," demanded Katy.

"Oh? Why?"

"Because it's mine."

"No, I don't think I will. That will teach you not to be careless with money. What if one of the servants had taken it?"

"But I knew you were in the room!" wailed Katy. "The servants wouldn't steal my money."

"Oh, yes they would! You are a wicked girl. I'll tell Mama you are teaching the servants to steal!"

Katy was not to be put out by the threat. "Mama, Mama!" she bawled at the very top of her voice.

"What is it?" Putli called from some recess of the house that was undergoing a ferocious scrubbing.

"Mama, Billy has taken my money and he won't give it back!"

Putli's voice came shrill and exasperated. "Stop teasing your little sister at once," and then, "Yasmin, go and stop those two quarreling."

Billy jumped up and down on the bed, chanting, "Careless Kitty. Careless Kitty," and just as Katy was lifting a jar of cold cream to throw at him, Yasmin came into the room in her nightdress, demanding, "All right, all right, now what's going on?"

"I left my money on the dresser and went out for just two minutes and Billy took it and now he won't give it back!" bawled Katy.

"Of course he will," soothed her sister. Yasmin was a plump, slow, light-skinned girl with nondescript features that had bloomed miraculously when she turned sixteen.

"Won't you, Billy?" she coaxed with conciliatory elder-sisterliness.

"She can't go around leaving money like that! I'm teaching her the value of money! She musn't be so careless."

"OK, OK, now that she has learned her lesson, give her back her money."

"I'll give it when I feel like, not when you tell me!"

A heavy, distended look came of a sudden into Yasmin's eyes. Billy gave an imperceptible start, and all at once his assurance slid off him and out of the window. He guessed the train of thought responsible for the strange look, and he knew also where it would lead. Even before his slow-thinking sister could marshal her thoughts, he looked about warily for a route of escape.

"You wouldn't happen to know anything about a ring, now, would you?" asked Yasmin craftily, closing in on him with eyes as narrow as a boxer's about to strike.

"What ring?"

"A gold ring with an emerald. My birthday present."

Billy knew the game was up. It was no use pretending innocence. It was a perilous moment. He flashed past her in a mighty leap and landing by the clothes-hanger fixed to the wall, he dug into the pockets of his gray shorts.

In the brief time it took him to clasp the ring, Yasmin, whirling about with a startled gasp, had him securely pinned by his ears. She turned them like doorknobs. Billy tried to wriggle out of the painful vice, kicking and punching.

"Katy, get hold of his legs," panted Yasmin, retracting her soft body as far as she could from the stinging blows.

137

Now there were two of them at him. But the resourceful Billy suddenly swung an arm and threw something that clicked and bounced and clicked again on the bare floor.

Both girls let go of him at once, searching the floor with their eyes, while Billy scooted from the room and up the stairs to the terrace.

The girls quickly recovered the two two-piece bits, and Katy, who wanted to buy a popsicle, rushed down to the hawker.

Yasmin, deceived by the click of the money on the floor, was left alone to ponder the deception. She had been sure it was the ring he had flung. She almost wept at the realization that her treacherous brother had escaped with it to the terrace.

Taking the steps two at a time, she climbed up after him.

Billy was crouching cautiously, three paces from the door, when Yasmin emerged. She shut the door and drew the bolt from the outside.

"OK, I've got you cornered now, you little squirt. I'm going to teach you such a lesson, such a lesson . . ."

Yasmin lunged forward. Billy, dodging her charge, just managed to slip from her reach. He skipped to and fro on the brick terrace, hopping to her and back like a willful monkey, his sister, patiently and inexorably crowding him into a corner.

Yasmin, arms outstretched, legs straddled beneath her cotton nightie, moved forward, menacing and confident.

Just as she thought she had him, Billy leaped to one side. In a single movement he scaled the three-foot parapet wall and dropped six feet onto their neighbor's mud-thatched roof. He knew she wouldn't dare the plunge.

Yasmin glared over the parapet. Billy danced beneath her, criss-crossing his nimble legs and waving his arms. His ears stuck out like a gargoyle's, and beneath his large nose the elfin split of his mouth curved ebulliently.

Yasmin's face was purple with chagrin. "You'd better hand over the ring if you know what's good for you!"

"Your fault. You shouldn't be so careless with jewelry. Do you know how much it cost? I showed it at Barkat Ram's and they offered five hundred rupees, and I can tell you, Papa did not pluck the money off a tree. Fat lot you care for your father!"

Yasmin, frustrated and enraged beyond measure, swung her legs over the parapet wall. She contemplated risking the six-foot jump and decided against it. Even if by some miracle she survived the drop, Billy would escape to the next roof and then the next.

"You mean, ugly, toad-sized grasshopper, if you don't give me the ring at once, I'll tell father!"

Billy's face sobered. He knew she meant it. His brown skin took on a dangerous, dusky hue. This was no longer sport. His father never struck any of them, and for this very reason his censure was unbearable and humiliating to the children. There was a tacit agreement between them not to complain to their father. Billy felt the provocation in this case was trifling. After all, Yasmin must know she would get the ring back eventually.

"I'm going to father," she repeated, and as she drew back from the parapet, Billy suddenly raised his fist in the air and shouted, "I'm going to throw it away!"

He swung his arm back, and Yasmin screamed.

"If you go to father, I swear I'll throw it away!" he shouted again.

"Then give me the ring. Please, Billy, please," pleaded Yasmin, shaken by his sudden fury.

Billy brought his hand down slowly, "Say you're sorry first."

"Sorry."

"Say, 'I'm careless, careless, careless, and I'll never do it again, so long as I live.'"

"I said I'm sorry."

"That's not good enough. Say, 'Sorry Billy, I'm so careless. I'll try to improve my bad habits.'"

"You monstrous little rat! Give me that ring before I kill you!"

"All right, if that's the way you feel, I'll throw it into the street."

"All right, all right, I'll say it! I'm careless, I'm careless, I'm sorry!"

"'And I'll try to improve my bad habits.'"

"And I'll try to improve my bad habits."

139

"Not like that! You are too proud to admit your fault! What will Papa say when he finds out you are so proud? It's no use. You'll never learn unless I throw the ring away."

Yasmin suddenly burst into tears—and Billy couldn't stand to see anyone cry. He felt trapped and choked and unaccountably sorry for his sister, and these baffling emotions charged him with the helpless fear of a wild thing at bay.

"Say what I told you—say what I told you to say, as if you mean it!" he screamed.

Yasmin knew when he reached this point he was not answerable for himself. Seeing her tears reflected in the agony of her brother's face, she was overcome by a wave of sisterly compassion. Docilely, timidly, she mouthed the words he demanded of her and held out her hand.

At once Billy was calm. "You promise you won't take revenge?"

Yasmin nodded.

Billy gave a puckish grin that stretched from ear to ear.

"Good girl," he condescended, and careful to maintain a safe distance from her legs—Yasmin was not above a parting kick—he tossed the ring gently over the parapet wall to her.

Chapter 25

When Faredoon Junglewalla, pioneer and adventurer, trotted into Lahore in his bullock cart at the turn of the century, there were only thirty Parsees in the city of over a million Hindus, Muslims, Sikhs and Christians. Twenty years later, the number of Parsees in Lahore had swelled to almost three hundred. Poor families had drifted in from Bombay and the area thereabouts to settle in the rich North Indian province, gratefully partaking of the bounty that was Lahore. And, of course, original sons of the soil, of whom Freddy justifiably considered himself a member, had enormously proliferated.

Freddy was the undisputed head of this community. He was also spokesman and leader of the Parsees scattered over the rest of the Punjab and the Northwest Frontier Province right up to the Khyber Pass. Freddy's willingness and ability to help, to give of his time, to intervene and intercede, were proverbial; his influence with men who wielded power was legendary. They said of him, "Oh, he has the police in his pocket." They boasted, "He has the English sahibs tamed so that they eat out of his hand." And this was no mean accomplishment, for the aloof, disparaging and arrogant British rarely became pally with the "natives."

Faredoon Junglewalla, toady, philanthropist and shrewd businessman, was renowned for his loyalty to his community and friends. People came from afar seeking his help in bagging prime jobs, securing licenses, contracts, permits and favors. They traveled two thousand miles from Bombay, expecting Faredoon to extricate them from "tight spots," as did Mr. Adi Sodawalla, whose brother, Mr. Polly Sodawalla, was languishing in a London jail.

Mr. Adi Sodawalla, pale, timorous and pleading, sat across the desk from Faredoon presenting his case.

"Tell me everything . . . every detail," insisted Faredoon.

Mr. Adi Sodawalla related the facts honestly and humbly. He

glanced every now and then at the heavy-lidded eyes that missed nothing, and he drew courage from the benign and understanding expression on Freddy's handsome face.

Mr. Polly Sodawalla, the subject of his brother's narrative, had voyaged to England with a suitcase full of illegal opium, which he had airily sent away to be deposited in the ship's hold with the rest of his luggage. On disembarking, he was too worn out by landing formalities to clear and take along his possessions. Carrying only the suitcase he had had in his cabin, he went to refresh himself at a hotel in Earl's Court. When he sauntered up to claim his luggage the next day, he discovered that one bag, dumped unceremoniously from place to place with the rest of his luggage, had split open, spilling its secret.

The reception committee of customs officers and policemen, patiently awaiting his return, welcomed him with flattering interest and marched him off to jail.

Interpol moved in. Mr. Polly Sodawalla could look forward to a long sojourn in His Imperial Majesty's prisons.

His brother, while relating the story to Freddy, had emphasized the freezing temperatures in dank English cells.

At the end of his tale, he anxiously watched Freddy sit back in his swivel chair, fold his hands on his chest and tilt back his head to gaze at the ceiling. He could see that Faredoon was angry.

"Cunt! The lazy, stupid cunt!" exploded Freddy slowly. His voice was bitter. "Do you know how much money your brother would have made if he had succeeded? At least fifty thousand rupees! Even a toothless baby would have known to clear the luggage first. But no. His Imperial Majesty was too tired, he had to go to a hotel to wash behind his ears first, he had to curl up on a sofa like a carefree lamb and fall asleep. He deserves to be in jail!"

"You're right, sir. I will break his teeth," quavered Mr. Sodawalla, holding aloft a puny fist for Freddy's edification.

"Now, had he been caught by a vigilant customs officer," Freddy continued, "had he been informed upon, he would have my sympathy. I can find it in my heart to help a misguided soul—but I cannot forgive a fool!"

"But he is my brother! I beg you, I implore you for our mother's sake to help him. She has not stopped crying since she heard the news. 'Oh, my son will freeze into a block of ice. Oh, he will die of pneumonia,' she wails, nonstop. My heart breaks to hear her. You shall have the entire family's undying gratitude—only you can save him."

Freddy pursed his lips. "Something will have to be done," he agreed. "Not for that indolent bastard's sake, but for the good name of our community. We can't let it get around that a Parsee is in jail for smuggling opium!"

Mr. Sodawalla sniffed, wiped his eyes with a huge, white handkerchief and raised grateful, supplicating eyes to his brother's anticipated saviour.

The Sodawallas were not well-off. Faredoon financed the entire rescue of the unfortunate smuggler from his personal funds. An emissary was dispatched to London with special documents. Influential connections were entreated and coerced. Faredoon worked incessantly, and at the end of two months Mr. Polly Sodawalla sailed from London, a free man.

But if Faredoon did not take a penny from the Sodawallas, he had no scruples about relieving Mr. Katrak, a diamond merchant from Karachi, of fifty thousand rupees.

Mr. Katrak, a man with a venerable beard, sat before Freddy, his trembling hands on a gold-handled walking stick. His son, Bobby, sat beside him with lowered head. He was a thickset youth of about twenty-four, his arrogant air momentarily deflated. Freddy approved of his open-faced, neatly groomed handsomeness, thinking he would make a good match for Yasmin.

Bobby Katrak owned a gleaming Silver Ghost Rolls Royce. It had stately dashboards, two horns that were elaborately curled, rising on either side of the tinted windscreen like silver cobras, and sundry silver fittings. He was given to dashing about at reckless speeds and had rammed the Rolls into an old blind beggar on a busy thoroughfare. Bobby had panicked and roared away at thirty-five miles an hour. Five men had noted his number. Even without it, his was, in 1920, the only Silver Ghost in Karachi.

The old beggar died the next day in hospital.

"I have told him again and again not to drive so fast," mourned Mr. Katrak. "How many times have I told you not to go over fifteen? But no! He wants to 'dhoorr-dhoorr' around at thirty-five and even forty miles an hour! Now look what you've got yourself into. I feel so ashamed having to give you all this trouble, Faredoon."

Freddy wagged his head and clicked his tongue kindly at Mr. Katrak's son.

"Bobby, you must do as your father says. After all, it is his privilege to guide you. Now, I don't think it is only your speed that is to blame. The first rule one must observe is to respect the law. You can never run from it . . . though you may get around it! You should have stopped and seized one or two witnesses. There must have been people who saw you were not to blame—with the aid of a little money perhaps? Then you could have reported the matter to the police. But you did not do this, and you have complicated things for yourself."

Faredoon turned to Mr. Katrak. "I talked to my friend—you know whom I mean. I pleaded with him that the boy is like my own son. He says he will try to get him off the hook. I convinced him it was not Bobby's fault, but since he did not report the accident, the charges are grave. Anyway, my friend promises to help. He might go to Karachi himself to arrange for a couple of witnesses—make a predated report at some police thana or other . . . but," and here Freddy's inflection rose to a thinly pitched, incredulous whisper, "the bastard wants fifty thousand rupees!"

Mr. Katrak turned pale. He looked at his son, whose head was hanging as low as it ought. He looked at Freddy again and wrote out the check.

Freddy gave Mr. Gibbons, who was now inspector-general of police, the ten thousand rupees they had agreed upon, and stowed away the remaining forty in his special kitty. This was the kitty he dipped into to help others—and occasionally himself.

When his old friend Mr. Toddywalla dropped into the office with his perennial tales of woe concerning Jal, his fifth son, who was once again in some kind of a scrape, Mr. Toddywalla was surprised and hurt that Freddy, instead of sympathizing and offering to scold the boy as usual, patted Mr. Toddywalla's hand kindly and said, "You don't know how lucky you are in the boy. As the English say, you have a 'black goat' in the family. I too have a 'black goat'—my Yazdi! He keeps giving me no end of trouble." Freddy sighed, thinking of the ridiculous scrap of notebook paper in his pocket. "And I thank my stars he will keep on being a 'black goat.' I can count on him as you can count on your Jal."

Mr. Toddywalla gaped in disbelief.

Freddy gazed soulfully at his bewildered friend. "In a few years all our children will be married. They will look after our business inter-ests . . . and we will have no cares. Tell me, what is a man without worry? Without challenge? He is but a useless, retired parasite waiting to die! But your Jal and my Yazdi, they will save us. They will always create some problem or the other, keeping our blood hot with anger and pul-sating with excitement. They will keep us alive!"

In his agitation, Mr. Toddywalla sniffed so hard on a pinch of snuff that he sneezed steadily for a full minute. He believed his friend had finally gone around the bend.

After Mr. Toddywalla's departure, Freddy took the envelope from his pocket and spread the crumpled scrap of paper on his desk. Once again he read the neat, slanting handwriting:

> *To the beauty of her eyes:*
> The eyes in your eye touch me deep down somewhere.
>
> They require me most casually
> To inquire into desire
> While the world holds us apart.
>
> They demand me
> Through the indolent glint of half-closed fire
> To sink deeper in the stupor of unfulfilled love.
>
> They urge me to
> Give from a depth in myself.
> What am I to do?

Freddy could feel an angry vein throb in his forehead. He was furious and horrified that a son of his should write such emasculated gibberish. As for poetry, "The Charge of the Light Brigade" he could tolerate, but this!

In a cold rage, he scribbled beneath the last line of the poem: "If you must think and act like a eunuch, why don't you wear your sister's bangles? And don't tear pages from your notebook!"

He tucked the notepaper into a fresh envelope and addressed it to Yazdi.

The strife between them was now intensified. Freddy was tight-lipped and stern, Yazdi sullen and uncommunicative. Neither of them spoke during meals, and the evening session of discourse stagnated. Freddy tended to be overly moral and angry.

A week later he received another poem in his business mail. On a scrap of paper was written:

> What makes me seek
>> And want to know
> Your nearness?
>
> Why does the uncertain void in me
>> Wish to perceive
> Your form?
>> Who are you?
> Remove the veil.
>
> An undecided deep am I
>> And thirst is a fever.
> Thankless of the blessings of Ahura am I
>> For I seek the impossible . . .
>
> How can I fight the maniac force of society?
>> Of my father?

146

That evening when Freddy went upstairs he found Yazdi alone in the dining room. Just as Yazdi turned his sullen, narrow back on him to skulk out of the room, Freddy called to him and handed him the creased envelope.

"I've corrected the gibberish. You seem to have wasted your entire education drooling over girls. Not one sentence is complete or correct!"

"You don't know English, father—let alone poetry," sneered Yazdi.

Freddy flushed. He prided himself on his English, and the contempt of his son wounded him more than he could have thought possible.

"And Rosy Watson?" he asked, "What kind of English does the whore speak?"

Yazdi glowered at his father. "How dare you slander a girl you haven't even met?"

"Met? I have not only met her, I have fucked her. She is a common little alley cat. It might interest you to know, Mr. Allen thought her breasts were like fried eggs."

Yazdi blanched. "You haven't met her—you are lying, father, lying!"

"Why don't you find out from Alla Ditta? Ask him. He might be able to arrange a rendezvous for you at the Hira Mandi as well!"

Freddy had been so carried away by his emotions that he hadn't noticed the effect of his words on Yazdi. Now he was frightened to see Yazdi cringe as under a blow. The boy turned pale, and Freddy thought he would faint. He reached out a hand, but Yazdi flinched like a lizard scraping against the wall.

"You liar! You liar!" he snarled and fled to his room.

He failed to come to dinner, and later they discovered he had slunk out of the house after dark and had returned only late at night.

Yazdi stayed closeted in his room for three days. He refused to answer to knocks and entreaties. He would not eat and accepted only a jug of water from his mother. Putli was distraught.

On the second day, Jerbanoo rocked the flat to its foundations by storming for one solid hour: God knows what her son-in-law had told the boy? He was so tender, so green, so sensitive—and didn't she know how brutal her son-in-law could be! How unfeeling, how selfish! Her grandson would sicken; he would die. Even now he was nothing but skin and bones and eyes. What kind of father was Freddy? Ask her! She wasn't afraid to speak out! He was the most unnatural of fathers! The most unnatural of sons-in-law! The most unnatural of husbands! He was a fiend! Oh, what had happened, what could have happened between those two? Jerbanoo went on and on until she wound down and subsided in a small monsoon of tears.

The residue of all this passion was curiosity. Jerbanoo had tried her best to coerce Putli into telling her what had happened. But even Putli did not know. She guessed it had to do with the girl, and curiosity ate Jerbanoo's very soul.

At last Billy, who always appeared to know everything, sidled up to her and hissed in her ear, "Yazdi mailed father two poems about his Anglo-Indian girlfriend!"

At the end of three days, Yazdi unlocked his door and calmly joined his family at the dinner table. But he was changed.

The family did not realize this at once. Yazdi, always inclined to be gentle, now appeared to glow with tenderness. He was inordinately considerate and kind. He spent hours kneading Jerbanoo's back and treated the servants with an unassuming humanity that was quite unnatural in those times. But the timidity, the wince that always had been close to the surface of his narrow frame, was replaced by a sheath of fine steel. He seemed entirely fearless—entirely self-contained.

The family treated him with tact, especially Faredoon. When he said he did not always find it convenient to return from school with Billy, no objections were raised.

He will turn out all right after all, thought Freddy with a surge of relief.

A fortnight after the fateful altercation, Yazdi returned from school barefoot. He had given his shoes to an orphan in his class.

Putli quietly replaced them.

A few days later he returned without his shirt and, the day after, climbed up to the flat in only his homemade underpants. He had distributed his apparel among four beggars near the Regal Cinema square.

The family discoverd that Yazdi had given up eating snacks at school. He spent his pocket money and the money he borrowed from Yasmin and Billy on the unfortunates.

Freddy clutched his forehead and groaned when Putli told him all this.

Jerbanoo had a fit at the thought of her grandson squandering money. Her acquisitive little heart was cruelly pained and suddenly full of sympathy for Faredoon. Her suggestion found favor with both Putli and Freddy.

"Send him to school in Karachi. The change will do him good, and he will have a chance to meet lots of Parsee girls and boys."

Yazdi became a boarder in a boys' school in Karachi.

And on the heels of this trouble, Freddy's stars, which had behaved so decently since the fire, once again turned on him.

Chapter 26

India is magic; it always was.

The word "magic" comes from "Magi," and Faredoon was a descendant of the magi, the wise men of antiquity initiated into the mysteries of medicine, astrology, mysticism and astronomy—disciples of Zarathustra.

Hinted at in the Gathas, Songs of Zarathustra, the knowledge is now lost to the Parsees. Legend says it was withdrawn when unscrupulous elements degraded the knowledge to sorcery.

In India there is still a cornucopia of ancient Aryan wisdom, of esoteric knowledge, of incredible occurrences. A lot of it is superstition and a lot of it is mistaken for superstition.

There is a real throbbing fear of black magic, and visual evidence of its craft is everywhere. There is Kali, the goddess of death and destruction and disease. And on days when she holds sway, mothers keep babies indoors. They warn their children not to step over broken eggs, little mounds of cooked rice, colored chalk or entrails of animals, which are strategically placed on sidewalks by evil adherents of the art. Brain and pigs' feet are not eaten on such days; or liver, or heart—for it is not only the vegetarian Hindus who believe in the black art, but all those who are of India.

There are ghosts and spirits and *dains*, witches disguised as women who give themselves away by their misshapen feet that point backwards. And when the witches remove their shawls of an evening, thinking they are alone, embers can be seen glowing from braziers built into their sunken heads.

There is the threat of the Evil Eye.

Then there are the mystics—Sufis, Sadhus, Pirs, Babas and Swamis—and the incarnation of saints, those dead ancients whose wisdom and miraculous knowledge set them apart in a bygone age, and their interpreters.

From among the latter was the Brahmin, Gopal Krishan.

Gopal Krishan was introduced to Freddy by Mr. Bottliwalla, who was still shy and still unmarried. They were in Freddy's office. Gopal Krishan held them captive by the sincere inflection in his soft, factual voice and by his fascinating tale.

Two years back, on a visit to Jhelum, the Brahmin had bought a betel-nut *paan* at one of the streetside stalls. The *paan* was wrapped in an old and moldy pipal leaf. He put the *paan* in his mouth. Just as he was about to throw away the stained, heart-shaped wrapper, he was struck by some lettering on it. The Brahmin was a Sanskrit scholar with a love of ancient languages. Intrigued, he held the faint lettering to the light of the sun and deciphered the script.

At his sister's house, where he was staying, and with the help of his books, he laboriously made out the text. It read, "You, the fifth incarnation of the scholar Rabindranath, will find me. You will unravel a whole treasure house of knowledge. Look after the treasure carefully. Use it for good. Do not exploit it for gold or fame. These *janam patris* (birth sheets) are fruits of a lifetime of dedication."

The next morning he again went to the betel-nut stall. The stall owner gave Gopal Krishan the few leaves remaining with him and directed him to the rag-and-paper man who had supplied him.

At the rag-man's, Gopal saw gigantic mounds of these leaves stacked beside dumps of old newspapers, empty bottles and iron scrap. They were marked with the same fine print. He bought the whole lot for ten rupees and had the leaves transported two miles to Lahore. Their large backyard, in which his wife washed clothes, stitched, and sunned herself in winter, was filled with leaves.

Miraculously, as if unseen hands were directing his picking, the first handful of leaves he picked up for study revealed the mystery.

Roughly translated, the messages read, "I, Pandit Omkarnath, reincarnation of the famous mathematician and astrologer Pandit Bhagwandas, have undertaken this task for posterity. Every child born in the land of the five rivers or man residing in the Punjab will have his future revealed in the *janam patris*. He will find good counsel and knowledge of herbs to cure ailments. My son Premnath will work out the charts, and I will interpret the future."

The pipal leaves were three hundred years old! Although moldy and discolored, they still retained flexibility, probably the result of some mysterious preservative.

Gopal Krishan continued, "Once again, miraculously, my fingers picked out my own *janam patri* and, later, those of my wife and children. I have since tried to sort out the leaves, as many as I could, but it never ceases to astonish me how easily I can find the *janatti patris* of those who visit me for advice. It is as if their presence guides my hand, as if their ordained visit coincides with the leaves I have sorted. Every now and then when I am troubled, I find a sheet to guide me. Each of us has several leaves that turn up as the need arises."

Freddy studied the modest, nondescript man closely. His somber black eyes were candid, his smooth-skinned, flat-nosed, round face gentle. The man had no pretensions in his getup: neither caste-marks on his forehead, nor the naked torso or shaven head of priests and soothsayers. He wore neither the beads nor the bizarre raiment often affected by fortune-tellers. He was dressed like any *baboo* employed in a business concern. He wore a white, European-style shirt and cotton coat over his dhoti, and his head was covered by a limp, unassuming turban.

Freddy found himself readily believing the man's story. For Freddy was of India, and though his religion preached but one God, he had faith in scores of Hindu deities and in Muslim and Christian saints. His faith taught heaven and hell, but he believed implicitly in reincarnation. How else could one reconcile the misery, injustice, and inequity of life in the scheme of things?

Gopal Krishan needed assistance in sorting out the millions of leaves. He needed space, shelves and money for all this. Quite a bit of his meager salary was contributed to this end.

Freddy was touched by the man's selfless obsession and was eager to find his own *janam patri*. Mr. Bottliwalla had already found two sheets regarding himself and had contributed generously to further the research.

"I will be honored to look into this," promised Freddy and made an appointment to visit Gopal Krishan's house after two days.

Freddy's somnolent lids flew open at the sight of the enormous dump of discolored pipal leaves in the courtyard. How could the Brahmin ever hope to sort them all out?

A rusty tin-sheet roof with bamboo supports covered the yard. "This is the best I could do to protect my legacy from the elements," explained Gopal Krishan shyly, indicating the roof.

Freddy did not comment.

"Come, I will take you to the sorting room where we may find your sheet."

Mr. Bottliwalla and Freddy followed Gopal into a long, roughly whitewashed room in which every bit of peeling wall space was streaked with wooden planks. The *janam patris* were neatly stacked and tabulated on the makeshift shelves. In the center of the room was a worn table with four cane-backed chairs.

Gopal noted Freddy's date and place of birth and began to search among the stacks.

Freddy sat bemused and anxious.

"He'll find something, don't worry," said Mr. Bottliwalla, adding, "He only took five minutes locating mine last time."

"How many of your sheets has he found?" asked Freddy.

"Only two."

"Were they truthful?"

"Of course! You'll see for yourself soon enough."

Gopal Krishan approached them, carefully holding a leaf the size of a man's palm. "I think I've got it," he said sitting beside Freddy.

Freddy felt exhilarated—as if he was on the threshold of an adventure.

"It coincides with your date of birth. It says your name begins with 'fuh,' that you were born to the south of the Punjab, and that you are of the Agni Puja (fire-worshipping) sect. It appears to fit in. I will read it out. Only you can confirm if it is yours."

Gopal Krishan adjusted his black-rimmed half-glasses low on his nose and, looking every inch the humble, careworn accountant he was, began to read and translate from the leaf. Two years of practice had made him quite proficient in the ancient language. Unlike written English, most Indian scripts are in shorthand.

"The owner of this *janam patri* is a singularly fortunate man," he began. "You will be endowed with exceptional grace and good looks. Tall and fair-skinned, you will enchant all who are privileged to meet you. You will shine like a star in the thoughts of men. Your community will look upon you as their leader.

"Your wife is the reincarnation of a Devi. She is a saint. You will be blessed with seven children. Three of them will be boys."

Gopal looked up at Freddy for confirmation and Freddy nodded. "That's right, seven children."

"Your young manhood will be sorely troubled by an older woman, but the trouble will be overcome. From this point onward you will do exceedingly well in business.

"You have a great attraction to fire, an intuitive understanding of its mysterious nature. You can draw upon its pure strength as few are able to. Its divine energy will always benefit you. Don't forsake it."

There was nothing to indicate how startled Freddy was by this revelation. There was no change in his demeanor as, for a brief moment, his mind dwelt on the fateful blaze that had given him his start in life.

Gopal Krishan looked at Freddy diffidently. "You light the holy lamp daily? You offer sandalwood and frankincense to the household fire as your religion prescribes?"

"Oh yes. We are a religious household."

"No doubt this has benefited you. In difficult times this reverence you show will always come to your aid."

Freddy felt the man was giving a slightly inaccurate interpretation of the message contained in the leaf. He let it go at that, but he knew what the *janam patri* really meant. It was like a delicate and secret communication between him and his *patri*.

Gopal turned his attention to the leaf.

"You will make a lot of money. You will give a lot away—of your money, and of your time. Your name will shine like lettering on the sky long after you are dead.

"You are fortunate in your children and in your grandchildren.

154

Except for a little trouble in your middle years, your relationship with them will be excellent and beneficial.

"One of your sons is the favorite of the gods. He will be a bigger man than even you. Good fortune will rest beneath the soles of his feet, endowing him with success at each step."

Freddy was exultant. He knew the *janam patri* could only mean Soli. His heart filled with joy and pride as the image of his handsome son smiled inside his eyelids. Soli was all any father could wish: considerate, affectionate, quick-witted and intelligent. Freddy was the most blessed of fathers.

Freddy hardly followed as Gopal Krishan continued to read the horoscope. He was too full of gladness and pride in his son's marvelous future.

Suddenly Gopal Krishan paused.

"This is not so good," he said. Then, clearing his throat and consciously assuming his matter-of-fact tone, he read, "Even the most fortunate of beings cannot escape sorrow entirely. You are lucky in that your sorrow will visit you in your middle years—you will have enjoyed living to the full and gained insight into the transitory ways of life and destiny. You will not allow bitterness to taint your days or sorrow to rob you of your joy of life. The gods take unto themelves those they love most. Consider yourself fortunate even in misfortune.

"What does all this mean?" interrupted Freddy.

"One of your sons will die . . . "

"Oh—who?" demanded Freddy peremptorily. All his senses were suddenly alert. He was sitting up straight in his chair.

Gopal Krishan read silently for a moment.

When he looked up, his dark, liquid eyes mirrored his sympathy. "Your eldest son will be lifted by the gods before he completes twenty-one years."

Color drained from Freddy's face. He gripped the table with white knuckles. He found it impossible to breathe. The room swayed and went dim.

"You are mistaken," he said, so faintly they could barely hear him. "Look again," he breathed in a stronger voice.

155

Soli was to complete his twenty-first birthday on the 22nd of December, just a month and a half away.

Gopal Krishan looked at Freddy in alarm. Mr. Bottliwalla, who knew of Freddy's love for Soli, grew fearful.

"It must be a mistake," he echoed feebly, trying to signal Gopal Krishan to agree with him.

"No, I don't think I'm mistaken—but one never can tell. We might find another sheet suggesting preventive measures or a cure for the disease.

"Then find it. Look for it now!" cried Freddy.

"Forgive me, Junglewalla Seth, I'm afraid I won't be able to. I've never been able to locate two sheets for a person on the same day. The *janam patri* reveals its secrets slowly—only when ordained."

"For God's sake, man," Freddy exploded. Then he shouted, "Rot! What absolute nonsense!" He stood up.

"But you have other sons . . ." said Gopal Krishan. How was he to know the other sons did not matter? Not when it came to a comparison with Soli.

"Please be rational," he begged kindly. He was touched and disconcerted by Freddy's reaction. "Look at it this way. Those who are plucked in youth and innocence are among the fortunates. It is we sinners who have to plod and labor through the whole span of a long life, rebirth after rebirth. This is your son's reward for his past virtue, for his present goodness. He is closer to blessed nirvana than you and I—eons closer. We must rejoice in his piety and advanced state and pray that his remaining incarnations be as short. For aren't we all striving for this? That we may pass quickly through our lives and at last reach perfect accord with the Supreme Source of all life?"

"You will excuse me," said Freddy by way of reply. "I am overcome by the message you have just read out. I must go."

Freddy, followed by his nervously apologetic friend, rushed from the house, not waiting even for Gopal Krishan to show them out.

Freddy climbed into his tonga and galloped all the way to his store. Mr. Bottliwalla watched their swift passage through the crowded streets with a hand on his heart and a prayer on his lips.

By the time Freddy reached home his mind, unable to accept even the possibility of the prophesied tragedy, had erased all the beliefs imprinted on it through the years. In a snap, as it were, his brain had embraced reason and discarded a lifetime of faith, superstition and supernatural conviction.

When he climbed up to the flat, Freddy had regained his control. He led Mr. Bottliwalla into the vacant sitting room and there engaged him in an eager, scathing and logical attack on superstition, astrology, reincarnation and all that rubbish. He decided not to mention anything about the *janam patri* to Putli. She was inclined to be superstitious and might take the nonsense to heart, he explained to Mr. Bottliwalla. And when Mr. McReady, the affable, bearded Scotsman from the Planning Commission, dropped in for a drink, he was surprised by Freddy's vehement tirade against the so-called saints, soothsayers and mystics of India.

Soli was out to dinner, but he and a college friend joined Freddy in the sitting room after dinner. Freddy raised himself to sit up in his armchair as Soli entered. He looked young and strong. Nothing could stem the force of his will to live, his irrepressible vitality. The man with his ridiculous *janam patris* was a charlatan and a joker!

Jerbanoo came into the room and started scolding Soli for not telling them he would be out to dinner. Soli gave her a bear-hug, raising his grandmother's unwieldy bulk a foot off the floor. Jerbanoo gave a delighted squeal and the family broke up with mirth, Freddy laughing loudest.

But the next day, and the next, worry gnawed at him. All of a sudden, an unreasoning fear would well up like a gaseous smog and clutch his heart. Then he would see Soli again, see the vigor in his handsome limbs, the joyous flash in his eyes and his warm smile, and he would know there was no truth in the prophesy. But it is not easy to shed a lifetime of instinctive faith in irrational beliefs. Had not Christ risen from the dead? Weren't there miracles? Something would miraculously change the course of the stars and thwart destiny. There could be a mistake in the *janam patri*. He tried to recall the particulars of a story in which a Mogul emperor had taken his son's death upon himself by praying. He would pray. There was black magic . . . the dark moments in Soli's stars could be transferred to some other member of the family . . .

And all at once Freddy put a stop to this trend of thought. It harbored the insidious ingredients of faith—his deadliest enemy since that stricken moment when he had believed the Brahmin.

Chapter 27

Katy rushed up and shouted gleefully from the landing, "Mummy, Soli's had a nasty fall! He tried to stand up on his bicycle. Serves him right for trying to show off!"

Putli, assiduously scrubbing a tomato in the kitchen, ignored her, but Freddy shot up from his chair in the dining room and hurtled head-long down the stairs to collide with Soli. Soli was on his way up to wash his bruises.

"You fell down!" he accused, breathless with anxiety and winded by the impact.

"Oh, it was nothing. Only a few scratches," said Soli, surprised.

Freddy went limp with relief.

"You should know better than try tricks on a bicycle at your age," he scolded, turning to remount the steps and finish his tea.

The next day when Soli complained of a headache at dinner, Freddy's spoon clattered to the floor. He jerked his head up to look at his son.

"You look flushed. Get into bed at once!" he ordered.

"I'm just catching a cold—it's nothing," protested Soli.

"I said, get into bed! Your mother will get you some hot soup."

As Soli stood up, Freddy added, "Putli, you'd better take his temperature."

"You might have let him finish his dinner," remonstrated Putli, astonished at her husband's behavior. He was as white as the tablecloth. Still, she followed Soli out of the room.

"My word! What a hue and cry over nothing!" gargled Jerbanoo through a mouthful of curried rice—and wisely eschewed further comment.

When Putli called, "His temperature is only 99 degrees," Freddy glared at Jerbanoo. "See? I could tell he had fever! I am getting a doctor!"

Freddy flung his napkin beside his half-eaten plate of fish curry and went to wash his hands.

"What's the matter with you?" asked Putli rushing after him. "It's only a cold. I'll give him some honey and brandy, and you see if he is not as fit as a horse tomorrow! If he is not well by tomorrow, you can get a doctor. All right?"

Freddy agreed reluctantly.

He did not sleep that night. Next morning when he discovered Soli had no fever, he was inordinately joyous. Soli wished to go to college, but Freddy ordered him to spend the day in bed and nurse his cold.

In his office Freddy decided he had to put a stop to his nervousness. He realized it was foolish to go to pieces like that. It came from listening to phonies and quacks.

The office mail that morning contained two personal letters from Karachi. Freddy slit open an envelope. A delighted smile crossed his face. The letter was from Mr. Katrak, formally proposing marriage between Yasmin and his son, Bobby.

"Putli will be pleased," thought Freddy, making up his mind to give her the good news after dinner.

Freddy had hinted at the desirability of such a match to Mr. Katrak when Mr. Katrak was in Lahore. Mr. Katrak had not capitulated at once and Freddy, despite the fifty thousand rupees he had taken off him, had had such pressures put on Bobby's case that Mr. Katrak was constantly in need of Freddy's assistance and intervention. All this was done most subtly, of course, and Mr. Katrak was not sure if Freddy had a hand in it.

Freddy had hinted again.

Mr. Katrak, grossly indebted to Freddy and uneasy about the cause of the prolongation and complications of the case, decided to try out the marriage angle.

And why not. The girl was quite pretty, well brought up and docile. Besides, Bobby had appeared to like her at the dinner Faredoon had hosted in Lahore.

That his stratagem had worked so well infused Freddy with a sense of achievement.

"Ah, but you don't know the part I played in all this romancing," he crowed that night when Putli smiled up from reading the letter. "I am like that charming, baby-god Cupid; I shot my arrows straight through their hearts."

"How is that?" inquired Putli.

"I had to shoot one into old man Katrak's first," was Freddy's enigmatic reply. He turned his back upon his staring spouse and disappeared into the bathroom.

The other letter was from Yazdi's guardian in Karachi. Yazdi appeared to have settled down at last. He was doing well at school and his behavior was very nearly normal.

It was a happy week for Freddy. The stars were giving him a respite.

Exactly a week from that day, Freddy was plunged into the throes of a nightmare.

At noon Freddy climbed up to collect some papers from the safe in his bedroom. The door to Soli's room was ajar and as he passed it he saw Soli, his head propped up on pillows, reading a book.

"What's the matter, son?" asked Freddy from the door.

Soli laid the book face down on his stomach and Freddy was appalled by the color in his face. His lips were as red as a mannequin's and two brilliant spots flamed on his cheeks.

"I had to come away from college. I felt dizzy," said Soli.

Freddy tiptoed into the room and sat on the edge of the bed.

"You did well, son," he smiled, but his hand on the boy's hot arm was trembling.

"Has your mother seen to you?"

"Yes, she's making cinnamon tea."

"Why didn't she send word you weren't well? Doesn't matter—I'll fetch the doctor."

Soli's feverish eyes sparkled with mischief.

"How can you expect mother to tell you anything if you make such a fuss? It's just the cold again."

"Try to get some sleep," said Freddy getting up. He laid a hand on Soli's forehead, gently pushing back an unruly wave of brown hair.

Soli glanced up at him with a good-natured mocking look in his eyes. He was incredibly handsome and, prone on his back with his face flushed, terrifyingly vulnerable.

Freddy removed the papers from his safe. On his way down he stopped at the landing to tell Putli, "I'm getting a doctor."

Putli continued to strain the cinnamon tea. All these days of Freddy's inordinate concern about Soli had begun to infect her.

"Have you taken his temperature?"

Putli glanced at her husband. He saw at once the worry she was trying to conceal.

"Little over a hundred and two," she answered, on the verge of tears.

By the time the doctor arrived, Soli's temperature was 103 degrees.

Dr. Bharucha was a short, rotund, middle-aged man with a kindly countenance and a brusque manner. He was Freddy's personal friend, and he held the family's confidence.

After examining Soli he remarked, "There's a slight congestion in his chest. Could be influenza, but one cannot be sure; so many infections start with a cold. Keep him on a very light diet and bathe his forehead in cold water if he gets uncomfortable. That should bring the temperature down."

Soli's temperature did not come down.

On the third day, Dr. Bharucha confirmed his first suspicion. "It is typhoid. Don't let him eat anything—just a sip of ice water. He's a sturdy young fellow. He'll pull through all right."

Now that the moment was upon him, Freddy withstood the diagnosis better than expected. But Putli's colorless complexion turned chalky. The fear in her drew fine lines on her dry skin and instinctively Freddy put out an arm to support her.

The children tiptoed in and out of the room to visit their brother. Seeing him unwell, Katy and Billy were suddenly self-conscious and awkward in his presence. The first few days, Soli attempted to put them at ease by smiling and joking. As he grew progressively more listless, they could see he had to make an effort to talk.

Freddy sent word to Mr. Bottliwalla, and together they went to see the Brahmin.

Freddy, who had ignored Gopal Krishan since their last visit, was apologetic. He placed an envelope containing five hundred rupees on the worn desk and said, "I'm sorry I couldn't visit you earlier—there was such a pressure of work. I've come at the first opportunity. I hope you will accept this little contribution. It is to help you with your noble task." And almost casually, he inquired, "Were you able to find any more of my sheets? My son is very sick."

Gopal Krishan studied Freddy's face gravely.

"Junglewalla Seth, I'd feel mortified accepting anything from you when you are so troubled. Let's keep this for easier times." He handed the envelope back to Freddy.

Gopal Krishan spoke with genuine sympathy. His manner of returning the envelope was so gracious that Freddy, instead of feeling hurt by the refusal, was deeply moved. His eyes filmed over and his face, always expressive, was eloquent with gratitude.

What the *patri* said was true: one could not help loving the man, thought Gopal Krishan. Aloud he said, "I have not been able to find your *patris* so far, but I will renew my effort and send you word as soon as I do."

Freddy got up submissively and took his leave.

That night he broke down. Sitting on his bed, he wept quietly. He didn't attempt to shield his face from Putli.

Touched by his anguish, Putli held him to her. She bent to kiss his eyes and face and hair in a way she had not done in a long time. She cradled his head and shoulders on her bosom and her sparse frame engulfed him in a caress that had the warmth and consolation of a sunlit ocean. Freddy drew freely of her strength and was recovered for another day.

Freddy climbed to the flat twenty times a day to see Soli.

Freddy stood by the bed. He was acutely conscious of the change wrought in his son in one week. Where once the outlines of his body beneath the bedsheet were those of a full-grown man, there was now only a tenuous frame of bones. Could a body waste so? The color still flaming on the young, shrunken face was garish. Soli's eyes appeared abnormally large in a mute and desperate appeal. Freddy stroked the forehead that was always burning.

The boy closed his eyes. He darted a bony tongue over his lips and breathed, "Water."

His voice is so thin and reedy it is like a sick woman's, thought Freddy, profoundly shocked. He went to a small table loaded with bottles of mixtures and poured a little water into a glass. He lifted Soli's head tenderly from the pillow and held the glass to his lips.

When Freddy came out of the room, he saw Jerbanoo sitting by the dining room window. A *mathabana* covered her peppery hair. She rocked back and forth, praying over her beads.

Sensing Freddy's presence, she raised to him her harried, questioning eyes.

Freddy shook his head and shrugged despairingly. On an impulse he stepped up to her and, enfolding her hands in both of his, lowered his head to kiss the beads.

Putli and Jerbanoo were in constant attendance upon the patient. Jerbanoo was indefatigable. She bathed his forehead, stroked his frail limbs and administered medicine whenever she could relieve Putli. She ran errands with an alacrity they had not expected of her.

All members of the family moved with conscious quiet, and even the insufferable Billy refrained from provoking his sisters. They were anxious to help and craved to do something for the sick youth. Hutoxi, Ruby and their husbands hovered about the flat, relieving Putli and Jerbanoo for an occasional night's sleep.

On the fourteenth day of the sickness, Soli took a bad turn. He moaned and thrashed about deliriously and alternately lapsed into a frightening, deathlike coma.

All eyes were red from weeping.

The doctor was summoned thrice that day, and late in the evening, when he left the bedside, Dr. Bharucha looked so solemn that Freddy rushed straight to the Brahmin, ranting, "Haven't you found anything yet?"

The mild accountant shook his head. Freddy, who was seldom violent, suddenly swooped down on the short man and seized him by his muslin shirt front.

"My son is dying. Do you know?" he hissed, shaking him fiercely.

"What happened to the *janam patris* that were supposed to prescribe a cure for his disease? What happened to the 'preventive measures' you were so sure you'd find, you blackguard?"

"I am sorry," stammered Gopal Krishan.

"You're sorry? You're sorry? My son will die tonight and you haven't even bothered to look?"

Just then, Freddy noticed the man's wife framed in the doorway. She was a short, stocky, nut-brown woman, and she looked at Freddy with the enormous placid eyes of her race.

Freddy came to his senses with a start. Releasing his hold on the Brahmin he stepped back. Gopal's thin shirt was torn below the neck.

"Forgive me," Freddy said, his voice hoarse with the emotions that racked him. "It is because I know my son will die tonight."

"There is nothing to forgive, sethji." Gopal Krishan placed a soothing hand on Freddy's arm. "You must not allow yourself to get so angry—you will only do yourself harm. Please return to your family and try to get a night's sleep . . . your son will not die tonight."

Freddy's eyes dilated with alarming intensity. He gripped the Brahmin's slack shoulders with fingers that bit into the flesh like talons.

"Oh, so he won't die tonight? So, when will he die? You have found something," he hissed. "You are hiding it from me, you bastard! I want to see it, whatever it is. Understand?"

"All right, since you insist. But let go of me, sethji."

Freddy let go of him. He followed Gopal Krishan into the room with the ancient leaves. He sat down, taut and impatient on the edge of a chair, and once again noticed the dark woman standing in the doorway.

Gopal Krishan put on his half-moon spectacles and, looking down his nose, began to scrutinize the faint lettering on the leaf. He moved the *patri* until it was directly beneath the weak bulb hanging from the ceiling.

"There is much that you already know," he said, looking up. "I'll translate the parts you want. It says you will be so upset during your son's illness, it will appear you have taken leave of your senses. Your son suffers from an illness that has no cure. The cure will be discovered after

165

the mighty war and after the upheaval that will turn the earth of the Punjab red with blood."

Gopal Krishan digressed. "It puzzles me, this reference to a mighty war and upheaval. It appears to crop up very insistently."

But Freddy made an impatient gesture with his hand and Gopal Krishan looked back to the sheet. He read silently for a while. He picked up a pencil and scribbled some calculations on a scrap of paper. "Your son will pass from this life in three days," he said, as a result of the calculations. "The writing advises you to be brave. Your loss is not permanent. He will be reborn in your family in a few years.

Freddy leaned his head on his arms. After a while he raised a red-eyed, chastened face and whispered, "Thank you, Punditji."

When Freddy reached home, Soli was in a coma and Putli was sitting cross-legged on the cold, bare floor of their room, weeping hopelessly.

Freddy lifted the unresisting, angular form of his wife and put her on the bed.

"Soli will be better tomorrow," he comforted her; and bit by bit he told Putli about the *janam patri*.

Freddy and Putli did not leave the bedside for three days. Their lips moved in silent prayer continuously. On the third day Soli's fever soared and by evening he was dead.

Freddy placed a trembling hand on his son's forehead. At last it was cool. It was the fifth day of December.

The body was bathed and dressed in old garments of white cotton. Freddy wrapped the *kusti* around his son's waist, reciting prayers. Because there is no Tower of Silence in Lahore, the body was transported to the Fire Temple. A room in the living quarters of the priest had been hastily prepared to receive the body.

Soli was laid on two stone slabs, and a corpse-bearer drew three circles around it with a sharp nail. Now none could enter the circle except the corpse-bearers.

On a white sheet spread on the floor, leaning against the wall to one side of the corpse, sat the stricken women. It was bitterly cold and the doubled-up blankets beneath the sheets provided protection against the brick floor. They wore white saris, except Jerbanoo, who sat next to Putli in her widow's black. Katy was in her school uniform.

Their heads covered, the Parsee ladies embraced the bereaved women and, after commiserating briefly, moved, weeping, to settle on sheets in front of the body. There was a hushed, grieved murmuring as they whispered amongst themselves.

Putli, her head almost hidden in her sari, wept soundlessly, hopelessly. From time to time Jerbanoo and Hutoxi leaned across to embrace and support her and to wipe her tears.

Someone brought them cups of tea, and Jerbanoo persuaded Putli to have a few sips. "Please, no more," pleaded Putli faintly. "I'll be sick."

Putli stared at the body as if she were willing it back to life. Catching her look, Jerbanoo sobbed aloud and blew her nose noisily into her sari. She gave a sudden start. She had not even watched to see if the corpse-bearer had drawn the circles around Soli properly. He must have, she thought, not really caring—and all at once the ritual she was wont to observe with hawk-eyes appeared meaningless to her. After all, Soli was dead and little else mattered. The priest and pallbearers glanced her way timidly, expecting her to call attention to some oversight with a significant hum, but none came. Not even when the oil lamp was placed momentarily in the wrong corner. Jerbanoo sat abstracted by her grief, and the priest, noticing her inattention, took special pains to see that each detail of the ritual was correctly observed.

The priest's dog, adopted by him because of the two eyelike spots above his eyes, was brought into the room. It was believed that his four eyes could ward off evil spirits and could detect the faintest hint of life— a precious faculty in pre-medical days when corpses were inclined to recover and sit up. Putli's staring eyes willed the dog to go up to the body, but as it shied away she knew she was being absurd. Soli was dead.

Late in the evening the sympathizers departed. The Junglewalla family and their closest friends settled on the sheets for the night.

The fire altar was brought into the room and placed on a white cloth on the floor. Sitting cross-legged before it, the priest began to recite from the Avestan scriptures. He chanted through the night and kept the fire alight and the room fragrant with sticks of sandalwood and frankincense.

At dawn the mourners started to come. All morning they came. Women crowded into the little room with the body. Men sat on benches on the veranda or stood outside the string of rooms that were occupied by the priest's family.

The compound between the priest's quarters and the stone building of the Fire Temple filled up with non-Parsees. Indian-Christians, Muslims, Sikhs, Hindus and a few British officials waited patiently to see the body when it emerged from its mysterious rites. Freddy came into the compound from time to time, bowing his ravaged face. From a small distance they offered their sympathy. They sensed they were not to touch him.

Yazdi came straight from the station at two o'clock and stood at the threshold looking into the room. The women sobbed afresh to see his sad, poetic eyes and gaunt frame immobile in the doorway.

Yazdi's shocked and unbelieving eyes raked his brother's corpse. The body was wrapped in a white sheet up to the neck and the small, white nostrils were stuffed with cotton. The flickering oil lamp cast a macabre light on Soli's face, distorting his features hideously. Yazdi gave a great inverted gasp that shuddered through his frame. Touching his arm, Freddy drew him away. Freddy held his son to him in a fierce embrace, and their bodies clung together, warming and comforting the flesh. Freddy kissed Yazdi all over his face, instinctively trying to protect him from the shock and pain the scene had given him.

At three o'clock the pallbearers came into the room carrying an iron bier. They placed it beside the body, recited a short prayer, "We do this according to the dictates of Ahura Mazda . . . ," and sat down to one side. They were swathed in white garments. Even their hands were gloved in white cloth tied at the wrists. White scarves bandaged their foreheads and the sides of their faces. The loose end of the scarf was wrapped around their necks right up to the chin.

Putli looked at these frightening men with fearful eyes—until she recognized her two sons-in-law beneath their grotesque white cocoons.

The other two men were Mr. Chaiwalla's son Cyrus and Mr. Bankwalla. Immediately she was touched and overwhelmed with gratitude. The number of Parsees was too small to warrant professional pallbearers and these men had volunteered for the task.

The prayers for the welfare of the departed soul were over. Now the mourners passed, one by one, before the corpse to have a last look and bow before it.

The dog was brought into the room once again.

Putli wept uncontrollably when the pallbearers draped a white sheet over the corpse, lifted the body onto the iron bier and hoisted the bier to their shoulders.

The women stayed behind. The bier, followed by the men, was carried out into the compound.

The mourners in the compound, who had waited so patiently all these hours, were surprised to see the white sheet covering Soli's face. There was a disappointed murmur.

Freddy saw the surge of faces through an unnatural vision. They floated up, one by one, out of the sea of his misery, to imprint themselves forever on his memory. These were the faces of friends—of people he had helped, of people who had aided him. There were neighbors and officials and merchants; there were princes and beggars. There was Mr. Allen, and Mr. Gibbons, and the Brahmin Gopal Krishan, and Harilal his clerk, and Alla Ditta the pimp, and the wizened face of the Irishman who had rescued Jerbanoo from the fire. There were college students and professors and the Brothers from St. Anthony's School. Caressing, loving hands touched him.

The bier was carried out of the gate, and Freddy saw that the street was filled with people to the end, where the hearse carriage and their tongas stood. They were familiar faces; all of them, at this moment, particularly dear.

On an impulse Freddy stopped the bier and with shaking hands removed the sheet from Soli's face. He kissed his son's cold, pallid cheek. Scandalized, the men of his community crowded around the bier. Once the sacred rites are performed over the body, people of other faiths are not permitted to look upon it. Someone said, "Faredoon, this is sacrilegious! Pull yourself together!" And Freddy, fighting desperately to keep his voice steady, said, "They have stood all this while to see my son: let them. What does it matter if they are not Parsees? They are my brothers; and if I can look upon my son's face, so can they!" The bier moved slowly through the hushed, bowed heads lining the street.

At the small graveyard Freddy saw his son quickly encased within four marble slabs and buried. When the mound of earth was smoothed over, a pallbearer clapped his hands thrice and men turned towards the setting sun to pray over their sacred threads.

The ceremony for the welfare of the departed soul went on for four days and nights. At the end of this, Freddy made the customary proclamation of charity. His family would construct a school in Karachi.

The entire family visited the site of the grave on the fifth day, and Jerbanoo declared, between sobs, "I want the plot right next to Soli reserved for me. Putli, promise you will bury me here."

Putli and Freddy looked at her dumbly. Coming from her the declaration was not only unexpected, it was an intrepid and selfless act of sacrifice.

And that is how the stars saw fit to deal with Soli.

Chapter 28

What Freddy had sensed in Yazdi on the day of the funeral when he held him so close was intuitive. Yazdi's acutely heightened sensitivity was strained beyond bearing; something within the boy was irreparably wounded. There was so much of the world he couldn't reconcile himself to; there was so much that was pointless, fiendish and unjust, like Rosy Watson's sordid profession, his father's unthinking brutality and Soli's death.

Yazdi once again withdrew into himself. His old symptoms returned. He was overly generous, overly kind. And when he once again returned from a morning's outing in only his underpants, Freddy decided it was time he was packed off back to Karachi.

The days were brisk and cool. There was excitement in the air and the bazaars of Lahore took on a festive look in preparation for Christmas. Confectioners, costumers, toy shops and shoe shops were decorated with colored paper and colored bulbs. And, at the corner of the row of commercial buildings, the Civil and Military Store was decked out in an enticing array of little Union Jacks and fancy streamers. Business is business, and even if the household was benumbed with sorrow, Freddy's store would not fail its customers. One did not forego a chance for profit merely because one was stricken.

It was too soon after the tragedy for Faredoon to cope with the shop. He secluded himself in his office, receiving only his close friends and devoting himself to the cause of those who were in need of his assistance. He was mellowed and enthused with altruism. He donated water troughs for tonga horses, benches for a seafront promenade in Karachi and funds for the graveyard at Quetta. He became interested in mysticism and studied the translation of the Gathas, verses in the Holy Avesta attributed directly to the Prophet. He was awed by the wisdom of the verse. The easy, loving tone of discourse between God and Zarathustra inspired him to give a series of lectures on the link he saw between Zarathustra and Sufism. He became known as a scholar.

All the responsibilities that Soli had gradually absorbed and the countless things that Freddy took care of were suddenly thrust on Billy's callow shoulders. He took to them like a duck to water. He was avidly interested and greedy to learn and picked up the trade as one born to it. Freddy accorded him a few desultory sessions of instruction and was taken by his grasp of things. He was quicker than Soli even. But it gave Freddy no more pleasure than if he had been instructing a uniquely gifted clerk. He had little pride in, and even less love for, this spindly, large-nosed gnome who had usurped Soli's rights.

Billy was on two months' study leave from his school, prior to his final certificate examinations in February. He spent his days in the store and his evenings studying beneath a lamppost out on the street to save on electricity, for he took his sudden responsibilities seriously—and his future commitment as man of the house. He lurked through the flat switching off lights, quarreling with the wasteful servants and criticizing expenses in the management of the household.

He curtailed Jerbanoo's tendency to forage in the larder for an in-between-meals snack.

"For God's sake! You are worse than your father!" she protested irately.

Putli, who impressed on Billy his duties as future provider now that Soli was no longer with them, was indulgent. Of all in the house she loved Billy most, and the vacuum left in her heart by Soli's death was soon absorbed by Billy.

Despite the festive trappings, the atmosphere in the store was gloomy, and not only because of Soli's absence. Billy had immediately introduced a series of stringent reforms. No one was allowed to be even five minutes late, or to loiter, or to pop out on brief personal errands. The small leakage of sweets and the occasional syphoning off of a bottle of spirits (attributed to breakages and ignored by Freddy and Soli) received Billy's full censure. His beady, alert eyes were ever ready to pounce upon the shop assistants, and the fuss he made if the least bit of stock failed to tally made them feel persecuted.

The festooned store was like a broken-hearted clown still grinning.

Bit by bit Freddy recovered from his grief. At Yasmin's wedding a year later his spirits, outwardly at least, were back to normal.

Jerbanoo had asserted herself against her new enemy, Billy, and had succeeded in cowing the sixteen-year-old to a point where he refrained from interfering.

With the departure of Yasmin to Karachi after her wedding, Katy was the sole recipient of Billy's dubious attentions.

Chapter 29

Yasmin was in her new home only a month when Freddy received the disturbing letter from her.

Yazdi, she wrote, confirming Freddy's worst fears, had become a college dropout. He squandered his allowance and fees on beggars. He drifted about the city and slept on park benches and pavements. He had not been seen for the past week and she suspected he had gone to help at a leper colony on the outskirts of Karachi. His guardian had not given the full details earlier for he did not wish to upset Freddy during the wedding, but he wanted to be relieved of his responsibility. He was very sorry. He had tried his level best.

Freddy heaved a deep sigh and stopped Yazdi's allowance. He stopped mailing the college fees as well.

For three months they had no news. When Yazdi showed up one evening, his head shorn like a holy man's and his lank frame in a tattered dhoti, Putli and Jerbanoo wept.

Yazdi wanted his entire share of the family money. He offered to compensate them with his permanent absence.

"As long as you don't see me you won't fret about me, and I promise I won't worry you again."

"And what will you do with the money?" asked Freddy.

"I'll feed dying children. I'll buy medicine for the sick left to decay like exposed excrement in those choked bazaar lanes. You prefer not to think about them. I've heard the tormented screams of children at midnight! Who are they? And the perverted monsters that torment them? You choose not to know. But I know nothing else. I see every morning the mutilated corpses of prostitutes found in the gutters and the agonizing pain of millions of futile, wasted lives."

"You can't expect to abandon your family and your home and be of use to anyone. Give yourself a chance, son. I will show you ways to be useful. Stay with us for a while and see how you feel. You'll find out what it is to be rich—not vulgar rich, but rich in the proper tradition. You already know that wealth imposes an obligation, and for every rupee you spend on yourself, you will be able to spend five on others!"

Yazdi fidgeted impatiently.

"Look son, you are one of the few favored individuals who are in a position to give. Tell me, are there many who have it in their power to give? No. The majority are condemned by their stars only to take! By disassociating yourself from the way of life you are born to, you are shirking your responsibility to those who are less fortunate!"

"But I cannot wallow in the luxury of this palace!" cried Yazdi, with a sweep of his hand accusing their modest flat. "I cannot eat a bellyful and sleep between silken sheets when my brothers have nowhere to stay!"

"What silken sheets?"

"Oh, you know what I mean, Papa! Leave me to live as I want. I know you think me mad, but leave me alone!"

"I don't understand you, son," said Freddy quietly. His face, belying the words, was luminous and sad with comprehension.

"Then you must try!" begged Yazdi. He explained how miserable he had been after Soli's death. His thoughts had tormented him, and at last, after all these months, he had come to terms with himself. He was at peace; he knew what he wanted. He had to live in harmony with the dictates of his relentless conscience. He could not survive in any other way. If this meant there was something wrong with him, he couldn't help it.

Freddy listened patiently. The next day, calculating a large sum as Yazdi's share, he put it in a trust.

As long as Yazdi lived he would not be able to touch the money, except the monthly pittance the bank was instructed to forward wherever he wished.

Yazdi wanted to leave at once. His mother sobbed and reasoned with him. His grandmother and sisters pleaded, but they knew it was hopeless.

175

He bade them good-bye and disappeared. They heard from him occasionally and learned of his wanderings from the forwarding addresses he sent to the bank.

Freddy gave up all hope for the recovery of his son's sanity, for it is insane to look beneath the surface of India; it is insane to look beyond the narrow confines of one's destined sphere.

Chapter 30

Lahore was rapidly developing into the commercial and social center that earned it the tribute "Paris of the East" during the Second World War. It was the seat of the government of the Punjab and of the administration of the North West Frontier Province.

Lahore's glorious winters attracted throngs of wilting holiday-makers from all over India, and pallid English women, their short, bright hair plastered in waves to their faces, alighted from carriages and shopped, arm in bold arm, with their pink-skinned male counterparts or strolled languidly between the rose bushes in Lawrence Gardens. Lorangs, Standard, Stiffles, restaurants with plush, extravagant bars and ballrooms came into being and were patronized by the British hierarchy and the Maharajas. But the sedate dancing that went on in these elegant halls offended Freddy's sense of propriety and prevented him from frequenting them. He limited himself to the traditional, and what he considered unpretentious, entertainment of the dancing girls at Hira Mandi.

Flowers bloomed all winter. Parks and billowing trees scented the air, and thousands of private bungalow lawns were lush green carpets.

The gardens in the Government House estate were particularly lovely, and, approximately four times each winter, Mr. and Mrs. Faredoon Junglewalla received enormous, impressively crested cards inviting them to formal tea parties on its gracious lawns.

Although the invitations were properly welcoming, they were more in the nature of a summons—and for Putli they contained all the jollity of a summons to her execution.

Freddy insisted she accompany him.

From the moment Putli saw the card she lapsed into a state of nervous depression that flowered into palpitating hysteria on the eve of the party. These compulsory appearances embittered her soul. How she implored Freddy to take Jerbanoo, who was quite agreeable to the sacrifice.

Freddy's pacific instincts soon guided him to the expedience of slipping her the news only an hour before the time of departure. It was a hectic hour for Freddy. He selected the sari and bullied and bustled his rebellious spouse until she was safely tucked into the tonga. Putli growled and muttered all the way until Alla Ditta, who served them on these gala afternoons, drove them through the imposing gates of the Government House. Then she froze into a mummylike state of terror.

As their tonga crawled behind the line of carriages and limousines in the drive, Freddy relaxed. From then on Putli's behavior was more or less predictable.

What revolted Putli most was the demand that she, a dutiful and God-fearing wife, must walk a step ahead of her husband. She considered this hypocritical and pretentious and most barbarous.

When they drew up before the entrance, Freddy handed Putli from the tonga with all the flourish of a courtier towards a cherished queen. It was a well-rehearsed bit, and Putli acquiesced with the verve of a zombie.

Freddy directed her along the long red carpets to the garden. He did not merely steer her. He prodded, poked and pushed her each step of the way. No one would have thought, to look at Freddy's affectionate arm encircling his wife, of the strength in it propelling her forward. Deep-rooted in the tradition of a wife walking three paces behind her husband, their deportment was as painful to Putli as being marched naked in public. Her legs beneath the graceful folds of her sari were as stiff as stilts.

No one guessed the surreptitious busyness of Freddy's fingers beneath the sari at her waist. A dutiful, husbandly pinch, a little up and to the right, was to remind her to shake hands. This signal proved a handy improvisation when Putli was introduced to the Governor.

They were standing in a small, informal group on the lawn when the Governor, accompanied by his *aide de camp*, sauntered up to them.

Freddy promptly presented his wife, and Putli, just as promptly, bobbed her head and said, "How doo doo?"

The suave, imperious Englishman had offered his hand and almost in the same gesture raised it to smooth his hair at the lack of any response from the oddly solemn little woman. But Freddy gave Putli such a fervent little pinch that her hand shot out, gamely hooked the astonished Governor's hand from off his head and shook it determinedly three times. Then she stood, staring with a dismal, forbidding visage, awaiting further instruction.

Once Freddy managed to ensconce his wife at a table, usually with a bunch of equally awkward Indian ladies, he was free to wander among his friends.

Every now and again a man—or a woman—is born so good-looking, so gracious, so exceptionally attractive, that all hearts surrender to them at sight. Freddy was such a man, and at forty-seven his appeal was still potent. He merely had to step into the presence of women, touch them, however briefly, with his hooded, hypnotic eyes, and there would be an excited flutter. That he remained oblivious of this, and unaffected, enhanced his desirability. Highborn ladies dreamed of braving the wrath of society and of tearing down racial and class barriers to abscond with him in abject, love-lorn subjugation.

Most of the distinguished guests at these parties were of a much higher social standing than Freddy.

Putli misbehaved only once. This was at her second attendance.

Freddy was talking to Peter Duff. Mr. Duff, in a zealous and patriotic attempt to penetrate the impenetrable tribal frontiers to the northwest of India, had married a tribal Khan's daughter, a comely, illiterate girl who had spent her entire life secreted within the tall mud wall of her father's fortress. Mr. Duff was now stuck also with a formidable collection of warlike, feuding in-laws. His Muslim wife spoke no English, and since he could not hope to provide her with an ancestral fortress, she was destined to spend the rest of her existence in her father's home in the mountains.

Peter Duff was regaling Freddy with an account of his hair-raising experiences as a tribal son-in-law when Putli came up from behind and gave Freddy a respectful prod.

Freddy whipped around with a start. "What's the matter?" he snapped.

"Home! I go. You go!" said Putli, obediently conducting the

179

conversation in English. She had been instructed not to speak their Gujarati vernacular in the presence of Englishmen.

"But we cannot leave until the Governor retires," Freddy tried to explain.

"Home to go! I go. You go!" she insisted.

Freddy took a firm hold of her arm and propelled her to a secluded table. He sat her down and patiently spelled out such a dire picture of ruin, disgrace, and business annihilation if they dared insult the Governor with their abrupt departure that Putli never again tried to get away. But she did not cease to hate the parties or resent being compelled to walk ahead of Freddy.

When Yasmin visited Lahore after an absence of four years, Putli was scandalized to see her push Bobby aside and rush forward to greet them like any bold English girl. Thinking the poor girl was carried away by her enthusiasm, Putli forgave her. But later, when she noticed Yasmin precede her husband down the steps and into the carriage, she took her aside to chide her unseemly conduct. What would Bobby and his parents think of her upbringing?

"But he wants it that way, mother," protested Yasmin loudly. "Anyway, it's stupid to walk behind your husband like an animal on a leash. Oh Mother! Hasn't Papa been able to modernize you yet?"

Bobby grinned at his mother-in-law, an impudent grin encompassing a challenging hunk of "generation-gap."

But Putli, funeral-faced, flaunted her chagrin by refusing to sit at the table until the men were served. As a practical demonstration of exemplary conduct, she trailed Freddy's unsuspecting passage through the house at an assiduous three paces until he felt hounded, removed his shoes in the sitting room and jumped to his every need with such alacrity that he was bewildered. Yasmin's conduct remained unaffected.

Having deposited his wife with her parents, Bobby returned to Karachi.

Yasmin's visit had been occasioned by Putli and Jerbanoo's impending journey to Bombay to find Billy a wife.

Chapter 31

Behram Junglewalla, Billy for short, was a taciturn, monosyllabic, parsimonious and tenacious little man. His tight-lipped, shrewd-eyed countenance instantly aroused mistrust—precisely because he was so trustworthy. Unlike his father, Faredoon Junglewalla, Billy's was an uncomplicated character. You knew right away where you stood with him and that his values, once you grasped the one-track bent of his mind, were straightforward. He was suspicious, and he exposed this aspect of his personality at once in any transaction. He was avaricious. His dealers knew exactly where they stood with him, and their faith in his cunning was seldom misplaced.

Billy had a simple vocation in life. *Money!*

He existed to make, multiply and hoard it. He was notoriously and devoutly penny-pinching. His one extravagance was a weakness for radishes, and, much later, for wine.

His frugality he might have inherited from an undiluted line of Parsee forebears. At the time of his marriage, he was twenty years old. His stars, swinging into full orbit, having exiled Yazdi and dispatched Soli, had launched Billy on his way to taking over Freddy's thriving commerce and to inheriting his considerable fortune.

Billy had grown to manhood, and his ears had grown with him. The lint-like cartilages had hardened and stuck out like teapot handles. His straggling, five-haired moustache now made a substantial smear beneath the bumpy crag of his nose, and above it triumphed the center part in his hair. Oil-glossed, blue-black, the hair waved away to end in a squiggly froth of curls.

Billy was a five-foot, eight-inch youth with a square jaw. He was cadaverously lean but without a particle of the irresistible allure that is the birthright of all hungry-looking heroes of romantic fiction. And Behram Junglewalla was the only promising progenitor of the

Junglewalla species. As such, his betrothal was planned and executed with the acumen of a new American cigarette being launched into the market.

All newspapers in Bombay and Karachi ran his advertisement, set in bold type, boxed in a chain of flowers:

WANTED

Tall, dark and handsome Parsee bachelor, having independent business in Lahore, wants to make a match
with beautiful, fair-complexioned and accomplished
Parsee girl of good family. Bachelor is rich, young, eligible. Wonderful opportunity for suitable girl. Dowry
no consideration. Write in confidence to P. O. Box No.
551, Lahore.

If a point was stretched, what did it matter? All is fair in love and advertising.

Letters poured in. They were written mostly in Gujarati. The entire family pored over them, scrutinizing them carefully. It was hard to believe there were so many rich and exquisitely beautiful girls. Soon they were able to read between the lines and separate the chaff from whatever else there was. Out of the hundred-odd letters, five were set aside.

Jerbanoo, her half-moon spectacles low on her pert, plump nose, subjected them to a final autopsy. Like a deep sea diver surfacing with the magic pearl, she ran into the bedroom waving an envelope in Freddy's face. "This is it! This is it! Do you know who the offer's from? Tear the others up!" she declared autocratically.

The letter was from Khan Bahadur Sir Noshirwan Jeevanjee Easymoney.

"He is one of the richest Parsees in Bombay!"

And not only was he the richest, he was also the most amazingly virile. He was renowned for the number of his progeny. No one could remember or keep track of the exact number of his children . . . Twenty, twenty-one, twenty-two? Who knew!

"From one wife?" inquired Freddy skeptically.

Jerbanoo, who knew everything about the personal lives and foibles of the prominent Parsee families, raised a solitary finger and nodded. "One!"

Her unwinking eyes round with pity, Putli groaned, "Poor thing! She must be as strong as a horse, but even then!"

"I think I met him once," reflected Freddy, trying to recall where. "Oh yes! It was at the Cotton Exchange in Bombay. Fine, imposing fellow. Dressed and talked like an English lord-sahib. Lots of personality—very impressive. But I cannot understand his answering our advertisement."

"And why not? We are an equally renowned and respected family. And boys from good families don't sprout on trees!"

Faredoon pondered Jerbanoo's spirited defense. "Perhaps. But I am sure he can find a suitable swain closer to home. Anyway, you'd better go to Bombay and find her. His sir-ship's kindly offering might turn out to be lame or blind or mad!"

Freddy left it at that and a terrible seed of doubt sprang up in the minds of both women.

Khan Bahadur Sir Noshirwan Jeevanjee Easymoney, who had married off fifteen daughters and still had three to go, was always on the lookout for eligible swains. Having been knighted by the King, he drifted in a rarefied atmosphere of lords, barons and sirs, far distant from the existence of Faredoon Junglewalla. The few inquiries Sir Easymoney made at his wife's insistence revealed that a lot of people had heard of the "chap," and what is more, considered him worthy. He gave her the go-ahead.

Postmen ran busily at either end delivering letters. Putli found Lady Easymoney's style charming. She was conversant in Gujarati idioms and flowery flourishes. She adhered to all the endearing, old-world formalities of letter writing. "We beg you to honor us with a visit," she wrote, "And you must bring your august mother, noble husband and beloved son with you." And, "Times have changed. Now the young ones wish to see if their ideas match!" She could think of no earthly reason why their offspring shouldn't like each other, considering they were both born of good families. But such were the curious demands of the modern generation!

The sarcasm was not lost on Putli, and she was extremely gratified.

Yasmin, who was childless, was sent for to keep house, and Putli, Jerbanoo and Billy were seen off by a sizable congregation of Parsees.

Billy insisted they travel third class. They journeyed two nights and a day, and on the second day Jerbanoo put her imperious foot down.

"Look. We are not dragging ourselves all this way to palm you off on some riff raff. Behram Junglewalla, you are on your way to marry Khan Bahadur Sir Noshirwan Jeevanjee Easymoney's daugher! Do you dare show your face stepping out of a third-class compartment? People will laugh at you! Ridicule us! Ha!"

Billy saw her point. At a station an hour's run from Bombay they transferred their hundred and one pieces of luggage, earthen water containers, food hampers and bedding into a first-class compartment.

Mr. Minoo Toddywalla, brother to Freddy's old friend in Lahore, and his wife received them at the Colaba Station.

Putli and Jerbanoo had visited Bombay before. It was Billy's first visit. As the Toddywalla's stately, four-wheeled carriage drove them through the bustling metropolis with its superb wide roads, tall stone buildings, buses and trams, Billy was filled with awe and the beginnings of an inferiority complex. In this city he felt like a country bumpkin.

Chapter 32

They were invited to visit the Easymoney residence on Wednesday, the 15th of September, at four o'clock in the afternoon—just two days away.

The 15th arrived and Putli was as flushed and excited as a bride. She spent hours deliberating on her choice of sari. Mrs. Toddywalla, unable to withstand her dithering, finally selected a cream-colored chinese silk with a blue and yellow border worked in petit point. Putli had to tie her sari three times before she got it right. She pinned the border to her hair with trembling fingers and gave her face a shaky daub of talcum powder.

"You look wonderful!" exclaimed Mrs. Toddywalla reassuringly on beholding her ghostlike house guest, and Putli cracked a feeble smile. Jerbanoo, too, was edgy, though she valiantly disguised her symptoms in a brusque manner. One of them would need to keep her head!

Billy was the most nervous of them all. He was already boiling in the mustard and green pin-striped suit that hugged his skeletal frame. His high collar chafed him, but he dared not poke his finger in for fear of upsetting the fashionable knot in his tie.

Mrs. Toddywalla's two-horse Victoria carriage was announced. She gave each of them a good-luck peck, deposited them in the carriage and waved good-bye.

Billy sat between his mother and grandmother, stretching his neck and gulping to ease the irritation beneath his Adam's apple. Noticing his nervousness, both women wrapped protective arms around his jumpy bones.

None of the passengers had eyes for the teeming life of the city, for the graceful sweep of the sea-framed Marine Drive. Each was immersed in his or her dreams and fears.

Jerbanoo was the first to notice that they were in a very quiet, very wealthy quarter. High walls partially hid a profusion of verdure, and here and there they caught a flashing glimpse of a stately, deep-set mansion.

The coachman, high on his perch up front, twisted around to tell them they were almost there. He stretched out his whip to indicate a turn, and they entered the Easymoney portals. It was a short drive through a cool, green haze of coconut palms and large-leafed creepers clinging to flaming gulmohur trees. They had an impression of fountains and white Grecian statues and suddenly they saw the house. "Monument" would be more apt a word to describe the massive, pink-stone and marble structure with its stout pillars and small, fly-screened windows.

The passengers disembarked, Billy all but undoing Jerbanoo's sari when he stepped on it. They smoothed their clothes and stood facing a lordly flight of gray-and-white marble steps.

A smiling servant ran down to give Jerbanoo a hand. He sported a stiff white turban and a red-and-gold cummerbund. His manner was so informal and deferentially friendly that Jerbanoo felt her assurance return. They ascended to the vast semicircular veranda supported by pillars, and they were halfway across the marble floor when a small, sari-clad form shot out at them from a carved doorway. The lady of the house was all smiles and flutter and welcoming dimples. Putli, expecting to see the stalwart Amazon who had produced twenty-two children, was astonished to behold this little thing.

Lady Rodabai Easymoney embraced Jerbanoo and held Putli, thudding heart to thudding heart, in a warm embrace. They were both of the same build and stature. It was a case of love at first sight!

In the few seconds it took her Ladyship to bustle up to them with outstretched arms, each particle of attire, every curve of her form, imprinted itself on Putli's mind. The blue georgette sari, the three strands of gray pearls, the six-inch band of gold on either hand, the crystalline twinkle of diamonds in her ears and the diamond, ruby and emerald rings. Her hair was pulled back in a knot as stern as Putli's, and Putli knew, instinctively, that here was a woman just like herself. She knew her Ladyship's beginnings, like her own, were poor. That her husband was not born to the wealth and laurels that were now his. And she also knew from her glimpse of the stringy, hard-worked hands with their blue, bulging veins, that she would be as tidy and meticulous as herself. More likely than not, her Ladyship washed tomatoes with soap.

Holding Putli's and Jerbanoo's hands, casting birdlike, approving glances at Billy, Rodabai led them into a handsome drawing room. It was a vast, cool room, lighted by crystal lamps and the sunlight that filtered through brocade curtains. One wall was hung with a huge French tapestry, and the dull gold furniture was of Louis XIV style. Carpets spread out beneath their feet a soft garden of Persian hunting scenes and flowers.

Jerbanoo and Putli exchanged significant glances and gingerly occupied their embroidered chairs. Their hostess hovered about them with a fluttery and anxious hospitality that put them at ease even in the overwhelming elegance of the room. What would they have? Could she get them some wine?

Jerbanoo, behaving with a dignity and restraint that became the nature of their mission, favored her suggestion. Fundamentally, Jerbanoo's role was that of observer and assessor. She had accompanied Putli to lend her imposing and corpulent support, very like the accompaniment of the double bass to a band.

"I would prefer something cold, please," said Putli, adding, "The same for my Behram, please. Knock on wood, he hasn't learned to touch spirits yet."

"My Roshan will be thrilled to hear that. She's the same," said Rodabai, rewarding Behram with a smile. She scurried from the room, a servant in tow, to see to their drinks.

"You noticed something? None of the 'bearer get this' and 'bearer fetch that' nonsense about her. Seems to be as straightforward and simple as we are!" remarked Jerbanoo, kindly, of their absent hostess.

Putli accepted her mother's observations with starry eyes.

The room filled up unobtrusively. There were two dour-faced, gummy-mouthed aunts, six or seven married elder sisters, and a smattering of children. Each scrutinized the groom.

Billy gurgled, gulped on his apple, stretched his neck like a swan disentangling a crick and squared his jaws right up to his ears. He was sweating profusely beneath the Brilliantine-slicked waves of his hair. What if he began to smell? What if a brilliant, oily trickle crawled down his forehead? His hands turned clammy.

The eldest sister brought in the girl. Roshan looked pathetically anemic and flat-chested in a welter of gold ornaments and a yellow sari. She glanced at them shyly and at once they saw, even in the dim light, that she was pockmarked. Keeping Freddy's doubts in mind, Putli had at times anticipated much worse. Her imagination had presented her with a string of hobbling, hunchbacked, harelipped monsters. This wasn't too bad. In fact she found the girl's expression pleasant and her features well proportioned beneath her passable disfigurement. Her subconscious ruminated on the dowry.

The girl was introduced to Putli and Jerbanoo and was led to a carved chair next to Billy. She sat with bowed head, demurely raising her eyes to answer the polite questions put to her by the visitors. She had a lilting, barely audible voice.

After an initial twinge of disappointment Billy found himself approving of her subdued deportment, and when she gave him a shy, slant-eyed look his pulse drummed.

Carts were wheeled into the room. They were loaded with pastries, Indian sweets and caviar sandwiches. Billy raised his eyes from the carpet to these invitations to his stomach, and his heart skipped a beat.

He had noticed a pair of smooth, well-rounded calves that curved with exquisite femininity into a pair of white tennis shoes. He looked up and beheld the most beautiful girl he had ever seen or imagined. She wore a white sporting outfit that outlined the firm globules of her behind and the tiny, Coca-Cola-bottle pinch of her waist. Above her waist protruded the most heavily gorgeous, upthrust pair of brassiered bosoms he ever hoped to see.

The girl smiled at Billy, and Billy, not trusting himself, slid his glance past her. His eyes confusedly sought the carpet like a homing pigeon's. But his vision was full of the perfect oval face, the swing of black, bobbed hair and the ingenuous, innocent eyes smiling at him from behind a pair of rimless glasses.

"That is my Tanya. She's just come in from tennis," said Rodabai, explaining the girl's informal attire. She sighed, "It will be her turn next, I imagine, but I'm in no hurry—she's only sixteen."

"Quite the modern little miss, isn't she?" said Putli with affectionate indulgence.

"Oh, yes! And how!" Her Ladyship pulled a droll and helpless face.

Tanya floated lightly on her wondrous, cream-brown legs and bent to kiss her mother and then Jerbanoo and Putli, before Billy's spellbound gaze. She swayed up to Billy and made room for herself beside her sister. Roshan sat back accomodatingly and Tanya perched sideways on the edge of the chair. She placed a negligent hand on Roshan's thigh and subjected Billy to a frankly inquisitive and impersonal scrutiny.

Billy's heart flew into his mouth and knocked at his teeth.

"Hello," she said, smiling once again.

"Hello," croaked Billy, gulping. Never had he seen such a sparkling set of teeth, such a bewitching smile, such a pair of lips!

He could scarcely breathe, and the thought flashed through his mind: just as well. What if his mouth smelled? In any case, to breathe in her presence was to pollute the air.

"So, you are to be my new brother-in-law!" exclaimed the girl conversationally.

Billy glanced at Roshan. She blushed, and he could feel color blaze in his own swarthy skin.

"You've been playing something?" he countered, pleased to have side-tracked the embarrassing demands of her statement. He marveled at himself for being able to say anything at all.

Tanya's round, puzzled eyes lit up. "Oh, you mean this?" she asked, flicking her skirt. "I've just been through a few sets of tennis! We have four courts at the back of the house. We have a swimming pool also. You must get Roshan to show it to you. It's lined with green marble. Do you swim?"

"Yes," answered Billy, and shifted his eyes. He recalled his two spirited attempts in the shoddy university swimming tank in Lahore. He had thrashed wildly and had almost drowned.

A damp inferiority descended on him.

But Tanya prattled easily, plying Billy with questions and teasing him in her exuberant, forthright manner. He soon felt quite at ease and exhilarated, entertaining the girls with witty snorts and a talented display of comical facial contortions.

Billy was overwhelmed by a ferocious urge to impress these rich, adorable girls. He hinted at his father's influence, at his family's wealth and position, with a subtlety that quite surprised him. And when he got a bit carried away and boasted, "My father is the uncrowned king of Lahore!" he promptly defused the bombast by adding, with a prim, sideways simper, "and I'm the queen!"

The girls roared. His timing was perfect and he kept on being funny.

At the end of it Tanya, who announced that her nickname was Tim, said, "Oh, you're a scream! I never would have thought it to look at you."

Billy beamed across his wide mouth to the tips of his ears. He looked like a rather attractive, swaggering gnome.

"Tim, what is your favorite color?" he asked her suddenly (they were by now calling each other Tim and Billy).

Tim stretched her picturesque legs and looked at the ceiling as if for inspiration. Abruptly she fixed her guileless eyes on Billy. "Blue," she said definitely. "I like blue best!"

"Blue is my favorite, too," said Billy seriously, coming to a decision right there. Truth to tell, Billy had never thought about the subject.

Jerbanoo, in her function as double bass to the band, had conducted herself creditably. She added the most impressive touch at the end when she slipped five gold Queen Victoria sovereigns into Roshan's palm.

When the time of departure came, Billy hugged his prospective mother-in-law, shook hands with all the sisters and aunts, and waved at them airily from the carriage. For all he knew, Jerbanoo and Putli were his fairy godmothers and the carriage Cinderella's pumpkin.

Chapter 33

During the ride home, Putli's and Jerbanoo's enthusiastic comments and conjectures passed over Billy's head, and next morning he mooned about the house calling everyone Tanya.

"What's this? Tanya, Tanya, Tanya! You're marrying Roshan, and don't you forget it!"

Jerbanoo was exasperated.

"No. I'm marrying Tanya," announced Billy, prancing forward on his buttockless frame and kissing Jerbanoo. He flitted over to his mother. "I'm marrying Tanya, aren't I?" he asked, bending impishly over her as she scooped coconut from a shell.

"Don't be silly," snapped Putli, choking on the coconut, hoping he was only teasing her.

"You're being silly, Mama! You seriously expect me to marry that dried-up, pockmarked, dying Bombay duck?"

Bedlam.

Billy's statement triggered a wild and confused controversy. He was lectured, reasoned with and admonished. He was wheedled, coaxed and intimidated. Even Mrs. Minoo Toddywalla pitched into the fray. Billy grinned, and Mrs. Toddywalla, not yet acclimated to his disconcerting habit, was irritated beyond endurance.

"Yes! And that's another bad habit you have!" thundered Jerbanoo. "No one in their right senses would marry you—and here is a perfectly lovely, well-brought-up child who is agreeable, and you call her a dying Bombay duck? Aren't you ashamed? Go have a look at your own monkey-grin in the mirror!"

"He can't help it. He doesn't mean to be rude," said Putli in defense of her grimacing son. She knew the more he was scolded the harder he grinned. Then she put what her heart so fervently hoped into words.

"Oh, Billy, you don't know your mind! It's just an absurd whimsy.

You'll meet Roshan again and it will pass. 'Phut'—like that."

But it was not a whimsy, and at the end of two hours she realized Billy was in earnest. He was stricken. He was in love. And he behaved like a cross between a bemused, bucking fawn and an obstinate billy goat, prancing and sighing and trilling and declaring his intent. If marry he must, it must be Tanya!

"Oh God," groaned Putli clutching her forehead. "What shall I say to them? How can I show my face to Rodabai? What will she think of me?"

"She will think your conduct disgraceful. She will think you un-grateful for kicking her golden offer. She will think Billy an ill-bred boob and you a spineless, witless mother . . . And she will never agree to any other proposal after this insult!"

The party broke up on Jerbanoo's analysis of the situation and our dauntless hero sailed away on a shopping spree.

He returned loaded with parcels, all containing articles of apparel in varying shades of blue.

His extravagance, his stupid prancing about and trilling, were so uncharacteristic of Billy that Putli began to be afraid. She recalled har-rowing incidents of suicide, of love-languished sicknesses and madness in her own family. Some of them she'd heard about, some she had wit-nessed, and she feared for her son's sanity.

And it is not surprising that Billy, twenty years old, bewhiskered and full-grown, was acting like a willful adolescent.

In the India of Billy's days, girls, like jewels, were still being tucked away and zealously guarded by parents, brothers, grandparents, aunts and uncles. Everyone kept a sharp eye out. Even the innocent horseplay of children was savagely punished, and a baby boy caught with his hand there was promptly spanked on that hand. There were no salesgirls in shops, and few women were to be seen on streets. There was but one coeducational school in Lahore and the only women a young man could talk to were those of his family.

In this repressed atmosphere, love grows astonishingly on nothing. It sprouts in the oddest places at the oddest times and takes the most bizarre forms. You can see the dusty toe of a woman peeping from her sandal and fall in love, even though her face and figure are veiled in purdah. You can fall for the back of a man's head or for a voice across your wall. Mir-taki-mir, a doctor, examining a woman's pulse, turned poet. All he saw was her hand—and he felt her pulse. Volumes, inspired and beautiful, describe her unseen face.

This is most so among the Muslims and among the majority of Hindus who keep their women in purdah. There is no purdah at all among the Parsees, but the generally repressed air of India envelopes them. Little wonder Putli was afraid.

In the evening the sun hung low and damp over the sea outside the Toddywalla bungalow, spraying the windows red. Putli sagged back on a stuffed sofa in their sitting room. Her face was puffy with anxiety and secret weeping. She ran a limp hand over her forehead murmuring, "Oh God, help me, help me . . . what am I to do?"

But instead of God, it was Mr. Minoo Toddywalla who finally put an end to her entreaties by declaring, "There is nothing for it but to do as the boy says. You can always try. The world won't come to an end."

"But the girl will not have him. Behram, you saw how modern and beautiful she was. She wouldn't want to go so far away. Lahore would look like a village after Bombay!" she cried, appealing to her son's reason.

Mr. Toddywalla looked at Billy's suddenly small and pinched face. His thin little neck sagged into his bony shoulders. The light was gone from his glasses, and Mr. Toddywalla felt sorry for the youth.

"Nothing ventured, nothing gained!" he declaimed, very much as Freddy would have, echoing the faint hope in Billy's failing heart. "You'll have to propose another offer, I'm afraid."

Putli was aghast. She and Rodabai had gotten along so splendidly. They had so much in common. Her Ladyship had even confided in her upon the delicate matter of her chronic constipation. Would she have done so if she hadn't felt, as Putli did, that they were twin souls?

Putli, with a gasp of surprise, had admitted that she was similarly afflicted. They had exchanged notes on purges, positions and potions, and Rodabai had shown Putli her glycerine syringe, a huge injectionlike glass contraption. The budding friendship was to be nipped because of Billy's obduracy.

The next day Putli sat before a mahogany writing desk to pen the letter. She gazed dolefully out of a window at the steely horizon of sea, and then she closed her lids in prayer. Her soul was timorous and she wished Faredoon was with her. A humid little wind curled about the papers on the desk. They were pinned down with glass, brass and onyx paperweights. At last, with a protracted, indrawn sigh, Putli licked the nib of her pen. She dipped it carefully in the blue inkwell provided by Billy. Her forehead furrowed intently as she wrote the first formal line on the blue-linen writing pad. The lettering was a bit shaky to begin with, but it became well rounded and firm as she progressed.

The letter started with apologies. So impressively humble, so imaginatively self-effacing were they, that anyone not knowing Rodabai would have thought her an ogre.

Putli joined her hands in supplication; she kneeled at Rodabai's feet; she was so mortified she wished to bury her face in ashes; she begged forgiveness. She had taken to Roshan at sight—she already loved her like a daughter—but what could she do? Her son had gone insane. He was enamored of Rodabai's younger daughter, Tanya. He refused to eat; he refused to drink; he wept and raved, and she feared for him. So besotted was he for love of the beauteous Tanya that he could not think of living without her. He threatened suicide. She had all but thrashed him.

Her eldest son, one of God's most beautiful people, was dead. Her other son had abandoned them and gone she knew not where. And now the life of her only remaining son was in Rodabai's hands—at Tanya's feet. She threw herself upon their mercy, begging for her son's life, for her son's happiness.

Behram wanted no dower. He wanted only the girl. And she would be welcomed though she came with nothing but the clothes on her back! God had been kind to Putli, and she was in a position to smother the girl with jewels and drown her in silks. She vowed to keep her forever beneath the vigilant care of her loving eyelids. The letter was sealed in a matching blue envelope, addressed and given to the coachman to deliver. Putli flung herself face-down on her bed in an open-eyed swoon of exhaustion to await her doom.

Chapter 34

Rodabai read the letter and gave a great sigh. It was always like this. This time though she had allowed her hopes to be raised. And now this letter.

For truth to tell, Roshan was twenty—three years older than Rodabai cared to admit—and two sisters younger than she were already married. Now Tanya would also be taken off her hands. Eligible boys were scarce, and she was not one to pass up a good offer. She had liked the stern-faced little woman who was the boy's mother, and the family was undoubtedly excellent. Still, she wished it had been Roshan.

She gave the letter to Tanya without comment and waited for her simple ruse to work. The letter had the anticipated effect. What girl, untouched, unkissed, and a guaranteed virgin at sixteen, can resist the heady flattery implicit in the anxiety of a young man threatening to transform himself into a corpse for love of her? And it was Tanya's first love letter. Indirect no doubt, written by the wooer's mother, but a love letter nevertheless. Its ardor gratified her. Her fancy soared and she fell in love with the scrawny youth who had made them laugh so much two evenings back.

She was most distressed, Rodabai wrote back, by the reputable Putlibai's message. Her distress was occasioned by her description of the pathetic condition of her worthy son, Behram. But she would be even more upset if Putlibai judged him too harshly. These were the ways of young love, and of destiny; and she prayed her thanks to God that the well- brought-up and dutiful youth had forfeited his heart to one of her daughters after all. It didn't really matter which. Both girls were equally beloved of her and she was equally happy with Behram's choice.

Alas, ever since the receipt of her letter, her Tanya, too, was off food and sighed for the love of the boy she had charmed so unwittingly. When fate behaved with such spirit to perform its wonders, it was a blessed omen. Blessed would be their married life.

She knew Putlibai's time in Bombay was short, and matters should be settled as quickly as possible. Would they come on Saturday afternoon with Behram? They could get the two formally spoken for at the "token money" ceremony and discuss further plans.

Billy was jubilant, Putli tearfully thankful. Jerbanoo was triumphant that this unpromising grandson of hers had proved himself worthy of such a girl—and from such a family!

Billy wore a cobalt blue suit, a sky blue shirt, a navy blue tie and matching socks, and blue suede shoes. He was made to stand on a small wooden platform which was prettily decorated with patterns of fish drawn in lime. Rodabai anointed his forehead with vermilion, touched vermilion to the toes of his shoes and pressed rice on his forehead. The ceremony was restricted to women, except for Billy. The sisters and a collection of aunts and cousins sang traditional ditties while Rodabai garlanded Billy. She gave him the little envelope containing the "token money." She gave him a heavy gold watch on a chain and told him to step off—right leg first.

Then it was Tanya's turn to mount the platform, and Putli performed the rites. She presented the girl with twenty-one Queen Victoria sovereigns, and everyone sang. Billy felt like a thinly stretched, blue glass bubble that would take to the air and burst. Never had he imagined Tanya in a sari: she was voluptuous, like a temple goddess—better. And the slip of skin showing at her waist was golden-fawn!

That evening they set the date for the wedding. Allowing for preparations, the earliest date they could fix on was an auspicious Sunday a month away.

The next day Lady Easymoney reserved three rows of seats in a cinema. Billy and Tanya sat in the middle, quite in the heart of the cozy hive of sisters, brothers-in-law, aunts, uncles, cousins and their offspring.

Towards the end of the movie, a tragic Hindu film called "Shakuntala," Behram held Tim's hand. Her fingers were short and stubby and her grip eager and endearingly probing.

Wires were dispatched to Lahore announcing the date of the wedding. Happy, newsy letters, full of instructions to bring this and that, were written to Faredoon, Yasmin, Hutoxi and Ruby, and the clan in

Lahore hurriedly prepared for the exodus to Bombay.

Jerbanoo and Putli worked a sixteen-hour day, visiting jewelers, sari shops, cloth merchants and tailors. Rodabai and each of her seventeen daughters were to be given sets of clothes: sari, petticoat, blouse, sudreh, mathabana, panty and a thin chain of gold. The elder sister also received a thicker chain and Rodabai a ruby-and-gold set of necklace, earrings and ring.

Tanya's four brothers, two of whom were studying in England, would get suit-lengths, shirts and cufflinks, and Sir Noshirwan Easymoney could count on receiving extras, like pearl studs and diamond tiepins.

Then, of course, there were dozens of outfits to be selected for Tanya: blouses and petticoats carefully matched, sets of jewelry and perfume.

Billy spent his mornings in a happily inquisitive and mildly interfering buzz and his evenings at the Easymoney monument.

He met Sir Easymoney briefly, only once, just before the household left on the cinema excursion. Sir Easymoney towered over Billy. He had patted him patronizingly and looked at him out of one black eye and one gray glass eye so cordially that Billy's knocking knees turned to jelly. Sir Easymoney had embraced Jerbanoo and Putli and ensconced his dapper frame elegantly in a sofa. His suit was from Savile Row, his patent leather shoes shone like mirrors and his long, gracefully crossed legs occupied an impressive amount of space in the room. Jerbanoo and Putli, thoroughly awed by his magnificence, gaped at their host like quiescently expiring lambs. Despite his British affectations he looked graciously and splendidly Indian.

Every evening, two or three sisters and their offspring accompanied Billy and Tanya on a sightseeing tour of Bombay. They drove in grand style in one of Sir Easymoney's carriages, with two flamboyantly liveried and tall-turbaned lackeys standing on boards behind the carriage and one up front, seated next to the coachman. Past landmarks, museums and galleries they drove, disembarking only on promenades. Here the sisters sat down on benches, and the children, accompanied by the lackeys, scattered to buy roasted lentils, ice cream and coconut water from vendors. Tim and Billy strolled up and down the promenades. When they were screened from the sisters' vigilant scrutiny by other promenaders, Billy quickly took hold of Tanya's hand. Once he even put an arm around her shoulders. They walked between the massive stone pillars of the Gateway to India, along Cuff Parade, Ducksbury, and Worli Sea Face.

Then one evening they decided to stroll all the way down the Marine Drive pavement to the crowded Chowpatti Beach. They told the sisters of their plan and the sisters, sitting on the seawall, nodded. One of them called after them, "Don't be too long."

Billy held Tanya's hand. On one side was the soft breeze, the sway of the sea, and on other the exciting rush of traffic. They kept to the seawall, winding their way between hawkers and strolling past stone benches. Billy noticed the thin, ragged length of a vagabond occupying a bench, a newspaper over his face. He felt himself infinitely lucky.

At the beach, their shoes dragging in the sand, they merrily sampled hot, spicy delicacies peddled on carts. They sat awhile on the sand until, reluctantly, Tanya said, "I think we'd better get back."

Once again they walked between the traffic and the sea, past benches, past the ragged vagrant—and suddenly Billy's heart thumped wildly and his footsteps faltered. He turned to look back at the bench. He had the impression that the newspaper had just been replaced on the face.

"My God!" said Billy.

"What's the matter?" Tanya was alarmed by the furtive look on his face.

"Just a minute," he said, turning hesitantly to retrace his steps. Now he knew why his eyes had twice sought out the nondescript man sleeping on a bench, one among so many equally threadbare derelicts.

He stood a pace from the bench, slightly stooping forward. "Yazdi?" he asked. "Yazdi?"

Yazdi slid the paper from his face and sat up slowly. A three days' growth of beard made him look wan and old.

"You saw me?" Billy was certain now that Yazdi had deliberately tried to hide behind the paper.

"How are you, Billy?" Yazdi asked gently. His eyes were as poetic as Billy remembered, but the fearless gleam that had come into them since his quarrel with Faredoon was intensified, giving him a look of fierce independence.

Tanya stood hesitantly behind Billy, and noticing her, Yazdi stood up.

"My fiancée," said Billy. "Yazdi, my brother."

Yazdi fixed Tanya with his intense gaze. Billy noticed his brother's bare feet and his starved face, and he suddenly grew vastly afraid that the girl's love for him would diminish at the sight. He was torn between his fear and the bond with his long-lost brother. Touching Yazdi's wrist briefly, he said, "I'll leave her with her sisters. They're waiting. Don't go away, I'll be back in a minute. I must talk to you."

Tanya, respecting his wish to be alone with his new-found brother, turned to go. "I'll go by myself. You stay here."

"I'm coming with you," insisted Billy, holding her hand. Over his shoulder he repeated, "Please don't go away—I'll be right back."

They hurried to the sisters sitting on the wall at the end of the walk, and all the time Billy held Tanya's strong fingers in his hand, he was aware of the feel of his brother's wrist. It had felt like a stick, almost brittle.

Billy ran back anxiously. He held onto the change rattling in his pocket and only slowed when he spied Yazdi still lounging on the bench. He knew he would never have forgiven himself if Yazdi had slipped away.

"Mother's here," he said breathlessly, sitting beside Yazdi. "We're staying at Mr. Toddywalla's brother's house at Colaba."

"I know."

Billy looked at him, bewildered.

"I've seen her a couple of times," said Yazdi, as if he were giving a perfectly rational explanation.

"You saw her? But you didn't greet her?"

"No," said Yazdi. "What's the use? She wouldn't understand my appearance. She would only be sad."

"Oh God," Billy grew excited. "You must see her!" He took out his creaky new leather wallet and removed all the notes. He crushed them into Yazdi's hands.

Yazdi accepted them with a thin, crooked smile and shoved them carelessly into his shirt pocket. "Perhaps I will get hold of a clean shirt and pants and visit you all."

"You must," begged Billy. "I'll give you more money. That's all I have right now." Seeing the amused, independent glint in Yazdi's eyes, he added facetiously, "Think of all the beggars you will be able to convert into lords!"

They laughed, relaxing with each other for the first time since their meeting. Four years had wrought their change on each.

"That's exactly what money's for," said Yazdi.

"Papa was wise to put your money in a Trust." Billy's tone was wry. Then a curious look crept into his face and he asked in an awed, subdued voice, "Are you a communist?"

"Maybe," said Yazdi. "Perhaps I'm a follower of Mazdak."

"Who's he?"

"The first communist. A Zarathusti ancestor. He realized centuries ago that all material goods, including women, had to be shared!"

Thank God Tanya was not with them, thought Billy; and, as if reading his mind, Yazdi said, "Your fiancée is very pretty."

"I'm not sharing her with anyone!" said Billy.

Yazdi chuckled. "So give me all your news," he said, smiling.

Billy gave him the news from home. He told him of Yasmin's marriage to Bobby, of Ruby's two new children, of Hutoxi's husband's hernia operation, of Jerbanoo and of Putli. He told Yazdi how dispirited their father had grown after Soli's death, and especially so after Yazdi's departure, and how he had to manage almost all the business. Billy had to travel to the stores in Peshawar, Jullundur and Rawalpindi. Their father only attended to the correspondence. Billy had passed his Bachelor of Arts examination.

"They are all coming for the wedding," Billy said proudly. "Hutoxi, Ardishir and their children, Ruby and her children. Her husband can't come; he's working on a construction project. But Yasmin's Bobby is coming direct from Karachi by boat. Papa and Katy will be here too.

You will see them all together in one go!" he exclaimed. They talked for half an hour and Billy got up after exacting a promise from Yazdi that he would visit them soon.

"I saw Yazdi today," announced Billy to Putli and Jerbanoo in the room they shared.

"Oh! When?"

"Where?"

"Loafing on the Marine Drive walk."

"How did he look?"

"Filthy, thinner . . . happy."

"What did he say? Did you take his address?"

"I asked. He said he didn't have any. He ate and slept where he could."

"Oh God! You should have brought him forcibly to us! Did you tell him father is coming?"

Billy nodded.

"You shouldn't have! Now he may not come."

"Did you tell him about Yasmin's Bobby?"

"Oh, my poor child! My poor child," wept Putli.

They did not sleep until late that night; but Yazdi never came.

Chapter 35

Billy's sisters arrived a week before the wedding. They were effusively welcomed and driven away by Lady Easymoney to her mansion. Each sister was accommodated in an extravagantly furnished room with crystal chandeliers, copious wardrobes, canopied beds and downy pillows.

Hutoxi and Ardishir were given two interconnected rooms on the first floor, one for themselves and one for the children. In the morning, when Hutoxi drew the lace curtains to look out of the window she received a shock. "Adi! Adi! Come here!" she squealed, urgently waving her hand to beckon her husband.

"What is it?" asked Ardishir Cooper drowsily.

"Come quickly! Come quickly!" she hissed, sotto voce.

Adi toddled over to the window and gaped in astonishment. There were acres of garden and trees beneath them, but what fascinated Hutoxi was the emerald swimming pool and the elephant kneeling before it. While they watched, he dipped the tip of his trunk into the pool and gave himself a shower. Half-hidden behind a clump of mango trees was a camel, and to their right, in a hedged enclosure, some deer and a peacock. Hutoxi rushed to the adjoining room to awaken the children.

Every morning the household descended to the chaotic traffic in the dining room to gorge itself on eggs, parathas dripping with butter, caviar, pickles, fish and cold cuts of meat. A dainty, marble-topped console held the wine to which the toothless aunts helped themselves because of its health-giving properties. Their husbands stuck to Scotch.

There must be at least a hundred people in the house, thought Hutoxi while they were being served breakfast at a mahogany table that could seat eighty. Each time they breakfasted in the house a bearer placed a freshly corked bottle of Black and White Scotch whiskey before Adi.

Cadaverous, false-toothed uncles, similarly served, spent hours breakfasting. At lunchtime they returned to the table to chew and ruminate, and chew and ruminate, like feeding cattle. They tottered through the corridors bleary-eyed and snored noisily all afternoon.

Barefoot servants carrying sacks of flour, sugar, rice and spices on their backs jogged through the dining room to the kitchen, making little warning sounds to clear the way. Her Ladyship darted behind them, and all over the house, with a bunch of silver keys jingling at her waist, her quick, hospitable eyes alert to the minutest comfort of her guests.

The house was never empty of guests, who often visited for six months to a year and frequently became permanent members of the household.

Freddy arrived four days before the wedding, and Bobby Katrak's boat docked in Bombay late that same evening.

It had been a frantic day for everyone. The *Mada-sara* ceremony occupied the entire morning. This entailed much stepping on and off the small, fish-patterned platform. After the prospective bride and groom stepped off and planted the mango sapling that was to guarantee their fertility, the sisters hopped up to be garlanded, stained with vermilion and presented with their set of clothes and thin strings of gold. The gummy-mouthed aunts and uncles, eagerly awaiting their turn, came next. They were also garlanded, stained with vermilion, and given small envelopes containing cash. Her Ladyship performed the honors for Jerbanoo and Putli, and last of all, with a great deal of coaxing, mounted the platform herself.

Sir and Lady Easymoney, some of the major aunts and uncles, and the Toddywalla household went to receive Freddy at the station.

Faredoon Junglewalla was welcomed with beaming smiles and garlands. Jerbanoo pushed herself to the forefront when Freddy emerged from the compartment. She waved her hands and energetically cracked her knuckles on her head to bless him, thereby compelling him to touch her feet.

Freddy was introduced to Sir Easymoney and they clasped hands in a warm, four-handed grip. Being the father of the groom, Freddy's position was a notch superior. The two men took to each other instantly, as their wives had, and Sir Easymoney, who normally refrained from fussing over his kin, exerted himself commendably on Freddy's behalf. That is to say, in between princely pinches of snuff, he directed his entourage to bustle about and see to the porters, the luggage and carriages. In the manner of his English counterparts, Sir Easymoney prefaced his instructions with an authoritative, "Now look here, old chap, why don't you . . . ?" and a hearty, "Jolly good."

Freddy, who long ago had given up his pajama and frockcoat, looked handsome in a brown suit—but not as debonair as Sir Easymoney in immaculate gray checks. And when Sir Easymoney removed his spectacles, Freddy observed the redoubtable glass eye glinting electrically in his swarthy, smooth-shaven face.

Later that evening the Easymoneys entertained the Junglewallas at a quiet dinner. There followed a cozy after-dinner chat in a leather upholstered and book-encased study. The younger members of the household had gone to receive Bobby at the harbor.

Sir Easymoney was expansive and cordial, Lady Easymoney tense in her anxiety to please. After dinner, in order to put his guests at ease, Sir Easymoney removed his eye, his coat and tie, and put on his pajamas. Freddy was coaxed into a pair of Sir Easymoney's pajamas, and the two gentlemen sank into identical swing-backed leather armchairs and raised their feet to matching stools. Four uncles settled in an attentive arc a little to one side, and their wives joined the women sitting primly in their elegant straight-backed chairs opposite the men. Sir Easymoney made a sign, and her Ladyship promptly placed two silver spittoons by the reclining men. A white-and-gold-turbaned bearer served the liqueurs.

"When I was with the army in the Sudan," began their host, launching the story about the loss of his eye, and Lady Easymoney started a conversation at her end about her various and variegated deliveries.

Chapter 36

"... The water was almost finished—a few of us had a little left in our bottles. My men were crawling and flopping, and then our scout shouted from the top of a mound that he saw date palms! Oh well, I can tell you, we crawled a bit faster!

"The oasis had a suspiciously deserted look. There was a small hamlet, but no sign of man, camel or dog. I knew it was not safe, going at it as we did—we should have taken some precautions—but my soldiers were half-dead with thirst. They flung themselves on the sticky mud around the pool. Even as I drank I knew we were surrounded by natives, concealed like wolves behind mud walls and mounds. They were Arabs—and there were only a handful of Muslims amongst us. We were the original non-believing kafirs! We were done for!"

At this point Sir Noshirwan Jeevanjee Easymoney shifted his position in the chair and adroitly freed the pinched fork of his pajamas. Then he passed a cordial volley of wind.

The pause was timed to kill his audience with suspense, the gestures to establish an informal camaraderie and to demonstrate that though he might be a Sir, and accustomed to the ways of British aristocracy, he was first and foremost a loyal and down-to-earth Parsee. He hawked phlegmatically and spat for good measure.

His audience did not move. The uncles leaned forward in their chairs as if they were listening to the story for the first time. The ladies chattered softly amongst themselves, debating the advantages of what they termed "cock-heeled" shoes over leather soles. Only Freddy reciprocated with a polite quantity of wind, anxious as he was to know the fate of the predecessor to the glass eye.

"Do you know what I did, old chap?" asked Sir Easymoney in English, turning his solitary eye upon Freddy. His nose was aquiline, and his chiseled, long upper lip permanently curved up at one end.

Freddy shook his head politely.

"My good man, I spread my blanket on the sand and kneeled down in the Mohammedan attitude of prayer, shouting "Allah-ho-Akbar!" a few times. I did not know what came after that, so I pretended to mumble under my breath, now raising my arms to heaven, now touching my nose to the blanket. My soldiers, following my lead, did the same.

"We prayed until we were out of breath—but it had to end sometime—and then bloody hell broke loose! Our uniforms, our guns, our rucksacks, blankets, bottles, shoes were pillaged. Some of us were wounded. My eye was gouged out in honor of my rank, but our lives were spared!"

"Jolly good shot! Jolly good shot!" chortled Freddy, appreciatively slapping his thigh. And in one go, he both congratulated his courageous host on his cunning and implied they were of a kind with his explosive use of "jolly good shots."

In the course of the evening Sir Easymoney gratified Freddy by acknowledging this. They were discoursing on the bigoted attitude adopted by some natives when he said, " . . . Now take you and me: one leg in India and one leg in England. We are citizens of the world!"

And jolly good for jolly good, fart for fart, the cultures of the East and West met in these two worthies . . .

Chapter 37

The Junglewallas left Bombay four days after the wedding. They took with them all of Tanya's considerable luggage. Billy and Tanya had already boarded a train for Simla on the night of their marriage. After a month of honeymooning they were to go directly to Lahore.

Five thousand guests had assembled to witness the wedding ceremony that took place on a flower-bedecked stage. Tanya, wearing a white, satin sari heavy with silver and pearl embroidery, sat demurely on a carved chair. Billy sat on an identical chair wearing a tall, dark pagri hat, white coat and pajamas. Two priests stood before them, chanting and throwing rice, coconut slivers and rose petals at them. Faredoon and Putli stood behind Billy, and Sir and Lady Easymoney behind Tanya, as witnesses.

The officiating priest eventually recited, "Say whether you have agreed to take this maiden named Tanya in marriage to this bridegroom in accordance with the rites and customs of the Mazda worshippers, promising to pay her 2,000 dirhems of pure white silver and two dinars of standard gold of Nishahpur coinage?"

"We have," answered Freddy and Putli.

"And have you and your family with pure mind and truthful thoughts, words, and deeds, and for the increase of righteousness, agreed to give forever and aye, this bride in marriage to Behram?" the priest asked the bride's witnesses.

"We have agreed," they replied.

Then the priest asked, "Have you desired to enter into this contract with pure mind and until death do ye part?"

"I have so desired," answered Billy and Tanya in unison.

After this the priest invoked the blessings of God on the married couple and advised them on how to conduct themselves properly.

The bridal couple were smothered in garlands and presented with thousands of envelopes containing money and gold coins.

It was a memorable wedding. Years after people still talked about it. Hedges had been leveled in the compound of the Taj Mahal Hotel to clear parking space for carriages and limousines. Openings were dug in the walls dividing the banquet rooms, reception rooms and lobby of the Hotel to accommodate guests and facilitate the flow of service. Flowers were commissioned from Bangalore and Hyderabad, cheeses from Surat, and caviar from the Persian Gulf. There was lobster and wild duck and venison. There was a bottle of Scotch and Burgundy for each guest, and ambulances, their motors idling, stood ready to convey the inebriated or overstuffed to their homes or to the hospital. Two hundred Parsee families, living in a charitable housing scheme and not invited to the party, were each given a sack of flour, a ten-pound canister of rarefied butter, lentils and a box of Indian sweets. There was a police band, a naval band, a dance orchestra and an orchestra that played chamber music. There was singing.

The revels continued into the small hours of the morning but Tim and Billy left their wedding reception at about ten, changed, collected their light luggage and went to the station. They were seen off by their immediate families. Someone gave Tanya a packet of telegrams just as the train was about to move.

Tanya and Billy waved their handkerchiefs until the station lights were a blur. Then Tim retracted her torso from the open window, wiped a tear from her eye and sat down. Billy sat down beside her.

"Well!" he said awkwardly.

The train gave a jerk, making a clatter as it changed lines—and abruptly brought Tanya to an awareness of her surroundings. The novelty of travel, of her brand new husband, the excitement of the alien and luxurious little compartment, all had their effect on her. She sprang up, enthusiastically switching on lights and fans and examined all the intriguing conveniences that could be pulled out or snapped in. She propped the folding table on its legs, put a glass in a slotted bracket and started unpacking. Laughing and prattling, she handed Billy things to put into the bathroom. Billy darted in and out of the toilet. He followed at her heels, bumping into her in the restricted space and apologizing gravely each time he touched her divine flesh.

Towels, mugs, soap and toothbrushes were organized in the bathroom; their bunks, one above the other, were covered with bedsheets and stacked with pillows, the doors secured and the window shutters pulled down.

Billy and Tanya read their congratulation telegrams. Billy was touched by Harilal's message. The old clerk's long telegram ended with a fervent " . . . May God grant you sons at His earliest convenience." Another telegram that delighted them was from Bhagwandas, an accountant Billy had employed a year back. It read, "I am bounding in delight that my boss is returning in couple."

All the telegrams were gone through twice. Now what? Billy was restless. There was a job to be done, almost ritualistic in its symbolism, and Billy despaired of ever getting down to it.

He tried out his bed on the upper bunk, rumpling the sheets in the process. He jumped down, adroitly clearing Tim's head, stretched his limbs and gave one of his exaggerated, roaring-lion yawns. Tim laughed at the peculiar face he pulled and at the roar and, throwing his nightsuit at him, commanded gaily, "Get into the bathroom and change into this. And lock the door from inside."

Billy emerged, grave and self-conscious in his crackling new cotton nightsuit, looking as if his hands and legs had more joints than normal. The overlong sleeves had three dentlike creases where they had been folded and pressed, and the diagonal indentation in his crisp pajamas conveyed the impression that he had an additional knee in his thighs, and an ankle in his calf.

But Tanya did not laugh. The occasion was too momentous and her concept of it too uncertain. And she loved her husband. She sat demurely, hands folded in her lap, the flesh above the scooped neck of her nightdress and at the sides of her cutaway sleeves swelling beneath the filmy material.

Billy tore his eyes away, trying to appear unaffected, but his covert glances gave him a shifty-eyed and exceedingly sinister aspect. He removed his glasses.

Tanya pushed past him saying, "My turn. I'll go to the bathroom now," and her bosom beneath the silken lace of her tiny bodice wobbled as delicately as dandelion fluff.

Billy plonked down on the bunk, wiping the perspiration from his face. He had been seeking the opportunity to be alone. Quickly he slipped the envelope, written all over in Putli's fine round hand, underneath the pillows.

They sat on the bunk swinging their legs. Tanya knew something was in the offing, but her anticipation was undefined. Billy's urges were more substantive, but he wondered how to get matters going. At this rate they would reach Simla unconsummated, a betrayal of their whole future. The speed, sound, and swagger of the train accelerated their urgency at each circumvolution of the hurrying wheels.

Billy cleared his throat. "Tim, may I kiss you?"

Tanya removed her glasses, placing them carefully on the table, and puckered her lips. Billy saw her for the first time without her glasses. She looked disquietingly childlike, and her small, uptilted eyes, for all the exuberance and cheek of her personality, were as ingenuous and trusting as a doe's. He touched the faint indentation made by her glasses on the bridge of her nose; he brought his mouth close and Tanya closed her eyes.

Billy drew back. "Not like that!" he said in a hoarse, plaintive whisper. His face was pinched and crumpled. "You don't want to kiss me?"

"But I kissed you," said Tanya astonished.

And suddenly he realized that he was the first man to ever kiss her and she knew no better.

"That's how you kiss your mother or father," he said, gluing his mouth to hers and forcing his tongue between her teeth. Her mouth tasted deliciously of minty toothpaste.

Tanya struggled, pushing at him with her hands. Desperately she bit his tongue.

Billy fell back with a cry. His eyes were smarting with pain and humiliation.

"What did you do that for?"

"You are a filthy sweeper-fellow! Haven't you studied hygiene? Poking your germs into my mouth!"

A chill ran up Billy's spine. If this was her reaction to a kiss, what would she do when he tried something else? Fortunately, he reflected, that at least would be away from her teeth. He lifted his pajamaed feet onto the bunk and leaned his head back. Tanya turned her face away.

"But that's how everyone kisses!"

"Hah!"

"OK, if it upsets you so much I won't kiss you again. OK?" Billy's tone was conciliatory. Tanya kept her face averted.

The engine blew a shrill whistle and there was a deafening rattle. Another train passed them. Tim turned about with a start.

"Just another train like ours," said Billy, putting his arms around her, and the tension between them was dissipated.

After a while, attempting a fresh approach, he said, "Look under the pillow. There is something there for you."

Tanya buried her inquisitive fingers beneath the stack of pillows and removed the envelope. It was sealed.

"What's this?"

"Read."

Tim read aloud, slowly deciphering the Gujarati script written on Billy's behalf. As for all auspicious purposes, the ink used was red.

"'To my beloved wife Tanya, the sum of 100 Rupees, for the privilege of undoing her tape—from your adoring and everlastingly devoted husband, Behram.' What on earth . . . ! What tape?" Tanya asked.

Billy blushed. "Your pajamas or . . . knicker tape," he said feebly.

"But I don't wear tapes in my pajamas or knickers! I wear elastic!"

Tanya jumped up, hoisted the hem of her nightdress clear to her chest and snapped the elastic in her flared rayon panties. "See?" she said, stretching the waistband with her thumb and letting it go, but not before Billy had a reeling glimpse of a dark, triangular shadow. Zap! Zap! The elastic stung her waist and she lowered her nightdress.

Tanya was in high spirits after this demonstration, but not Billy. He felt his family had conspired to show him up to this girl for what he was—a boy who had his antecedents in the jungly villages of his forefathers. Obviously a tape was a vulgar, outmoded article, used by no one except his own fossilized family. The girl would talk to her sisters, and they would laugh at him. He felt betrayed and vaguely inferior, as when Tanya talked of her tennis courts and her swimming pool, or of the elephant her father gave her on her eleventh birthday, or of the crystal reading lamps specially imported from Vienna when her brothers sat for their Matric examinations.

Tanya tore open the envelope and waved the hundred-rupee note victoriously. She retrieved her crocodile-skin handbag from the rack and encased the note with an exultant and proprietory snap.

Her pleasure at the gift mollified Billy a little. But the persisting gloom of inferiority and his sensational glimpse of black hair aroused him to an ungovernable frenzy of excitement. Losing all self-control he suddenly flung Tanya back on the embankment of pillows, flung himself upon her and pressed her with his weight.

Once again she surprised him. He had expected her to throw him off. Instead, her body relaxed. It molded itself to his shape and then grew rigid with anticipation.

This proved too much for Billy. He went to the toilet to wash.

Ever since babyhood Tanya had been safeguarded by a battery of nannies, sisters, and aunts, and by her mother. No man, old or young, servant or guest, was above suspicion. To judge from their attitude, all males were only awaiting the chance to commit unspeakable atrocities.

There was some justification for this, considering that most servants were celibate for months on end, visiting their villages and wives only once a year.

This repression worked both ways. A gigantic conspiracy was practiced by an entire society to keep its girls ridiculously "innocent." The wealthier the family, the more ignorant the daughters. This carefully nurtured ignorance had a high market value in the choice of a bride. Tanya, although she was intelligent and intelligently brought up, had remained totally innocent of the fundamentals of sex. She always had been dumbly in love with someone or other, obsessed and devastated by emotion and utterly confused by the undefined cravings of her body.

When she was only six years old, Tanya had once gone to a festive *mela* accompanied by her nanny and a man servant. On the way back she wept with exhaustion, refusing to walk another step. The servant picked her up and sat her on his shoulders. She enjoyed the ride, holding his head and dangling her feet on his chest until they found a carriage for hire. At home she was full of prattle about the *mela*. Scarcely anyone listened. Suddenly Rodabai was all ears. "What did you say?" she asked, swooping down on her. Tanya repeated that when she was very tired, the kind servant had carried her astride on his shoulders.

Rodabai placed a trembling hand on her palpitating bosom and screamed. The servant was summoned, scolded and sacked. The nanny was stormed at and only forgiven when she fell at her Ladyship's feet swearing that she would never allow such a thing to happen again.

Then, when Tanya was ten, some cousins visited from Poona. Among them was a randy thirteen-year-old who fell in love with her. At least that is what her precocious nine-year-old brother suggested. "What a sissy! Why does he always hang around you—is he in love or something?"

Her cousin taught her to make bows and arrows and flattered her with unexpected attentions. He exerted himself to do this and that: opening doors, vacating his seat and valiantly braving the ridicule of other young persons for her sake. He also led her, conspiratorially, into empty rooms. Once inside, he laid her on a bed and swayed his body full-length on hers. She enjoyed the rhythm of his movements, the exciting intimacy of their fully clothed bodies, and lay docile beneath.

One day her withered, gray-haired nanny walked in on them. Tanya never forgot the accusing and sharp glower she directed at her cousin. He raised himself on his hands and knees with a sickly, sheepish smile. The sari-attired nanny stood there, glaring at the boy, her face quaking with wrath. There was no need for her to speak. The boy slunk from the room without a backward glance.

Tanya realized guiltily that she was absolved of any part in the crime. It was all the boy's fault. And fortunately the nanny never repeated the incident to Rodabai. This, until tonight, was the sum total of Tanya's carnal knowledge.

Billy was entitled to a lot more premarital experience. As a male it was incumbent on him to be knowledgeable in matters of sex.

Billy had visited the Hira Mandi girls three times, read the Kama

Sutra and discussed sex with his friends in a somber and illuminating exchange of detail.

If Faredoon was meticulous, Billy was systematic. His mind worked in bracketed numericals. Tabulating the collective wisdom of the Kama Sutra, his own experiences and those of his friends, he had tenderly resolved on a phased plan of action for the marriage night. Phase one was to arouse and stimulate Tanya, phase two to consummate the marriage, and phase three, the details of which were still vague, to establish an idyllic relationship with his wife. He did not expect too much, but convinced of his superior and gentle wisdom, she was to become his loving and obedient slave.

Tanya had unnerved him by her disconcerting reaction at the start of phase one, titled "erotic kiss." Fortunately this was offset by her subsequent response to his unscheduled leap on her person.

Billy spent enough time in the bathroom to resuscitate his initial resolves concerning the possession of his bride.

By the time he emerged, Tanya was impatient for a repeat performance.

"Why did you change your pajamas?" she demanded, surprised.

"Felt like it," replied Billy lightly, concealing his dismay at her naïveté.

Tanya made room for him on her bunk. Billy lay alongside and commenced stroking her; he was still on phase one. Tanya's breathing became heavy, her eyes drowsy. Scrupulously avoiding the "erotic kiss" and anxiously alive to her responses, he planted chaste little kisses on her hair and face. He delicately stroked her bosom and stomach and, emboldened, inched his trembling fingers beneath the rayon panties.

But this Tanya did not allow.

Billy was aware of the vulnerability of the clitoris. His friend had gravely pronounced it the "key to the door of paradise." Gradually, stroking her, shifting this way and that, he wedged his left shank between her thighs. He noticed the difference at once. Tanya's breath came short and soft, her eyes became searching, intent, as if listening for a faint, faraway sound.

Tanya felt an astonishing surge of excitement in her body. She knew nothing but the wondrous haze of desire and the instinctive compulsion that the momentum must continue and take her, she knew not where, to some mysterious summit. She felt excitement prickle in her fingertips and beneath the skin of her forehead.

Now, thought Billy. He removed his leg.

But this was unbearable to Tanya. Twisting, throwing Billy back, she turned to grip his shank to her thighs and Billy, thinking all her exertion was directed to bite him again, shielded himself with his hand and tried to retract his legs. He could not go far on the narrow bunk, and Tim gripped his bone-hard shank between her thighs and, holding him in a moaning, palpitating vice, moved against him. She moaned and Billy was frightened and elated. He obligingly held his thigh at the awkward, hurtful angle she wanted, gazing at her face and at the wondrous abandon of her body. "Oh," she moaned, "Oh? Oh?" questioning the reality of her marvelous experience and growing rigid again and whimpering and slowly going limp on him.

Tanya lay exhausted, her head on his chest. Gently extricating his leg, Billy caressed her back and felt her skin quiver slightly, involuntarily, beneath her thin nightdress.

Tanya raised her face, still heavy with the wonder of it, flushed and damp. "Billy," she whispered, "Billy, I love you."

Creeping her five-feet, two-inch length up over him she kissed his lids, his moustache and, running her fingers through the tangle of his hair, his mouth.

Billy felt the scented weight of her bosom brush his face—and he knew that the consummation could wait.

Chapter 38

The train squealed to a halt, awakening Billy. It was cold, the beginning of autumn in the plains of northern India, and he judged from the change in temperature that they were already halfway to Delhi. He switched on a small reading light at his head. It was three o'clock. An odd lavatory stench pervaded the compartment. The bathroom door must have opened while they slept.

Deciding to get a blanket he climbed down quietly. He crouched by the holdall, rummaging in the dark. The stench was overpowering. Billy reached to shut the bathroom door and was surprised to find it closed. He stepped up to Tanya's bunk and switched on the dim overhead light.

Incredibly, the bedsheet covering Tanya looked faintly blotched and damp: she had wet her bed! Tanya stirred in her sleep and Billy hastily turned off the light. He stood stunned and still in the dark. When the train moved again, he closeted himself in the bathroom.

Billy sat on the closed toilet seat pondering the phenomenon. No wonder there was so much linen in the suitcase! He remembered the expression on Tanya's face when he had remarked on this as they made the beds. It had not struck him then that she was embarrassed. She had averted her face, ignoring his comment, and had asked him to fetch her a drink of water.

Billy would not risk covering her with a blanket. Let her keep her secret as long as she wished. He was filled with compassion. There was a big, aching hollow of tenderness in his heart and a devouring mist of love.

Leaving a blanket on top of the holdall within Tanya's reach, he stole up to his bunk.

When he woke up again, slivers of glare cut the darkness where the shutters did not exactly fit.

Tanya heard him stir. "You up?" she inquired.

"Ya," he mumbled. At once alert, he sniffed. There was no smell.

He looked over the edge of the bunk. The sheets were innocently white where they showed beneath the blanket. Tanya was propped up against the pillows. He noticed she had changed her nightdress.

"Slept well?" he asked.

Tanya nodded. "You?"

"Like a dead donkey."

Tanya laughed. Abruptly she drew her legs from the coverings and, swinging them up, pushed his bunk with both feet. "Get up! Get up, you lazy lump!"

Billy's bed almost collapsed. He jumped off it to wrestle with her. He spanked her bottom and she automatically attached herself to his ears. They were less self-conscious with each other than the night before.

When Billy went to the bathroom he saw a large, neatly wrapped brown paper parcel in one corner. He knew it contained the soiled sheet and nightdress, and he wondered when she had wrapped it.

Chapter 39

In Simla, at an altitude of 8,000 feet, autumn was well advanced by the end of October. They saw flaming chinar and walnut trees, dark green Himalayan mountains thick with fir, and a towering tumult of hills and precipitous valley gorges.

The forest earth was coated comfortingly with russet mattresses of decaying pine needles. In the amber twilight of autumnal trees, the dank, fragrant air was kissed with the promise of coming snow. The tortuous Mall ran grayly down the spine of Simla into slushy, monkey-infested bazaar lanes. Cheap hotels and wayside tea stalls beckoned, and away from the bazaars stood the high-walled government buildings.

Simla is a retreat of the wealthy, but already most shops were shuttered and barred for winter. The bulk of frolicking visitors had descended to the cooling plains, putting an end to the short, lively season. The hill station had a secluded atmosphere—just right for those who wished for a more private holiday. Soon visitors, too, would be gone, and mountains, bazaars and buildings would be wrapped in thick sheets of snow, preserving the city like a house in which chairs and sofas are covered during the absence of its owners.

They unpacked in the luxurious suite of rooms reserved for them at the Cecil Hotel. Billy was awed by the sumptuousness of the furnishings and by the salaaming attendants. Since his visit to Bombay and his association with the Easymoneys, Billy had not ceased to wonder at the extravagance natural to them. He never lost his dismay at the flaunting of wealth and possessions, not even when he became one of the richest men in the country.

Tanya, accustomed to luxury, took the hotel in her stride. Prodigality was her birthright. When she made a caustic comment about the bathroom fittings, Billy was shocked and disquieted.

Billy's desultory attempts at the resuscitation of his carefully phased plan of action were continuously dashed by the unpredictability of the girl he had married. Their intimacies advanced, but the longed-for consummation did not take place until their third day in Simla.

That fateful, darkly overcast morning, they decided on an excursion to Jacco Hill, a famous monkey sanctuary sacred to the Hindus. They had been told in Bombay they must visit it; the spectacle of thousands of swinging, scampering and chattering monkeys would entrance them.

Arming themselves with a packet each of peanuts and timidly approaching strangers for directions, they located the track that led to the top of Jacco Hill.

The path, twisting through the underbrush of a pine forest, was deserted. Heady with a sense of adventure, they enjoyed their solitude, shouting and caterwauling to make their voices echo in the gloomy, overhung stillness.

Not a leaf stirred. Not a sound from the town that all at once appeared to have been left miles behind. Tim grew apprehensive.

"Billy, let's go back. There is no one here. I don't like it."

"What's to be scared of, silly? Don't you want to see the monkeys?"

"I don't like it all alone. They might attack us—like that big brute who snatched the banana from my hand at the station. And it's going to rain. Let's go back."

"Scaredy cat. Scaredy cat," taunted Billy. But noticing the outrage on Tanya's face, he sobered his grin. "There'll be plenty of people once we get there. It can't be dangerous, or they wouldn't have allowed us to go."

Still, despite the brave inflection and reasonableness of his words, Billy was infected by Tanya's trepidation.

They trekked for more than an hour. The underbrush grew thicker beneath larger trees and the path narrowed until they felt as though they were in a subterranean tunnel. The brooding stillness was accentuated by the gritty crunch and slip of their nervously hastening feet.

Then they came to a yellow board with an arrow pointing the direction. Beneath the arrow was written "Jacco Hill."

"There we are!" exclaimed Billy, and lugging his panting bride by the hand, he helped her up the last steep bit of incline to the top.

They were at the edge of an undulating plateau. After the confined horizon of mountainsides and forest, the vista spread refreshingly open before their eyes. Even the pines stood further apart. But there was no one in sight. No man, bird or monkey. Only the towering, brooding pines and a threatening emptiness. The sky was slaty, showing a turbulence in the upper reaches, a frantic scudding of chimney-smoke clouds.

"No monkeys?" said Tanya, disappointed and at the same time relieved. She cast a quick, searching eye over the trees, hoping to spy a baboon and fearing she really might. The atmosphere was threatening enough without their brutal, wizened faces. And yet they knew the monkeys were there, hidden in treetops, following their every move—a thousand inquisitive eyes. Billy and Tanya felt like intruders in an unintelligible realm, wild and alien.

But having come so far, they had to go ahead. With faintly fluttering hearts, hand in hand, they took timorous steps to explore the plateau.

They came upon small stone structures, little make-believe temples, as if masons, halfway in the process of constructing dollhouses, had become serious and turned them into Mandirs with spiraling cones and sacred decorations. There were offerings of fresh flowers and sugar at the mouths of these dollhouse Mandirs. Some had small, darkly sinister interiors that could not be deciphered, and Tim half-expected to see a monkey or two lurking in the shadows in worship of the monkey-god, Hanuman. Some, like shallow concrete caves, were permeated with light. Before these lay enormous foot imprints cast in cement. They were eerie—just a pair of bodyless feet to remind one of the presence and passage of mysterious deities.

A breeze rustled through the pine tops. There was a distant thunder, approaching fast—a zigzag of lightning. Then the wind lashed the pines and moaned down the mountains. The storm broke. They were soaked instantly by a solid press of rain. Lightning electrified the green gloom of the swaying forest, and the deafening crash of thunder reverberated among the trees.

Fighting the wind and rain the honeymooners ran to the edge of the plateau, seeking the track they had come by. Billy spotted the yellow board. Tanya, her cashmere cardigan and blue silk sari darkened by the wet, was barely able to see through her rain-splattered glasses. She attempted a diagonal shortcut behind a crop of boulders. Unused to the uncertain terrain, her legs skidded and she splashed down in the mud. She heard Billy's anxious, "Are you hurt?"

Billy caught her from behind, trying to lift her, and the weight of her flesh pressed on his thin, hairy arms. He was seized by a sudden languor, a debilitating passion. All at once he was unable to support her. In an entwined, slush-soaked tangle they fell on the gritty ground.

There was a renewed peal of thunder. Billy was kissing her, impatiently fumbling with the buttons of her blouse and feverishly pulling the sari up over her thighs with the other hand. Tanya's legs, exposed to the elements, trembled. And all this in thunder, lightning, and torrential rain!

Forgotten were the thousand pine-veiled monkey eyes, forgotten their fear of solitude. Tanya was panting. Billy was on her, nuzzling her large, firm, rain-washed breasts. Tanya squirmed, instinctively widening her legs, her childlike eyes ecstatic. There was a change in his caress. Billy adjusted his body over hers in a new way. Holding himself with one hand, stroking her hair with the other and kissing her, he groped. Tanya clung to him, arching her body to his. Struggling to enter, Billy feared he might push too hard or too awkwardly, and Tanya, wriggling with artless enthusiasm, was no help. Then the forest resounded with a spectacular explosion of thunder and Billy, startled out of his wits, banged in as if lightning had struck his buttocks.

The marriage at last was consummated!

The month in Simla was over. Billy leaned an elbow on the counter, raised his spectacles over his forehead and holding the sheets close to his denuded eyes, scrutinized the bill item by item.

"We sent for coffee only twice. I remember. You are charging three times."

The counter clerk dragged his eyes from Tanya's chest and focused them dreamily on Billy.

Billy repeated, "We had coffee only twice. You have charged three times. Why?"

"I will correct it, sir," said the clerk, extending a delicately apathetic hand towards the bill.

"Wait," said Billy, "better do all the corrections together."

He added the figures. "There is something wrong with the total!"

The clerk withdrew his eyes from Tanya's bare midriff and reluctantly turned them to Billy. His gaze was blank.

"Your total is wrong," repeated Billy and, losing his temper, he almost shouted, "I am talking to you. Look at me! You have no shame?"

The clerk lowered his lids with a mildly penitent lassitude.

"Let me have the bill, sir."

He glanced over the numerals, adjusted the coffee payment, the total, and presented the new figure to Billy. "You are right, sir. The accountant made one mistake of twenty rupees in the total."

Billy eyed him reproachfully and with a bleak, "don't you dare look at my wife" glower, he drew two hundred-rupee notes from his wallet. The clerk took the money and sauntered towards a safe to fetch the change.

"Button up your cardigan!" said Billy in a fierce whisper.

Tanya obediently buttoned herself up. The fluffy mohair covering her bosom and waist, if anything, accentuated her voluptuous curves. Billy was more and more put off by this unforeseen concomitant of his wife's beauty. He wished for the tenth time he were a Mohammedan and could cover her up in a *burqa*. Sensible people, the Muslims, he thought.

Chapter 40

A big surprise awaited Billy at Lahore. The returning honeymooners were welcomed and hugged and driven straight from the station to a new house in one of the better localities of Lahore, across the poplar-lined canal.

The house was a gift to the newlyweds from Faredoon!

Billy gaped as they trotted up the drive. There was a sunken oblong lawn between the driveways leading to a burnt-brick bungalow with a projecting portico. The frontage on either side of the portico was flanked by two doors which led left to the bathroom and right to the kitchen. It was a deep house with a narrow façade. Faredoon had selected it more on account of its shape than for any other consideration. Such houses, Gopal Krishan had told him, were dynamic and lucky. They were known as "tiger-faced" and were governed by the challenging and powerful spirit of these beasts. Its occupants would amass wealth and power as secret and secure as the hidden depth of the house.

Secret?

Because secrecy in good fortune, riches, health or happiness is a virtue in India—to flaunt any is to invite the evil-eye of the envious.

Had Faredoon wanted a house for himself, Gopal Krishan would have advised him to choose one of the broad-fronted elevations patronized by the spirit of the cow. "Cow-faced" houses were also lucky; they conferred peace and contentment upon the inmates—attributes that did not count for much with an ambitious bridegroom who had yet to make his mark on the world.

Small, square houses, with neither depth nor width, were for small, square people.

A staff had already been engaged. The cook, bearer, gardener, washer-man and sweeper salaamed welcome as soon as the tonga came to a halt in the portico.

Billy had tears of gratitude in his eyes. His face was stretched in an indelible and quivering grimace.

Putli performed the honors on the veranda. Tanya and Billy bowed as she swung a silver tray containing water and uncooked rice around their heads. She tipped its contents at their feet. She sacrificed an egg. Circling it seven times over their heads, she broke it on the floor. Then a fresh coconut: she whacked it vigorously until it cracked and spilled its water.

Having propitiated the spirits and having done whatever was humanly possible to insure the couple's happiness, Putli stained their foreheads with vermilion and led them through the freshly garlanded portals.

The veranda opened into the sitting and dining rooms. Behind these were the two bedrooms, and behind these a receding hive of rooms that Faredoon prudently had locked up. Billy could divide them into two independent flats and rent them out at his convenience.

The house was furnished with essentials. Putli had thoughtfully left the selection of those things a woman likes to choose for herself to Tanya. Tanya's luggage had been unpacked and arranged, and ornamental articles from her dower had been placed on show in the drawing room.

The bearer, tall, crisp-turbaned and smiling, bowed. Lunch was ready.

Tanya played at housekeeping with enthusiasm. She embarked on wild shopping sprees, bringing home tongaloads of drapes and furnishings. She bought lamps and lampshades, figurines of china, vases, coir mats and carpets.

She spread bolts of velvet and brocade in a blaze of color on sofas and chairs for Billy's selection. She climbed up on stools and hung lengths of silk from pelmets for Billy's approval.

"Such rich materials don't quite suit our house," explained Billy, frantically tactful. "Simpler fabrics would be in better taste."

Tanya obediently returned the rejects and brought home simpler materials. Billy selected the cheapest.

The moment Tanya caught on to Billy's enthusiasm for the least expensive, she accosted him point blank.

"Billy! Don't say the brown goes with the purple only because it's cheap!"

Billy grinned wickedly.

They were in love, and they compromised. Tanya was given a reasonable sum to furnish the house. She could do as she pleased so long as she did not exceed it. But money simply drained through the gaps in her stubby, broad-knuckled fingers.

Novelty fascinated Tanya. She had an engineer's passion for acquiring unusual things and experimenting with them. Gadgets, knick-knacks, an imaginative flyswatter, egg whisk or can opener, would enthrall her as much as fancy cars and costly electrical equipment. She was like a child with a new toy—like a scientist at a discovery.

She was to carry this enthusiasm into widowhood and old age, never losing her attraction for the marvels of technology. They were, for her, part of the wonder of life.

"Old? Old?" she rebuked Jerbanoo once, when Jerbanoo entertained her to a soliloquy on the worthlessness and misery of her great age. Tanya was thirty at the time.

"You're not old!" she protested. "What is eighty years in the span of millennia? A hundred years of life is nothing: a snap of the fingers—like that—over in a second. If I live three hundred years, then maybe I will get fed up with life and feel old. You are young!"

What is it to be as enamored of life, vulnerable to its charms and extraordinariness at seventy as at seven? Tanya, ninety-three when she died, retained her capacity for enchantment to the last breath.

Chapter 41

A way of life was imposed upon Tanya and Billy by the locality in which they lived, by their independent bungalow and by their new possessions. They made friends with modern couples equally determined to break with tradition. It amounted to no more than a fanatical faith in the ways of English society in India and a disciple's knack at imitation. They were not of the masses, this young crowd. If their wealth did not set them apart, their ability to converse in English certainly did. They were utterly ashamed of traditional habits and considered British customs, however superficially observed, however trivial, exemplary. They entertained continuously at small, intimate "mixer" parties where married couples laughed and danced decorously with other married couples. "Mixer" parties were as revolutionary a departure from Freddy's all-male get-togethers at the Hira Mandi and Putli's rigid female sessions as is a discotheque from a Victorian family dinner. The parties were fashionably cosmopolitan, including the various religious sects of India: Hindus, Muslims, Sikhs, Christians, Europeans and the Anglo-Indians.

The Behram Junglewallas acquired a large circle of friends, many of whom later were invited chiefly to further Billy's business ambitions.

Tanya was born to this life, eager to socialize and an adept hostess. Billy, inferiority complex and all, eagerly accepted the social challenge.

But there were pitfalls.

Billy plunged into the social revolution with the blithe confidence of the uninitiated, confident that the rules of the game would adhere to the British concept of "fair play." He was not prepared for the competition Tanya unwittingly generated.

Billy, who no more expected his friends to covet his wife than to covet his soul, was bewildered by the extraordinary attention Tanya received. He was hurt. This, he thought confusedly, was not "cricket." He studiously avoided looking at his friends' wives, never addressing them in preference to their husbands, who had no such scruples. They ogled Tanya unabashedly. They took her side if she ventured the mildest contradiction, and they fawned on her until Billy bristled.

Secure in her love, firm in her loyalty, Tanya reveled in the attention. She blossomed in poise and bloomed in beauty. She became daring in her attire and tied her sari in a way that accentuated the perfection of her body. She took to wearing a little makeup and outlined the astonishing loveliness of her lips . . . and Billy could not understand why.

"Tanya," he said one day, "don't look straight into people's eyes. I know you don't mean anything—but men misunderstand. They get bad ideas."

Tanya made a valiant effort to accommodate his wishes.

A year later, when Billy said, "Look Tanya, I've explained all this before. Don't look so directly into men's eyes," Tanya protested.

"But I can't help it, darling. I have to look at them sometimes! Look, I have small eyes and I wear glasses—they can hardly see them!"

And yet another year later, when Billy once again expressed concern, she retorted, "OK, so you don't want me to look at their eyes! So where do you want me to look? At their balls?"

By some quirk of nature Tanya was still childless. It was a source of great anxiety to all the Junglewallas.

But the single fact that racked Tim and Billy out of their infantile honeymoon gaucheries and plunged them into the headier commitments of matrimonial maturity was money!

Never was a man so parsimonious—or a woman more extravagant.

They had momentous scenes when a refrigerator, or gadget, or piece of jewelry was to be returned. Billy could not forgive Tanya's impulsive spending. He brooded over it. It lacerated his sensitivities. It aroused a gigantic conflict between his passion for his wife and his passion for money. Money, being his first love, triumphed.

It was as impossible for Tanya to curtail her spending as it is for a person with hay fever to stop sneezing.

Jerbanoo, ever ready for battle and finding things too dull at the flat, jumped into the fray. She had an unerring instinct for quarrels, and as soon as she sensed a juicy one brewing, she hauled herself off to spend a weekend with the couple. She took up for Billy. She added fuel to the fire and toasted her boisterous little heart in the glow. She couldn't for the life of her understand the willful and wanton desire to throw away money. It was sinful the way modern wives let things go in the kitchen . . . they gave the cook whatever money he demanded as if they had no more sense than sheep. Thank goodness she had trained her own granddaughters herself! Even now, though they were married, she wouldn't hesitate to whack the demons of wastefulness and laziness out of them.

At the flat she worked upon Putli. "Do you know what that dumb, senseless daughter-in-law of yours is up to now?" she began. And though Putli made excuses for the girl to Jerbanoo, she couldn't help chiming in herself with an occasional criticism.

Tanya could not stand it. Her life was being dominated by a bunch of foulmouthed misers! She threatened to write to her father of her misery, and Billy had a hard time pacifying her after Jerbanoo's turbulent visits. Tanya became abusive. She dredged out a rather anemic vocabulary of swear words, senseless and droll in themselves, but uttered with such vehemence that Billy was shocked.

"Don't you dare say such things about my mother!" he thundered sanctimoniously, once, during the heat of battle.

They fought in English, with an odd Gujarati word or sentence thrown in.

"OK, I won't say anything about that silly fool. But what about that damn daughter-of-a-mule grandmother of yours? Even if you shut my mouth by force I will say what I have to about her! Look what they've turned you into—a little cheapskate! And she has the cheek to criticize my upbringing! I will not stand for it!"

"Cheapskate? I'm a cheapskate? And may I tell you what you are? You are a spoiled brat! So pampered that you weren't even potty-trained! You still wet your bed! Imagine a full-grown donkey like you wetting her bed!"

The blood drained from Tanya's face. She slumped on the mattress, all exuberance gone and in a state of acute shock as if Billy had shot her. He had never let on that he knew of her nocturnal weakness. Now he had dealt the brutal trump!

Tanya buried her flushed, tear-ravaged face in the pillows. Her body was aquiver with sobs. This quarrel, barely three years after their marriage, was a hallmark in their relations. It dealt quite a blow to the lingering honeymoon, and it was the first time Tanya wept.

Instantly, Billy was beside himself with concern. He could not bear to see her cry. "I'm sorry," he choked, "I didn't mean to tell you ever. I never meant to throw it in your face like that. I promise you, I'm sorry. I will never say it again. It is your secret—no one will know. Please, please, forgive me."

Tanya heard an unaccountable sound. When she ventured a tearful peep, she beheld Billy sobbing as heartbrokenly as herself.

Her tears dried up. She gaped at him open-mouthed.

Billy wiped his eyes. "Please don't ever cry like that again," he pleaded brokenly. "I cannot see you cry. I will do anything you say—but don't cry."

Tanya determined to cry as often as possible.

All tempers subsided for a bit when they learned that Tanya was at last expecting. The family was thrilled, and Billy was ecstatic. Tanya was inundated with kindly advice. Putli stuck pictures of chubby-cheeked English babies all over the house. A dozen blue eyes peered at Tanya whenever she swung open her cupboard doors. Framed photographs of dimpled infants in cute poses hung from walls. There were three in the bathroom alone. Nor could Tanya look into mirrors without observing the babies stuck in corners.

There was an endless repertoire of stories in which swarthy parents had produced European style offspring. Tanya, initiated into the secret since as long as she could remember—her sisters had undergone the same ritual—contemplated the pictures faithfully. Billy was skeptical.

"The baby will look like me or Tanya. How can it look like an Englishman?"

Then Putli, or Jerbanoo, or Hutoxi, would ask, "You don't believe me? You remember Bacchmai Mehta, how dark she was? And her husband was like charcoal! But she had faith. She looked at the pictures of beautiful babies and when her Keki was born I couldn't believe my eyes. I was there. He had blue eyes, I tell you—blue eyes! His skin was white, his hair was like sawdust!"

Almost all the pictures were of infants who looked like little boys.

But Tanya produced a girl. After the initial disappointment everyone agreed it was most fortunate. It was a sign that Laxmi, the Hindu goddess of wealth, sought to favor them.

She was a delicate, brown-skinned baby and Tanya, who was not too adept at managing her, came in for a deal of indignant and righteous criticism.

Everything she did was wrong. Putli's criticism took the form of corrective advice; Jerbanoo's was more directly expressed.

Life once again became intolerable for Tanya. Trouble came to a head when she bought a new layette for the baby when she was six months old.

The family bore down upon her. Couldn't Putli knit? Couldn't Jerbanoo, Hutoxi and Katy sew? Was Tanya so high and mighty and hoity-toity that she preferred garments made by God knows what kind of dirty hands to their efforts? And the shame of it, throwing money away!

That sultry evening, Tanya quietly sent for a hired tonga and rode off to visit Freddy. In his office she let herself go and gave full expression to her hysteria. Freddy soothed his daughter-in-law and she returned home assured that her troubles were over.

And indeed they were—at least as far as interference from Putli and Jerbanoo was concerned. Freddy was genuinely fond of the girl. He knew the injustice she was being subjected to, and of course, the fact that Jerbanoo was so firmly against Tanya aligned him to her as nothing else could. He solved the problem with characteristic ingenuity.

He was very sentimental that night, almost tearful. He praised Putli, extolling her goodness, going into rhapsodies about the hard work she put in for the family. He choked and managed to squeeze forth a convincing bit of tenderness and appreciation for his mother-in-law as well.

Jerbanoo grew wary. She looked at Faredoon with apprehension, wondering what he was up to now.

"Both of you need a break," he announced sentimentally. "I've been thinking. What have I ever really done for you? I have been too busy—selfishly engrossed in work—and you have stood by me without a murmur! But at last, I am in a position to show my gratitude. The children are settled: Billy is looking after the business very well. The Theosophists are after me to give some lectures in London and I feel I can take six months off and take you for a holiday to England."

Jerbanoo's suspicions subsided at this grand declaration. She and Putli were all atwitter with excitement. Had Faredoon broached the subject less tactfully, Putli would have refused. How could she possibly think of leaving the house alone for six months? Who would look after her grandchild? Tanya was totally incompetent. What about Katy? There were any number of excuses she might have produced.

"Well, what do you think?" inquired Faredoon, beaming like a benevolent sheikh.

Jerbanoo concurred wholeheartedly. To visit England! A misty and glorious fantasy! She couldn't believe her ears!

Putli put forward a few half-hearted objections: what about Katy? They must think to settle her future first. But they could see Putli was taken by the idea, and Jerbanoo made short shrift of her objections.

The children helped them brush up their limited English vocabulary.

And that is how Jerbanoo came to be let loose upon an unsuspecting London.

Chapter 42

Putli and Jerbanoo had almost identical fantasies about the land of their rulers. Their thrill was imaginative. They envisaged an orderly kingdom under the munificent authority of a British monarch based on their knowledge of the gigantic statue of Queen Victoria, cast in gun-metal and protected by a canopy of marble, in the center of the garden in Charing Cross in Lahore. Her gun-metal Majesty had austere features and imposing rolls of flesh. She had a crown on her head and carried an orb and a sceptre. Her steel-trimmed mantle flowed voluminously about the throne.

Then there was the marble sculpture of the Consort astride his towering horse, bearded, haughty-eyed, a sheathed sword resting aslant his high-fitted boots.

To them, England was a land of crowns and thrones; of tall, splendidly attired, cool-eyed noblemen and imposing, fair-haired ladies gliding past in gleaming carriages; of elegant lords in tall hats and tails, strolling with languid ladies who swept spotless waterfront promenades with trailing gowns, their gestures gracious and charming, marked by an exquisite reserve.

Had someone suggested to them that Englishmen, too, defecate, they might have said, "Of course . . . they have to, I suppose," and their exalted opinions would have been touched by doubt. But since such suggestions were not ventured, the England of their imaginings was burnished to an antiseptic gloss that had no relation to menial human toil.

When they boarded the ship at Bombay in November, a month after Freddy's dulcet gesture, their pulses throbbed enchantedly—I am going to England! I am going to England!

As the ship neared their destination, Jerbanoo's heart expanded with mounting elation. She strutted about the deck, thrusting out her seal-like, overcoated chest. Faredoon found her supercilious expression painful to behold.

The effect of their imminent arrival on Putli was exactly the reverse. She shrank into herself, alarmed at the prospect of associating with a race so awe-inspiring and splendid. Her mouth pressed into a thin, anxious line, her face compressed into a sharp triangle and her eyes became more staring and humorless than ever. She snapped nervously at Freddy at the slightest pretext.

They had had their first disturbing confrontation with reality on the ship when they beheld Englishmen scouring the decks and waiting upon them. Within two days of landing in London their disillusionment was complete.

They saw grubby Englishmen in ill-fitted woolen garments scurry past with faces that betokened a concern with the ordinary aspects of life. They saw meek, unassuming men with mournful, retiring eyes and men with the sly, cheeky eyes of street urchins. They saw seedy-looking Englishmen sweep roads, clean windows and cart garbage. They met salesgirls, clerks and businessmen—all English, all white-skinned and light-eyed, on a footing of disconcerting equality. And the expression on the faces of Londoners was no different from that stamped on the faces of a cross-section of India. Where were the kings and queens, the lords and ladies and their gleaming carriages? Where were the men and women with haughty, compelling eyes and arrogant mien? They realized in a flash that the superiority the British displayed in India was assumed, acquired from the exotic setting like their tan.

Above all, they saw Mr. Charles P. Allen, on whose household they descended, scrub out his toilet bowl with a little, long-handled brush. This was the final blow! This, and the fact that Mrs. Allen had no servants except for an insolent and slovenly maid who came for an hour each morning.

Mr. Allen had invited the Junglewallas to stay with them. Mrs. Allen, having lived long enough in India for a glimpse of its domestic intricacies, was justifiably apprehensive. Their children, Barbara and Peter, were married and living separately in London.

Mrs. Allen had changed greatly since they last remembered her in Lahore. Her stylish languor and patronizing air as a commissioner's wife were replaced by the bustling abstraction of an overworked housewife.

Her blue eyes were diffident, her face beginning to show a pallid, large-nosed gauntness. She had permed her hair into a dull, red fuzz.

Mr. Allen's corpulence was less abundant, and the beguiling flash of pink thigh was tragically sealed up in flannel knickerbockers.

They lived in a square, gray-stone house in a row of similar houses in Finsbury Park. The house had the complicated and ingeniously contrived levels that can only be found in England. The three or four top levels and the attic were let to students. Mr. and Mrs. Allen occupied the ground floor and the Junglewallas were given two rooms on the half-landing to the first floor.

The hosts were overwhelmingly hospitable, their guests charmed and overwhelmed—except Jerbanoo.

She could not reconcile herself to what she considered Mrs. Allen's treacherous degradation. She remembered her surrounded by lackeys trained to jump to her bidding. She recalled her parties on flower-banked lawns. And just as she could not relate the superior Mrs. Allen to the inconsequential drudge doing all the dirty housework, so she could not reconcile her fantasies of England to the commonplace Londoners. She felt greatly betrayed, her idols toppled, as it were, with a thunderous crash, leaving nothing but a pulverized residue of contempt—scorn that turned up her nose in the air and her mouth down at the corners! She maintained this disdainful expression throughout her stay in London.

Poor Mrs. Allen, closeted with Jerbanoo while the household frolicked about London, received the full blast of her scorn. Soon Jerbanoo felt it demeaning to address such an inconsequential person as "Mrs. Allen," and took to calling her hostess "May-ree." Mr. Allen became "Charlie."

Mr. Allen, Faredoon and Putli went to lectures, to the theater, and sightseeing and shopping from dawn to dusk. Jerbanoo, unable to stand the pace, went with them occasionally in the evening. She spent her time at the house tormenting Mrs. Allen, meddling with her chores and generally making herself obnoxious.

Every morning she descended from the half-landing with cautious, leaden thumps that boomed up to the attic, and Mrs. Allen's heart sank. Jerbanoo would waddle into the kitchen and thrust an armful of clothes at Mrs. Allen. "Here, May-ree. You wash little little?"

Then she would step back into the dining room, drag a chair a few belabored inches to the tiny fire grate and shout, "May-ree! Stool!"

Having appropriated the best chair in the room and the entire warmth of the grate for the day, Jerbanoo raised her legs to the stool. Muffled in woolly scarves and cardigans, she proceeded to issue orders.

"May-ree, tea?" After the breakfast tray was lapped up, "Finish! Take away!"

And if a rare sun was out, "May-ree, sun, sun! I out." Mary, trailed by Jerbanoo, would carry the chair out, pop in and fetch the stool.

If nothing else, Jerbanoo certainly exercized her smattering of English monosyllables, and by the time she left England she was able to construct adequate small sentences.

Mary, obliged to be dutiful at her husband's insistence, accommodated the old lady. She was a naturally easygoing person, worn placid by her stay in India. There she had also absorbed a compelling sense of Indian hospitality that is both profuse and slavish. She was willing to indulge her guests.

But Jerbanoo did not content herself with merely making demands. She meddled. "Why you not make curry today?" "Why you not cut onion proper?" "Why you not rinse OK? I not drink with soap!" "No chili? I no digest!"

Sometimes her remarks were India-personal, India-insulting, "Why you not wear nice long gown? Silly frock. It shows you got a terrible leg." "Why you not have bath! Water bite you?" "You sit, you drink teacup every two, three minutes. Mind, demon of laziness make your bottom fat." And once, "Why you got no breast?" she asked, reproachfully thrusting her own abundance forward and patting Mary's flat chest. "Not good. Poor Charlie!"

Jerbanoo touched, tampered and tinkered with everything, poking her inquisitive nose into cupboards, drawers and larder, drawing things out for inspection. Often she summoned Mary from her work to inquire. "May-ree! May-ree! What is this?"

At the end of two months, Mary's patience wore thin. The rain had not let up for four days. It had been a particularly trying day. Mary unwisely tried to counter the offensive by adopting Jerbanoo's methods. "Why you so fat?" she fired, "Why you so meddlesome? Why you so lazy?" And Jerbanoo snubbed her by snapping, "Why you poke your nose into me, Miss?"

Jerbanoo called Mrs. Allen "Miss" whenever she wished to be especially offensive.

A little later, when Mrs. Allen bent forward to adjust the fire, Jerbanoo jacked up her skirt with a fork from the dining table to examine her underwear.

Mrs. Allen snapped around, whipped the fork from her hand and stood red-faced and glowering. She was trembling, too enraged to utter a word.

"Shame, shame, shame! You wearing such a small knicker?" tut-tutted Jerbanoo.

That evening Mr. Allen knocked anxiously on the locked door of his bedroom, a door that had never before been locked, and discovered his wife in hysterics. The next day he had a quiet little chat with Faredoon. "It's not that we don't like your mother-in-law, old chap. It's just that she keeps Mary at her beck and call. You know, things are different here—we don't have bearers and chokra boys. The old dear just doesn't understand. And," he said, lowering his voice and blushing solemnly, "I'm afraid she gets a bit personal every now and again."

"My dear friend, don't speak one more word. I understand. It will be fixed!" assured Faredoon.

Jerbanoo was banished to her room on the middle landing. She was allowed down only when Faredoon or Putli were in the house.

That evening when the decision was conveyed to her, Jerbanoo descended for supper in a huff. She dragged her slippered feet more than usual, sniffed, moaned, snorted and sat down making as much noise as possible.

Mrs. Allen's face was red and puffed. She met nobody's eye and spoke primly and only when absolutely necessary.

Mr. Allen carved the roast. He stood to dish it out and he served Jerbanoo a generous helping of beef, gravy and potatoes.

Jerbanoo glared at the mealy potatoes as if they were cockroaches.

She stabbed them with a fork and set them aside on her sideplate with a sour expression of implacable displeasure.

The atmosphere round the dining table was strained. Putli sat mute and staring. Faredoon and Mr. Allen attempted to converse with a heartiness that did not ring true.

Mary and Putli got up to clear the dishes. Her stomach full, Jerbanoo sat in slightly mollified umbrage before her mess of bread crumbs and spilled gravy.

"Why don't you help clear the table?" asked Faredoon. "Your legs been amputated or something?"

Jerbanoo flashed him a look of pure venom. "Why you always poke your damn nose into me, Mister! Why?" she bawled.

But Faredoon was more able to cope with her questions than poor Mrs. Allen had been. He directed a rebuking, lawyerlike finger at her. "Because you like to poke your goddamn nose into everybody's business! Tell me, you don't cook, you don't wash, you don't help at all— you are a no-good guest. Why?"

"I have a chance? No. I never have chance!"

"All right then. I give you your chance. Tomorrow you do all the cooking."

Mary, overhearing the conversation in the kitchen, cried, "Oh no! There's no need for her to cook, really." She was horrified at the thought of the devastation Jerbanoo would wreak in her kitchen.

"O yes, yes!" called Faredoon. "She will give you a holiday. You two visit your children."

Mary would not have it. But Charles later persuaded her to change her mind. They would spend Saturday with their daughter and invite both Barbara, Peter, and their families to a dinner cooked by Jerbanoo.

There were four days to Saturday.

The morning after Mrs. Allen rebelled, she once again heard the dreaded thuds on the staircase. She was aghast. She rushed to the landing and beheld Jerbanoo almost halfway down.

"No! Get back! Back to your room, back!" she squealed with such firmness and ferocity that Jerbanoo's advance was checked.

Mary stood at the bottom of the staircase waving her hands. "Up you go. Up! Up!" And Jerbanoo, turning submissively, lumbered up to her room.

In the evening Jerbanoo declared that she was homesick. She missed her grandchildren. They must return at once. She could not bear the cold any further.

"I want to go back to my Lahore. I don't want to die in a foreign land," she declared whenever she got hold of Putli or Faredoon alone.

Saturday came. Mr. and Mrs. Allen drove away to spend the day at Barbara's. Putli remained in the house to assist her mother, and Freddy did the shopping. Putli's assistance consisted of preparing the entire dinner. Jerbanoo directed and messed up pans. Curry rice, a sweet-sour and spicy shrimp stew, and onion salad were ready. Only the cutlets remained to be fried.

Jerbanoo, ready an hour before their guests were due, descended to fry the cutlets.

She fried half the lot and placed the dish on the dining table.

The meaty fumes, drifting up the house, penetrated Faredoon's nostrils and teased his appetite. His stomach growled. He came down, tiptoed into the dining room and began eating the cutlets. Halfway through the fourth he was caught red-handed. Jerbanoo stood like a grisly and hostile apparition in the kitchen door.

Faredoon wiped his mouth guiltily. "Umm, nice cutlets," he gurgled, attempting flattery.

Jerbanoo, eyes glowering, smoking frying pan in hand, remained motionless and avenging in the kitchen door.

Faredoon turned and retreated up to his lair.

The obese apparition advanced to the dining table and stuffed its mouth with cutlets.

When the doorbell rang Faredoon and Putli were still upstairs. Jerbanoo opened the door partially and, presenting a most injured face to the party stranded outside in the bitter wind, said, "He eat up all and all of my cutlace!"

It was beginning to snow.

"Oh?" said Mrs. Allen, trying to edge past Jerbanoo. "You haven't met Pete's wife, have you? Sheila, meet Mr. Junglewalla's mother-in-law."

"'Ello," Jerbanoo nodded briefly. "He eat up all and all of my cutlace," she repeated and, having made her point, retreated a step. The family squeezed through the constricted space and Mrs. Allen led them, wet and shivering, into the sitting room.

When they were all seated, Jerbanoo waved her arms and, altering her refrain somewhat, wailed, "All and all of my cutlace he eat up."

"Oh, really?" responded Sheila with bewildered and polite sympathy.

Fortunately Faredoon stepped in just then and brought order to the room with his handsome and pleasing presence.

The cutlets were relegated to the background until they sat down to dinner. Then it started again, a lavish, helpless spreading of hands, and, "He eat up all and all of my cutlace! All and all of them he eat up!" until the dish, holding just enough cutlets to go round once, was presented. Jerbanoo sniffed pitifully at the sight.

"Jolly tasty," said Mr. Allen sampling a bite.

"One by one, he finish all!" accused Jerbanoo belligerently. She glowered at Freddy, patted her chest, and emitted a series of gratified belches.

Fortunately the remaining dishes were ample, and the curried rice and shrimp stew were devoured with relish.

Jerbanoo's satisfaction at having disgraced Freddy over the cutlets lasted no more than a day. Her demand to return to Lahore grew more insistent. She hated being penned in her room. The single window overlooked a gray, perpetually drizzling sky, a tiny back garden and the soot-grimed backs of buildings. She felt trapped and, like a caged tigress, she enacted tempestuous scenes.

One dull, foggy morning Mary once again heard the disquieting descent. She heard a few thumps and abruptly they stopped. She rushed to the staircase to discover Jerbanoo sitting abjectly on the third step from the top. Before Mary could utter her usual "Up up!" or "Back

back!", Jerbanoo swayed and, in a small, defeated voice, said, "I feel fainting."

Mary relented. She helped her down and sat her on the chair by the fire. She propped up her legs and tucked her in a blanket.

For a solid hour Jerbanoo sat subdued and ruminative.

Mary relented further. She handed her a cup of tea and a few jam tarts. "You comfortable?" she inquired, and Jerbanoo nodded gratefully.

Mary felt she had wronged the old lady. She felt guilty at having confined the poor soul to her cheerless room. Just when she concluded she had been too hard on the old dear and must allow her down every day, Jerbanoo called, "May-ree? What you cooking?"

"You're getting stewed beef and dumplings for supper," answered Mary cheerfully.

"Dumplings!" snorted Jerbanoo in a way that left no doubt of her opinion on dumplings. "Phhooo! We give our servant dumplings, he spit out!"

Mary's face clouded. It grew set and thin-lipped. She recalled the swarm of wrongs she had almost forgotten, the mean antics and mischievous cross-examination Jerbanoo had subjected her to. Never again would she feel an ounce of pity for the old devil, she promised herself. As if to reinforce Mary's decision, Jerbanoo reverted to all her old aggravating tricks until suppertime.

The next morning when Mary heard the thuds and rushed forth to see Jerbanoo languish on the steps piping feebly, "I feel fainting," she galloped up. "Oh no, you don't! You're no more likely to faint than I am. Back! Back!" she barked, hoisting Jerbanoo resolutely to her feet and depositing her in her room.

This was more than Jerbanoo could take. She brooded for three days and nights. She thought of staging a scene and toyed with the idea of jumping from her window.

Willfully, consideredly, she plotted her last-ditch stand against the enemy.

Jerbanoo spent the next day in acute discomfort, valiantly controlling the major call of nature. By evening she was in such anguish that the mere thought of food nauseated her.

When Putli called at her door to announce supper, she unexpectedly answered, "I think I will remain light tonight." Putli expressed concern at her unusual resolve, and Jerbanoo roared, "Can't you ever leave me alone?" At such fervor, Putli turned pale and fled headlong to the supper table.

Jerbanoo switched off the lights and settled herself as comfortably as she could in the circumstances. She waited until she was quite sure the household was slumbering. At midnight she opened her door carefully and, looking to the right and to the left, she tiptoed to the center of the landing. She spread a newspaper on the floor and squatted in the half-light of a dim bulb.

Having performed her feat, Jerbanoo escaped undetected to her bathroom. She washed herself from the brass jar she had brought with her from Lahore and fell into a dreamless sleep.

Jerbanoo awoke to a commotion of unusual activity on the wooden staircase. There was much movement: up and down, to and fro. She sat up. Her crime had been detected, she guessed correctly, by one of the students. She recognized the voice of the student who dwelt in the attic. He sounded hysterical. She identified more voices. Her face lit up with anticipation. She was like a child who has lit a fuse on a firecracker.

Then it came, a shrill voice: "Good heavens!" followed by a siren-like wail.

More feet galloped to the landing from all levels of the house. And Jerbanoo realized it was not a solitary cracker she had ignited. It was an entire fireworks!

Mary shrieked an eerie and inarticulate string of words. She banged on Jerbanoo's door. Jerbanoo ducked deep in the bed and covered herself up to her ears. Almost immediately she heard banging on Faredoon's door. Mary shouted, quite distinctly this time, "Mr. Junglewalla! Mr. Junglewalla! I will not stand for this! Mr. Junglewalla, open at once!"

The door must have opened. Mary could be heard exploding again. "Look at this mess! Look at it! The woman must be insane!"

Jerbanoo heard Mr. Allen exclaim, "What the bloody hell's going on here?" and then, "Hey, what's this!"

She heard Faredoon echo his exclamations and she shut out the senseless clamor by plugging her ears with the eiderdown.

There was more banging on her door, more roaring and jabbering, and Jerbanoo emerged from her eiderdown to hear Mary scream, "This is the last straw! I will not have that . . . that demon in my house another minute! Get her out! Get her out!"

Finally the clamor eased. The fireworks display had spent itself.

Jerbanoo got out of bed, shuffled into her slippers, washed and began at a leisurely pace to pack her suitcase. Since she had initiated the action, deliberately and in full command of her faculties, she was quite prepared for the consequences. She crooned tunelessly to herself as she emptied the cupboards. There was a triumphant little sneer on her face.

At midday Faredoon led Jerbanoo, disgraced and seemingly penitent, to a cab. Their departure was forlorn. No one waved good-bye. Mr. Allen was not home and Mrs. Allen had acknowledged Faredoon's warm and apologetic farewell with an icy nod. Tight-lipped, she had averted her face at Jerbanoo's passage.

Faredoon once more felt his life blighted by the ignominious appendage attached to him. After an initial rampage he maintained a resigned and bitter silence. He sat huddled in the cab in a storm of gloom. Next to him Putli stared ahead with a terrified expression. Jerbanoo was surprisingly subdued and acquiescent.

The cab deposited them at a hotel in Oxford Street. As if to bless the shift, late in the afternoon the sun peeped out and bestowed a prolonged and freakish spell of Indian summer on London.

Jerbanoo's spirits bucked up. She was delighted at the change of scene. She hung over the third-floor balcony of their hotel room for hours on end, watching crowds in the glamorous hub of London's shopping center. Often she rode down the elevator and thrust her squat, tanklike way through the crowds in Regent Street, the Strand and Piccadilly. She jabbed her nose at shop windows and her umbrella at people who did not have the telepathic foresight to move out of her way. She attracted a lot of attention. This was in the days when Londoners were still intrigued by the bit of sari that covered her head and showed below her coat. Attention to her was as dope to the addict. Her inherently robust confidence scaled new heights. She bullied shop assistants, scowled bearishly on fellow loiterers and snubbed whoever ventured, out of kindness, to address her. She refused Putli's invitations to go with them. "I am quite content to be on my own," she declared. "I can do without somebody's 'don't do this' and 'don't do that'!"

Faredoon was content to leave her alone. He and Putli were once again enjoying their outings and encounters in London. Mr. Allen had approached him, and things had been smoothed out between them.

Jerbanoo crossed streets with the effrontery and nonchalance of an armored tank. She took the squealing of brakes and the breathless stares of motorists as her due. And she got away with it, until one afternoon a bus roared on unheeding of her small upturned palm signaling it to stop. It would have flattened her but for her high-pressured, last-minute dash. Her sari billowed like a sail from the rush of breeze generated by the nearness of the bus. She gasped for breath, and each gasp increased her fury.

A young constable, conspicuous in his blue uniform and helmet, stood among the pedestrians on the pavement. Jerbanoo spied him. She crossed back and beckoned the hapless bobby with a bullying finger.

"Why you not take bus number! You only decoration?" She roared so belligerently that the bobby, who had bent his stringy length to hear what the little old lady wished to convey, straightened like a man shot in the back.

"Why you wear fancy uniform? Why you wear gold button and belt? For decoration?"

A motley group of Londoners with polite and non-commital countenances gathered around them.

The fresh-faced bobby stared down at Jerbanoo dumbly.

"You want decoration on road?" Jerbanoo inquired of the onlookers. "I bring flower vase from my house—I bring little china statues." She turned to the bobby. "You not flower vase, you not china statue. You policeman! Why for you not take bus number? Why? I nearly dead!"

Suddenly she gave the astonished bobby a shove. "Go catch bus. Go. Go. I pull out driver's tongue! I poke his eye! Go!"

An onlooker tittered politely. Taking his cue from him, the bobby drew on his reserves of good-natured calm, put a dauntless arm round the tank and humored, "Sorry, Mum. I'll catch that rotten driver!" And he strolled away.

The onlookers melted into the evening rush. Wary of buses, Jerbanoo prepared to cross the road again. She was mollified by the use of the words "sorry" and "Mum." She was delighted by the bobby's assurance, and though she was shrewd enough to know nothing was meant to come of it, his brave treatment of the episode tickled her vanity. Back at the hotel, when she narrated the story of her brush with death, Faredoon was despondent. "Another golden opportunity gone," he reflected glumly.

Chapter 43

Their hotel did not provide attached baths. This bothered Jerbanoo. There was one bathroom at the end of their corridor and three tiny lavatories. Jerbanoo, who was used to bathing twice daily, was restricted by the long lines, the expense involved and by Faredoon's injunctions to bathe only once every three days.

This alone would not have chafed Jerbanoo as much as the lavatory facilities. The tiny cubicles offered nothing but flush bowls and toilet paper. There were no taps and no water.

Jerbanoo was used to washing herself thoroughly each time she evacuated. For a while she managed by carrying water in the brass jar she had brought with her from India. The arrangement was unsatisfactory. She grumbled, but she would have tolerated this foreign inconvenience had Faredoon not intervened.

Faredoon was acutely embarrassed to see his mother-in-law march up and down the corridor armed with the old-fashioned water container. The jar looked like a handleless, pot-bellied kettle. It was carved all over and it had a long, artistically curved spout that Faredoon particularly despised.

He felt that the combination of his mother-in-law and the kettle created a spectacle. He forbade her its use.

"What will all the Englishmen in the hotel think of me? What will they think of that funny brass teapot? They will really wonder what you do with it! And I'm ashamed of the mess you make with all that water."

Jerbanoo was stunned. She couldn't believe her ears! "Have you lost your self-respect? Don't tell me you dry-clean yourself! Don't tell me you have forced my daughter to dry-clean! Oh God! That I should live to see this dirty day!"

For all her protests, Faredoon refused to give an inch. Jerbanoo, seeing he was in one of his pig-headed moods, gave in. She would not take her brass pot to the toilet any more, she promised.

Jerbanoo was brought up to believe that cleanliness is Godliness, and she refused to fail her religion. The moment Faredoon and Putli left the hotel she scooted across the corridor with her jar. But she was dissatisfied. She felt cruelly cheated of her daily bath.

One truth about Jerbanoo must be made clear: she could not be riled without arousing a perilous hornet's nest. And Faredoon, foolish despite his experience, had touched a most tender spot. The inconvenience that she had been prepared to tolerate suddenly became intolerable. She found the little toilet bowl increasingly thwarting to wash over, the restricting space in the bathing cubicle unbearably claustrophobic. She felt ill-tempered and dirty.

Jerbanoo's longing for the spacious, cemented bathing parapets of Lahore waxed into a phobia. She craved this one facility above all else. And one sunny morning (the spell of Indian summer having continued), hanging from her balcony, she was struck by an idea. She wondered at herself for not having thought of it earlier.

The balcony was about eight feet long and five feet wide. It was walled in at both ends. The wrought iron railing in front was worked in an intricate design that provided enough privacy. In any case the windows in the building across the street appeared to be permanently shut. If peeping Toms ventured to peer at her through its dingy panes, it was their lookout and their disgrace!

On a day when Faredoon and Putli were not expected until evening, Jerbanoo filled a small tub with water from the tap in their room and placed it on the balcony. She fetched her brass jar, stripped to the bare minimum and, squatting in her mid-thigh drawers and homespun bodice, proceeded to bathe to her heart's content. Drainage was no problem. Since the balcony sloped away from the room, the water drained onto the street.

The room immediately beneath theirs must have remained unoccupied for some time. Because on the fifth day its occupants protested.

Jerbanoo was splashing about happily when she heard a furious voice bellow: "Blimey! God, we're being flooded!"

She was a bit startled at the proximity of the voice but did not realize it was directed at her. Suddenly her ears picked up the words "water" and "balcony" and she stopped her merry splashing to listen.

"What the hell's going on up there? Do you hear me? Stop it—whatever you're doing!"

Jerbanoo realized someone wished to speak to her.

Quickly she draped a towel round her shoulders and peered over the balcony into the red, wet and choleric face of a bull-necked Englishman.

He seemed to have located the one small space immune from the waterfall and was leaning dangerously back from his balcony. If he was disconcerted by the brown, fuzz-haired face peering at him he did not show it. His middle-aged wife, wet and mouse-eyed, peeped up.

"Where on earth is all this water coming from?" he demanded.

Jerbanoo was an expert at thinking on her feet. Assessing the explosive situation, she pointed a prophetic hand at the cloudless sky and thundered, "Rain! Rain!"

Having said her piece she retreated from the railing and set to clearing the balcony. She had the air of one who has dealt satisfactorily with a sticky problem. Jerbanoo was quite unprepared for the violent knock on her door a few minutes later. Still in her wet drawers and bodice, she opened the door to the choleric Englishman. She recognized him at once and, all but slamming the door on him, restricted him to the threshold.

"Come on, what's going on up here? You washing clothes or something?"

Jerbanoo glowered. "You not poke your nose into me, mister, I not poke my nose into you!"

A fair enough answer, one would think, but the Englishman was not content.

"Look! If this bloody nonsense doesn't stop I'm going to complain to the management. What the hell are you up to, anyway?"

Jerbanoo was stung to the quick by his rudeness. "Get out! Get out! Fool!" she shouted, trying to squeeze him from the door. The man stood like a rock.

"I'm getting a bobby to find out what's going on up here," he threatened and, noticing the uncomprehending look on the fierce old lady's face, explained viciously. "Bobby, you understand? Policeman! Policeman!"

Jerbanoo's face registered understanding. It also registered scorn. "Go! Go!" she said, pushing him contemptuously with both hands.

"Look here, you damn witch. You'd better tell me what's going on up here or I'll get you locked up!"

Jerbanoo reconsidered. She decided to hit this despicable man with a white lie.

"You want to know?" she asked, and her voice despite its malice rang with authenticity. "I tell you! I wash my bottom. I no dry-clean like you dirty Englishmen. I wash my bottom!"

The Englishman's purple face turned shockingly pale. He crumpled visibly and Jerbanoo banged the door on him. He took his wife and fled the hotel within the hour—but not before he had lodged a violent protest with the management.

The management considered the problem in all its aspects and seriously approached Faredoon, who decided it was time he returned his charges to Lahore.

And so the Junglewallas returned to India in early March, a full month and a half ahead of schedule. They discovered that Tanya was again expecting.

Chapter 44

Tanya had had a hard time during the absence of her enemies. Ironically, she missed them. Her deliverance from Jerbanoo and Putli had only allowed a freer and more direct development of friction between her and Billy. They felt stranded, Tanya defenseless against Billy's stinginess and Billy helpless before her extravagance.

Billy was expanding the business and doing well in diverse ventures. Tanya knew he was making a lot of money and she could not comprehend his strange attitude. They battled furiously. They argued, each desperately trying to make the other see reason, but their battles ended in a baffling stalemate.

Tanya was sick two mornings in a row. Billy took her to see Dr. Bharucha. He confirmed what they suspected. Tanya was pregnant.

Billy was solicitous to the extent of telling her to look after herself while he spent all day at work. Each morning he asked her, was there anything she wanted? and thriftily brought back only those items on her long list that were absolutely essential.

Tanya asked for money.

"What do you want with money? I'll get you anything you want—you've only to ask!"

Considerate of her delicate condition, Billy took over the chore of household budgeting. He inspected the account of purchases presented by the servants and advanced money directly to the cook. Tanya was relieved of the burden of receiving any money at all.

Tanya's own money was prudently locked up in securities that neither he nor she could touch.

Tanya became miserable, and then despairing. She tried to attract Billy's sympathy. She got dizzy spells. She had cravings. She craved pomegranate and pineapple—Billy offered her radishes.

Billy came home for lunch every afternoon. He allowed himself an hour in which to eat and rest. This midday homecoming was ritualistic.

The clamor of his bicycle bell on the drive alerted the tense household. Tanya, and later the three children, gushed forth to the portico to kiss and greet him as he locked his cycle. In summer he was relieved of his sola hat, handed a glass of ice water and led to the bathroom to wash. In winter there was a flurry to take his overcoat and muffler, pat his icy hands and adjust the coal brazier closer to his feet.

Then he sat at the table before a salad bowl and selected a long, white radish. Laying the radish on his plate, its leafy crown overflowing, Billy attacked it with his knife. Slash. Slash. Slash. Three precise clicks on the plate and the crunch of crisp vegetables crushed between energetic molars. Slice. Slice. Slice. And again the loud smacking crunches. He came home preoccupied and he ate without speaking.

The cook peeped from behind the kitchen door. As soon as the radishes were consumed, he served a piping hot and frugal meal.

After lunch Billy retreated to the bedroom, tied a handkerchief around his eyes and fell asleep flat on his back. He was up within the exact time limit he had set himself.

This never varied, except that the clamor of the bicycle bell was to be replaced by the toot of the Morris Minor he acquired in 1940.

At this moment in our story in 1929, Freddy, Jerbanoo and Putli are in England and Tanya is expecting.

Tanya has eaten. She finds it difficult to keep Billy's late lunch hours. December is bitterly cold in the high-ceilinged, whitewashed, brick-walled rooms, and Tanya has slept curled up beneath a heavy quilt. She has awakened to the slice and crunch of Billy beginning to feed. Slipping out of bed guiltily, she has wrapped herself in a shawl, duty-bound to keep her mute husband company during meals. She sits across the table.

Suddenly she says, "Don't do that!"

"What?"

"I feel sick. I can't stand that noise! Why do you make such a performance of eating radish? It's only radish!"

"It's good for the liver. Here, have some," offers Billy. "Much better for you than pomegranate. You won't feel sick."

Tanya strikes out, and the proffered plate flies clattering to the floor.

"I want pomegranate!" she pants. "I want pomegranate!"

Billy is hurt, his faced closed and sullen. Tanya has grown to dread this expression. It could bode the onset of a non-speaking spell that once lasted a full week. She had not been able to penetrate his ice. Confused and terrified, she saw him turn into a monstrous stranger. She could not relate the grim set of his mouth and his accusing, suspicious eyes to the gentle lover she had married.

The cook now replaced Billy's plate, and he began slicing through another radish with the harsh showmanship of an award-winning actor.

Tanya watched his scowl as he worked his gnashing jaws, and suddenly she threw up.

Billy didn't even glance her way.

Tanya wobbled to her room, stretched out on the bed and told the baby's maid in a faint voice, "Call sahib, I am going to faint."

The maid delivered the message and Billy, scared out of his wits, rushed to his wife's bedside. This was a new stratagem reserved by Tanya for dire emergencies.

Billy patted Tanya's hands, rubbed her feet, laid wet towels on her face, wrung his hands in anguish and sent servants on futile errands to fetch this and that. His frenzied efforts delighted Tanya. She almost wept beneath her swoon-closed lids.

The moment she emerged from her faint, Billy flew to her side, penitent and pale-faced and all lover!

"You don't love me any more," she whispered.

"I love you. I love you, darling," he all but sobbed, and it did Tanya good to hear the words she had despaired of.

Dr. Bharucha arrived. "What's the matter?" he asked, sympathetically.

"I want pomegranate," whispered Tanya.

It was the season for pomegranates. Bazaars rang with the cry of vendors promoting the fruit. Fruit stalls were red with its colorful abundance.

"I'll get you all the pomegranates you want," cried Billy.

Billy jumped on to his bicycle and pedalled furiously to the fruit shop at the end of their road. The price was too steep and he went on to the Mall. The price was still too high!

Billy rode through crowded bazaar lanes, bargaining and offering outrageously low bids. He abandoned the bazaars and pedaled all the way to the fruit mandi. Picking his way through swarms of flies, slush, straw and rotting fruit, he at last found what he sought.

Three hours later Billy returned with the cherished fruit and proudly presented Tanya three yellow-brown pomegranates the size and shape of crab apples.

"Get away! Get away from me!" screamed Tanya, flailing her arms and scattering the pomegranates like ping pong balls.

"But darling, I searched all over."

"Don't tell me that!" screamed Tanya. "Lahore is full of beautiful red pomegranates and you can find only this?"

"But red ones are no good for you: they don't have any strength. These have vitamins. Ask any doctor."

"I don't care, you brute!" cried Tanya. "I didn't ask for vitamins. You wander all over for three hours and get this? I should have guessed!" Tanya jumped from the bed like a fury. She pounced on a pomegranate that had bounced off the wall and rolled beneath a chair and hurled it, smashing through a window. She was red-faced and perspiring. Billy could not restrain her. She pounced on another hapless pomegranate roosting by the dressing table and flung it out of the window. Billy was terrified. He feared for the unborn child. "I'll get you what you want!" he screamed and scooted from the room.

He returned in three minutes and he found Tanya propped up in bed. Her hair was wet with perspiration and she was gasping with wrath and hatred.

"There, is this what you want?" he said, placing a large red pome-granate on her lap. He retrieved it promptly, in case she decided to smash it, too, through the window.

Tanya continued her curious gaping.

Billy peeled the fruit, gathering the juicy, blood-red kernels into a bowl. "Here," he said holding the bowl under her chin.

Tanya averted her chin.

Billy sat on the bed stroking her hair. He scooped the kernels into a spoon and fed her.

"Phew! Don't ever scare me like that again," sighed Billy, holding Tanya in his arms that night. Then he leaped out of bed in his rumpled nightsuit and teased, "Should I show you how you acted?" and proceeded to mimic Tanya's hysteria.

"Get out! Get out!" he cried, sotto voce. Prancing on his thin, knobby legs, waving awkward arms, he threw an imaginary pomegranate through the window. "Craaash!" He imitated the sound of the fruit smashing through the glass.

Tanya laughed.

Billy rolled his eyes up, hung his jaw slack and made a helpless, rueful face that recalled to Tanya's mind the halcyon days of their courtship and honeymoon. He was once again the joker who enchanted, the wooer who wrote tender notes on blue paper, who once, in Simla, did not visit the toilet all day for fear of offending his loved one's delicate sense of smell, the passionate lover who consummated his marriage despite the ferocious battery of thunder!

Billy's renewed ardor lasted a full month. But it was, as before, an infatuation. The infatuation having run its course, he reverted to his true love, money. Tanya was helpless against her fascinating rival. Reacting like an abandoned mistress, she attacked his passion for her adversary, and he hated her for it.

They were both raw with wounds. But Billy's will and tenacity were greater than Tanya's, his effort more single-minded. And Tanya finally gave in to his tyrannies. The only way to please Billy was to be absolutely submissive, and he was getting harder to please.

By the time Faredoon returned, they had established the pattern of their life—and the pattern grew more rigid and constricted with the years.

Noticing Tanya's strange docility, Faredoon at once grasped the situation. He felt sorry for the girl but he retreated quietly from their affairs in the hope that Tanya's buoyancy would help keep her spirits high. Putli, too, noticed a change, but only Jerbanoo dived into their affairs, inquisitively ferreted details, and left a trail of discord that once again had Tanya up in arms and fighting back with courage.

Tanya produced a boy. When the child, robust and fair complexioned, was a year old, Faredoon suddenly realized that Soli was reborn. The *janam patri's* prophecy had materialized! He trembled for joy, and a happy mist crept into his eyes. He watched the child grow, reliving each precious moment of Soli's childhood.

This event brought on the last phase of Faredoon's life. He lost his sense of challenge and striving and was content to leave the entire management of their business to Billy. He devoted himself to altruistic deeds, holding audience in his office room. He advised those who sought his advice, and having long established a reputation for impartiality and sound judgment, he arbitrated in innumerable disputes. The sphere of his authority and influence was wider than ever. And Billy encouraged Faredoon's altruism. It enabled Billy to draw from a well of goodwill he had neither the time nor ability to develop. He used people obliged to his father and helped them discharge their obligations.

Chapter 45

The pattern of Billy's life was set, his tyrannies established. He governed his household with an authority that was inviolate. Lacking confidence in himself, he found it necessary to command, demand and order about. He required stringent discipline and prompt, unreasoning obedience.

Billy's tyrannies began with sunrise. His eyes opened and urgent signals were transmitted throughout the house by Tanya. The newspaper was rushed to him. With it, Billy hurried to the thunderbox, which he commandeered for the rest of the morning. Since the bathroom was in the front of the house he had a clear view of the drive, part of the portico, and the garden. Billy never closed the bathroom doors. He sat screened from the outside by a thin, reed curtain. The children briefly popped in and out, the children's maid fetched toothpaste or towels, and the bearer sailed in with a cup of tea on a tray.

Now Billy's thunderbox, being part of the dower received from Sir Noshirwan Jeevanjee Easymoney, had to be special. It was! It was large, it was carved, and it was inlaid with brass. When the lid, which was also the backrest, was shut, it looked like a chest.

Enthroned, Billy sipped his tea and read the newspaper. As soon as the cup of tea was emptied, it was replaced by another. Often Billy sent for his ledgers and scrutinized them on his princely perch.

This was the hour of his business audience. Those who wished to see him at his house and at his leisure visited in the morning. One by one the contractors, land agents, purchasers and dealers would cough outside the reed curtain, say, "Salaam, Sethji," and state their case. Billy could see them clearly; they could only see the shadow of Sethji, newspaper outspread, seated on some kind of box. If he switched on the light they could see more. And, of an occasional evening when it was dark outside, they saw Sethji in all his glory, lean shanks gleaming between pajama top and pajama bottom, brass inlay and carved thunderbox! Sometimes there were small conferences, with Billy coyly negotiating with a group of men from behind his reed curtain. In fact, Billy's thinking was sharpest at this hour. Here he initiated some of his best deals, including the deal in iron that, at the onset of the war, zoomed him into a billionaire. Billy was as thrifty with his time as with his money.

Billy bathed, transmitting a battery of unspoken signals. His clothes were laid out, his breakfast prepared, and the moment he walked into the dining room, the cook put his buttered egg on the stove. The egg had to be just so, otherwise Billy would walk away, egg untouched, and the household was disgraced.

The morning routine never varied, except the day the thunderbox was replaced by the flush system and the morning when Jerbanoo, hoisting the curtain, announced, "Have you heard? I just heard on the radio: England and Germany have made war! We are going to fight!"

Billy clinched the iron-scrap deal within an hour of the news.

The house relaxed with Billy's departure to the office. The children suddenly became boisterous, servants shouted to each other and Tanya went for her bath.

To train a household to the extent that they seek only the master's well-being and approbation is no mean achievement. Whereas Freddy governed his house with the aid of maxims, putting his foot down only if someone's conduct was absurd or destructive, Billy kept his foot down all the time. He tyrannized his house, governing chiefly through Tanya. His commandments were directed at her. They were, in order of preference:

Thou shalt not spend money!

Thou shalt not waste.

Thou shalt give me a minutely detailed account of expenses.

Thou shalt obey thy husband and jump to his bidding.

Thou shalt bring up thy children to obey and to love me more than they do you.

Thou shalt never require anything.

Thou and thy children shall not disturb me.

Thou shalt switch off all lights and fans.

The commandments continued endlessly. Few, like Billy, have the overriding tenacity to enslave.

Tanya lived on her toes and on edge. She gave of herself obediently because she had the soul of a romantic. They make good martyrs. She gave in because Billy had been the first man to satisfy her—and the only one she was permitted to love. The tradition brooked no deviation. Besides, Billy was so rich that her father's wealth appeared paltry. She was the wife of the richest man in the land!

Tanya was always missing things: a watch from the bathroom shelf, a bit of jewelry left carelessly on the dressing table, money. In the earlier days, nervous of Billy's lectures, she carried out a frantic search in his absence. When he returned, she affected the carefree nonchalance of a housewife to whom nothing untoward had happened and not like one who had lost a diamond ring. Billy watched for telltale signs of agitation like a cat playing with a mouse.

Soon Tanya learned to accost Billy directly. He forced her into adopting the strategies of a courtesan. She coaxed, wheedled, pleaded and sweet-talked him until Billy returned the hidden treasure. In fact, these were the only times Billy relaxed and enjoyed being with Tanya, and she finally learned to be as careful of her belongings as Billy wished.

Chapter 46

It was a fierce day in June. The heat already had killed all the flies and mosquitoes in Lahore, and it took a daily toll in scores of human lives. Temperatures ranged between 118 and 119 degrees Fahrenheit in the shade. It required an effort to stir, and people moved their limbs as little as possible, sitting up or reaching for a glass of water carefully and calculatingly, like misers who have to pay for their indulgence in hard cash. Mostly they slouched in darkened rooms, panting like fish expiring in shallow waters.

The roads were deserted between noon and three o'clock.

Afternoon sunlight pierced a slit in the curtains and stabbed Faredoon. He awoke and turned his face from the glaring shaft of sunlight, gaudy with inflamed particles of dust. He got up to secure the curtains, and he lingered a moment to look at the sun-dazzled road. Although it was past four o'clock, car bumpers, cycles, hoardings, tonga shafts and even the asphalt on the road flashed and reflected the implacable fury of the sun.

Faredoon felt a weariness in his flesh. He adjusted the curtains and went back to bed. He felt a hot, dry fever in his bones, a brittle, aching fatigue that was not of the June heat—and he knew the end was near.

It was 1940. Faredoon Junglewalla was sixty-five years old.

In the evening Freddy forced himself to the supper table and then to the sitting room. He was distracted and listless. Hutoxi, Ruby and Ardishir had dined with him. Katy and her husband (she was married to a boy from Amritsar who had established a successful hardware business in Lahore) dropped in later for the usual after-dinner assembly. Seeing that Faredoon was weary and unanimated, they talked among themselves and left early.

Faredoon spent the next day in bed. Putli took his temperature. It was 99 degrees. She sent for the doctor. "It's nothing, just a touch of heat," said the doctor.

Faredoon had been in bed a week. Late in the morning, seizing an opportunity to be alone with him, Jerbanoo popped in.

"How long is this circus going to carry on? It's all very well to lie flat on your bed with everyone waiting on you hand and foot, but let me tell you something: if you don't use your limbs, your hinges will get all jammed up!"

Freddy looked at her equably. "I am dying."

"Dying? Bah!" snorted Jerbanoo. She moved closer and peered sharply into Faredoon's face. "Nonsense!" she said, "You look like a healthy beetroot!"

"Nevertheless, I am dying."

"So what!" said Jerbanoo. "So am I! So is Putli! So is everybody! We all have to go sometime!"

Faredoon propped himself on his elbows and stared at Jerbanoo with a curiously dispassionate and enigmatic intensity.

"What are you looking at me like that for?"

"Know something? I give up. Congratulations! You have won. You will outlive me," said Freddy quietly.

"What does it matter—you go first, or I go first? No one lives forever!"

"Yes . . . but you look so indestructible—so devilishly pink-cheeked and healthy—I don't think you will ever go."

Jerbanoo was sorely grieved. Faredoon knew better; to tell someone at her age that they looked as if they would live for ever was to tempt providence—to cast an evil eye.

"Oh God, oh God. Does no one know how I suffer? How sick I really am? No! And that's because I suffer in silence! But my days are numbered. I feel it! I feel it! Oh, I'll be gone before you," she cried, squeezing out a tear or two. She groaned and moaned piteously, endeavoring to counteract the ominous effect of Faredoon's envious words.

"Seems to me we've been through all this before," sighed Freddy wearily. "You ought to have gone ten times by now."

Jerbanoo was enraged. Her glowering old head wobbled from side to side as if palsied. "All right. All right. If that's what you want, I'll bury you first!" she cried. Turning her copiously rounded back on Faredoon, she stalked from the room.

Faredoon wondered at himself. It was strange for a man who had lived as zestfully as he to be resigned to the cessation of life. There was a curious languor on him. Every moment in his last days passed lucidly and bright as in slow-motion scenes. A sense of fulfillment and contentment settled deeper on him and he no longer feared death. He had lived, he had savored all the surprises, joys and sorrows that fell to his share, and it now did not matter if he died. Faredoon knew he would continue to exist—in his children—in a prosperous dynasty of future Junglewallas!

And yet Faredoon felt an urge to leave a greater part of himself behind. Not in their memories—he knew few would remember even in a year that a man called Faredoon Junglewalla ever existed—but he meant to linger in his influence on their minds. He proceeded to reiterate inexhaustibly his rough and ready views on the benign motivation of needs and wants. He talked to each of his children at length, in his bedroom, subtly injecting the lessons of his experiences and the rich fruit of his reflection. "It has taken me a long time to comprehend Evil—and Good—and a lifetime to catch just a glimpse of the *Path of Asha*, God's grand plan for man and the cosmos. Yes, the strength of God comes to the man of good action, and such a man is gifted, progressively, with the Good Mind, the Vahu Mana, God's own mind . . . Thus spake Zarathustra!"

In this way he felt he had a stake in the direction of their future, a stake in endless generations of Junglewallas.

One evening, gathered around him in the bedroom, the family found him animated as of old, yet perturbed by the trend of events in India. He was stirred by talk of rebellion, self-rule and independence from the British, and most of all by the role of a few Parsees in all this. He stated his opinions with a vigor and prophetic emphasis that infected his listeners. They saw in him not the white-haired, wasted, resigned old man, but the man he once was!

Yazdi had been telegrammed. They never knew if the message

reached him. Faredoon leaned back on the pillows. A ceiling fan creaked around and around and ineffectually stirred air that the heat had congealed into a transparent glue. Billy, Ardishir and Bobby Katrak, who had arrived from Karachi with Yasmin, lounged at various angles on the bed, their sweating faces turned to Faredoon. Hutoxi, Ruby, Yasmin and Putli sat alert on chairs they had carried in from the dining room, ready to jump up if Faredoon required anything. Tanya and Katy talked softly on the balcony.

"Do you know who is responsible for this mess?" asked Faredoon, not expecting an answer, and his listeners waited for the rhetoric that usually followed. "I'll tell you who. That misguided Parsee from Bombay, Dadabhoy Navroji! Things were going smoothly; there has always been talk of throwing off the British yoke—of independence—but that fool of a Parsee starts something called the Congress and shoots his bloody mouth off like a lunatic. 'Quit India! Quit India!' You know what he has done? Stirred a hornet's nest! I can see the repercussions.

"What happens? He utters ideas. People like Gandhi pick them up—people like Valabhai Patel and Bose and Jinnah and Nehru . . . and that other stupid fool in Karachi, Rustom Sidhwa, also picks them up! What does he do? He sacrifices his business and abandons his family to the vicissitudes of chance and poverty. He wears a Gandhi cap, a handloom shirt and that transparent diaper they call a dhoti. He goes in and out of jail as if he were visiting a girl at the Hira Mandi! Where will it get him? Nowhere! If there are any rewards in all this, who will reap them? Not Sidhwa! Not Dadabhoy Navroji! Making monkeys of themselves and of us! Biting the hand that feeds! I tell you we are betrayed by our own kind, by our own blood! The fools will break up the country. The Hindus will have one part, Muslims the other. Sikhs, Bengalis, Tamils and God knows who else will have their share; and they won't want you!"

"But where will we go? What will happen to us?" asked Bobby Katrak in half-serious alarm. The question, in varying degrees of concern, was on all faces.

"Nowhere, my children," said Faredoon, sinking back in the pillows. He raised his gaunt, broad-wristed arms in a slow, controlled movement and rested them on the headboard. The bedsheet was crumpled at his feet. He was wearing loose cotton pajamas and a sleeveless V-necked sudreh. His skin was a pale yellow-brown. The hair of his chest and armpits had turned white. His veins were prominent and blue-throbbing. An inward look of triumph and assurance suddenly veiled his eyes. Faredoon said softly, "We will stay where we are . . . let Hindus, Muslims, Sikhs, or whoever, rule. What does it matter? The sun will continue to rise—and the sun continue to set—in their arses . . . !"

Bapsi Sidhwa, who belongs to the small Parsee community, was born in Karachi, Pakistan, and grew up in Lahore. She graduated from Kinnaird College for Women, Lahore. An active social worker among Asian women, in 1975 she represented Pakistan at the Asian Women's Congress. Sidhwa has taught in the graduate program at Columbia University in 1989 and prior to that at Rice University and at the University of Texas at Houston. Married and with three children, she resides in the United States but travels frequently to Pakistan.

Bapsi Sidhwa is the author of *The Bride* (Jonathan Cape Ltd., 1983; St. Martins Press, 1983), *The Crow Eaters* (Milkweed Editions, 1992; St. Martins Press, 1982; Jonathan Cape Ltd., 1980), and several short stories. Her work has been translated into German, French, and Russian. Sidhwa was appointed Bunting Fellow at Radcliffe/Harvard in 1986-87 and was awarded a National Endowment for the Arts grant for Creative Writing in 1987. In 1991 she received the *Sitara-i-Imtiaz*, the highest honor in the arts that Pakistan bestows on a citizen, and the *Liberatur* Prize in Germany for *Cracking India*.

Titling in Ondine type
and 11 point text in Trajanus,
typeset by The Typeworks.
Printed on acid-free Glatfelter
by Edwards Brothers.
Designed by R. W. Scholes.